THERE MUST BE A PONY

IN HERE SOMEWHERE

Also by Kara Swisher

aol.com

THERE MUST

BE A PONY

IN HERE

SOMEWHERE

The AOL TIME WARNER DEBACLE
and the Quest for a Digital Future

KARA SWISHER

with LISA DICKEY

CROWN
BUSINESS
NEW YORK

Copyright © 2003 by Kara Swisher

Published by Crown Business, New York, New York.
Member of the Crown Publishing Group, a division of Random House, Inc.
www.crownpublishing.com

CROWN BUSINESS is a trademark and the Rising Sun colophon is a registered
trademark of Random House, Inc.

Printed in the United States of America

DESIGN BY BARBARA STURMAN

Library of Congress Cataloging-in-Publication Data
Swisher, Kara.
There Must Be a Pony in Here Somewhere: The AOL Time Warner Debacle
and the Quest for a Digital Future / by Kara Swisher.—1st ed.
Includes index.
1. America Online, Inc.—History.   2. AOL Time Warner—History.   I. Title.
HE7583.U6S853 2003
338.7'61004678'0973—dc21   2003012082

ISBN 1-4000-4963-6

2 4 6 8 10 9 7 5 3 1

First Edition

To Louie and Megan

and

To Shar

CONTENTS

AUTHOR'S NOTE

Of the myriad problems plaguing the AOL Time Warner merger, perhaps one of the bigger problems was the lack of disclosure among the many players about motives, business prospects, and simple emotions. Save for the legendary entrepreneur Ted Turner, who became the voluble weathervane of the deal, very few in this story were as forthright as they needed to be to make the merger a success.

With that in mind, I thought that some of the first words to the reader of this book should be about disclosing things about myself. Thus, I think the reader must be made aware that my partner—Megan Smith—had been a top executive at a dot-com company called PlanetOut, which has had a longtime investment from AOL. AOL made its initial investment long before I met her, although—as is the typical practice with startups—it continued to invest in follow-on rounds after we met. I obviously had no involvement in these investments, and Megan no longer has an operating role at the company. Finally, she also worked briefly at a nonprofit literacy organization created by an AOL Time Warner board member, but is no longer employed there.

Second, I based most of this book on my own reporting and on interviews I conducted in 2002 and 2003 with a plethora of key sources from both companies, as well as throughout the Internet and media industries. I also used my own reporting from my first book, *aol.com,* for the early chapters on the history of AOL. But, for background research, I also relied on several books, magazines, and newspaper and online accounts. I have tried to include noting these sources wherever pertinent in the text of the book itself, instead of buried in footnotes, so I could give proper credit where it was due.

But I would be lax if I did not mention a few in particular here. Among books, I would give special credit to the incredible work done in: *Ted Turner: It Ain't As Easy As It Looks* by Porter Bibb; *Master of the Game* by Connie Bruck; *Burn Rate* by Michael Wolff; and *Bamboozled at the Revolution* by John Motavalli. Among newspapers, magazines, and online sources, I would especially point out: *Wall Street Journal, New York Times, Washington Post, Business Week, Time, Fortune, Wired, Industry Standard, New York, New Yorker,* News.com, and the Dow Jones News Service.

And now to the really important part of any book-writing project—thanking those who have helped me pull this off once again. Here, I must give the most appreciation to Megan Smith, who has endured this endeavor with the equanimity that is her hallmark and the kindness that is at the heart of her nature. From being encouraging while I complained to being wise when I was foolish to being quiet when I ranted, she has been the perfect partner, most especially for her loving care of our son. Thanks too to Louie, whose ever-present smiles and laughter have become like oxygen to me and whose life is a constant reminder of what truly counts.

My mother, Lucretia Carney, who clipped out every story on AOL Time Warner she could find, provided the kind of support and love that never waned. And thanks too to the rest of my wonderful family, as well as my extended one, including my very best friend Joe Brown, Ed Daly, Mark Clark, Silvia Rivera, Cosmo, and, *sigh,* my dear departed Bo.

Huge kudos and much credit for this book must go to Lisa Dickey, who apparently lost her mind temporarily when she agreed to take on both AOL and me for a second time. She has been an invaluable sounding board, an honest voice, an excellent editor, and the finest of friends.

At the *Wall Street Journal,* I could not have done this project without the support of Steve Yoder, Dan Hertzberg, Paul Steiger, Gordon Crovitz, and many others. Of everyone at that august newspaper, though, Walt Mossberg has been my mentor and friend in so many important ways. Leslie Walker and Laura Blumenfeld of the *Washington Post* have also been valued colleagues and friends.

Thanks to all at AOL Time Warner and throughout the online and media sectors who agreed to talk to me for this book. I extend particular appreciation to those who spoke on the record, since doing so was so uncommon in this complex story. For those who wanted to remain nameless, I thank you for the information, but I still wish you had gone on the record. I also would be remiss if I did not thank those at AOL Time Warner whom I bugged for an entire year with annoying fact-checking queries and endless requests for interviews and information, especially John Buckley, Kathy Bushkin, Trish Primrose, and Ed Adler. I promise you all, I will never again write a book on AOL. (Well, unless something even *more* newsworthy happens in the future.)

And this book would have never occurred without the help of my agent Flip Brophy, my *aol.com* editor Jon Karp, and Crown publisher Steve Ross.

Finally and especially, I extend the warmest thanks to my editor, Annik LaFarge. There is no such thing as a great reporter without a spectacular editor, so any credit I get for this book goes to her too. Any criticism, of course, is all mine.

KARA SWISHER

I'd like to thank Kara Swisher, who gave me my start in books by hiring me to help her with *aol.com* in early 1997. Thanks also to my many clients since then—you know who you are, and I appreciate your entrusting your books to me. To Barbara Feinman, Deborah Grosvenor, and Laura Einstein, thank you for your advice and help over the years. To my parents, my brother David, and my Uncle Pitt—you can't pick your family, but if you could, I'd certainly have picked you all. Finally, to Shar Taylor, thank you for all the help, loyalty, and love you've given me over the past five years. Your support has meant everything to me.

LISA DICKEY

THERE MUST BE A PONY

IN HERE SOMEWHERE

We are all at a wonderful party, and by the rules of the game we know that at some point the Black Horsemen will burst through the great terrace doors to cut down the revelers; those who leave early may be saved, but the music and wines are so seductive that we do not want to leave, but we do ask, "What time is it? What time is it?" Only none of the clocks have any hands.

ADAM SMITH, *The Money Game*

Prologue

WHAT IS THE SOUND OF ONE DOOR SLAMMING?

When the door slammed in my face from 3,000 miles away, I knew Steve Case had actually managed to pull off the heist of the very new century.

Luckily for me, it wasn't a heavy wooden door, but a virtual one. Many virtual ones, in fact, being banged shut by different high-level executives at America Online Inc. almost immediately after I pinged them electronically. I had done so because an unusual number of them were logged on to the online service in the wee hours of Monday, January 10, 2000.

How did I know this? The digital footprints were unmistakable, right there on my "Buddy List"—an electronic who's-where on AOL that allows you to keep track of anyone on the service. Once you see that someone is online, you can send an email or, more immediately, an instant message—or IM, as it had come to be known—that pops up directly on the recipient's screen. As a helpful feature, when someone on your list logs in, there is a sound of a door opening. And, when he or she leaves, there is, naturally, the sound of a slamming door.

It's all very silly and very AOL, mostly used by teens, one tool of an elaborate digital social scene that had made the service incredibly popular with them in a few short years. IM'ing had also become widely employed by its legions of users who like to participate in a bit of racy online sex chat every now and then, yet another massive and loyal audience AOL had used to transform itself into a Wall Street wunderkind. But I assumed it was not for some electronic after-hours party that a bulk of AOL's management hierarchy had gathered in the digital ether in the dead of night.

I wasn't AOL exec-fishing just for fun. I had signed on immediately after getting a call near midnight at my house in San Francisco from a fellow reporter at the *Wall Street Journal*. Peter Gumbel of the Los Angeles bureau had just gotten a killer tip, when a stunned source had called him late at night and told him that the giant entertainment behemoth Time Warner was merging with AOL. This was an unbelievable piece of news, both for the massive financial numbers it would surely involve and the enormous reverberations it would have throughout the media and Internet world.

More important, Peter's source had told him that AOL and not Time Warner was going to hold the majority stake in the new company. This would be the clearest signal that the online upstarts—which had burst on the scene in the late 1990s and whose market valuations had climbed to incredible heights—had reached the apogee of power and influence. Even in the midst of what turned out to be the Internet's frothiest moment, this was still a jaw-dropping idea. Time Warner was one of the world's most important media companies, with such wide-ranging and iconic properties as *People* magazine, Bugs Bunny, and CNN. Despite its hot stock, AOL had only a single dial-up online access business. As I would later write, a company without assets was buying a company without a clue.

Nonetheless, it was exactly this kind of "transformational" deal that had been a long-held dream of AOL's chairman and chief executive, Steve Case. He had, in fact, told me as much when I had first met him in 1995 as a technology reporter for the *Washington Post*. In a drab office in a nondescript building behind a car dealership in Vienna, Virginia, the peculiarly calm and unusually baby-faced Case declared that his near-term goal was to be one of the biggest and most powerful media and communications companies in the world—and very, very soon.

My first thought—since he did not appear to be an egomaniac, like so many executives I had interviewed—was that he might actually be insane. At the time, though, I only nodded politely and, as he chattered on, began to calculate how soon his perpetually rickety company would declare bankruptcy. At the time, most people thought that would be the ultimate fate of AOL, given its precarious financial state for much of its volatile history.

Still, I soon learned that Case had been spinning his impossible scenario to many visitors, which was why most reporters who covered AOL considered him a bit of a crank. Besides predicting the inevitability of world domination by his tiny business, he also never seemed to let up on endless pie-in-the-sky speeches, mixing in references to "convergence" and "interactive" and all sorts of other computing hoo-ha and linking it with the future of all mass media. From a cruddy little office, far from any canyons of power and influence, this seemingly out-of-his-league businessboy had decided he was going to be the king of the world. You might excuse anyone for being skeptical.

In fact, the company had found itself at the edge of disaster so frequently that one of its first executives, a brassy Vietnam veteran and restaurateur named Jim Kimsey, had taken the punch line of an old joke popularized by Ronald Reagan and made it into an unlikely mantra for AOL. It concerned a very optimistic young boy who happened upon a huge pile of horse manure and began digging excitedly. When someone asked him what he was doing covered in muck, the foolish boy answered brightly, "There must be a pony in here somewhere!"

Kimsey's version was a bit earthier. "C'mon, there must be a pony somewhere in this shit," he had crowed when times got particularly tough in 1984 to egg on his dispirited corporate troops. They were justifiably dubious, given that the online services offered by the company weren't selling, it had burned through most of its cash, and creditors were poised to snap up what little was left. Such crises would become a familiar refrain for AOL over the years—a history that was punctuated by a lot of shoveling of a lot of manure.

But had AOL *finally* found the pony?

If one of these Internet highfliers was actually able to buy what was considered the finest traditional media company on the planet, this was an incredible scoop. So, Peter Gumbel had called reporters in various cities at the paper to get a critical second and third confirmation that such major stories required. I had tried making calls to AOL people I knew at first, but no one answered. This was not surprising since most of my relationships at the company took place online. So I dialed into the AOL service to see if I could email someone.

I quickly began to type in the online monikers of any executives I knew from my years of covering the company and from later writing a book, *aol.com,* about its turbulent history. Thankfully, unlike other big company executives and their legions of public relations obstacle-creators, many online business leaders loved kibitzing back and forth with reporters via email in what I can only guess were efforts to charm us into loving them for their accessibility. Frankly, it worked a lot of the time, so they freely handed out their email addresses and were always very easy to locate instantly. It was true that night, too. It soon became clear that pretty much everyone in any position of power at AOL was signed on to the service.

"We know," I wrote in a flurry of initial instant messages, attempting to be as vague as possible. "Tell all." I hoped this would produce a response of some kind from someone, especially since instant messages were hard to trace and had always been an easy way to make first contact with company sources. Instead, I got a very unusual reaction.

Slam. Slam. Slam. Slam.

The people I had IM'ed were signing off the service as soon as the little message bombs I sent had exploded onto their screens. Moreover, many started to actually block my messages, which can also be done to those on your Buddy List you want to avoid. The technique was usually used by those who needed a tool to deflect creepy online chatters, which I now seemed to have become to the top rank of AOL executives. But since several of my missives had gotten through before being declined, their belated door slamming seemed like the online equivalent of some poor sap running away from pursuing TV cameras. I couldn't imagine they could be quite this dumb, but the online names skittered off my Buddy List as fast as I could hit the return key to send more messages. It appeared as if I had them digitally nailed!

But I didn't really. Their skittishness only proved they were up to something, which might not involve a multibillion-dollar deal. They could be putting the finishing touches on some hyped-up advertising shakedown that was de rigueur for AOL in the boom years, as they plucked all the low-hanging venture capital investments from newbie Web startups dying to go public and needing to punch their AOL-deal ticket to get there. Or perhaps AOL was rearranging its management structure, which the company did regularly over the years, shifting from one chameleon color to another in order to please investors. They could even be acquiring some lesser company like eBay, a deal that had been rumored for a while, in an effort to keep up their fast-paced growth that was always at risk of faltering and bringing down the whole breathless show. Lord help us, Steve Case may have decided to run for president, for all I knew.

Gumbel called back, wanting to know if I had gotten a confirmation. Um, no, not yet, I replied. But, I ventured, they're all online, slamming doors on me right and left and even blocking my electronic missives! Barred virtual entrances? Bounced emails? Gumbel was justifiably frustrated, since this was not what one of the finest business newspapers in the world could rely on to confirm such a major story. Imagine explaining this to the top editors at the New York headquarters: Well, we couldn't get a second source, but there was that curious rash of online door slamming and email blockage. New-economy companies might be able to suspend the basic rules of their business, but new-economy reporters could not.

For a story this big, as the *Washington Post*'s Ben Bradlee used to say, I hadn't got it. Thank goodness for better and faster reporters than I. Our media reporter in New York, Martin Peers, had reached someone from Time Warner by phone. Not given to lurking online at all hours, the source had confirmed to him that the deal was indeed happening and added more details. And with that, a 228-word story on the stock-for-stock merger was then raced onto the *Wall Street Journal*'s Web site and the Dow Jones news wires, since it was too late to actually print the news in the flagship *Wall Street Journal*.

This was a little ironic. Just the Friday before, Peers himself had asked Time Warner's spokesman Ed Adler if such a deal was even a possibility, after a *Los Angeles Times* year-end retrospective had included a widespread Wall Street rumor that AOL had recently tried to make a hostile bid for his company. Adler actually had no idea what his boss, Time Warner CEO Gerald Levin, was up to even though the deal had nearly been struck. Naturally, he had dismissed the notion as bogus to Peers.

I had, too, even though it was completely possible because of AOL's gigantic market cap. At the end of trading on January 7, 2000, it stood at a remarkable $164 billion—almost twice the $83 billion value of Time Warner. That absurd number had even caused me 10 days earlier to suggest—in an annual column I did for the *Journal*'s Marketplace section prognosticating what would happen in the year ahead for the online world—that AOL should buy anything it could get its hands on. After talking over the possibilities with Silicon Valley venture capitalist Stewart Alsop, a longtime AOL watcher, I wrote on December 30, 1999:

> *For America Online, look for a bigger ball game.... Experts say AOL must think even bigger to transform itself into a true global media company rather than remaining what is essentially a glorified online service with mostly American customers. Some analysts suggest AOL might look for a merger with a big traditional media company, which would offer a variety of distribution and content arms.*

In the original version, I had even specifically mentioned Time Warner by name, along with Viacom, as possible AOL targets Stewart and I had thought seemed most likely. But those names were expurgated in editing in order to make me look less stupid, since it was clear that such a deal would never happen. They'd have better luck if they tried to buy France, my editor had even joked to me. Simply put, the idea of AOL actually being able to pull off such a coup seemed too ridiculous to print.

Now, as dawn approached, it might still be silly, but it had turned out to be true. And, soon enough, the business world would be waking up and journeying down an unknown path of uncertain direction.

Just then, the tinny sound of a single door creaking open sounded on my computer. An IM from a high-ranking AOL exec popped up with a ping, signaling the now unnecessary additional confirmation. Even in the truncated text, it was full of exactly the kind of glee and gloating that would later wreak havoc on the merger. "Yes. We bought Time Warner. Unbelievable. We won."

It was unbelievable, for sure. But of what exactly had been won, I was a lot less certain. Had AOL found, at long last, the proverbial pony? Or—as it had always been the case throughout its capricious corporate history—that much more familiar pile of manure?

Begin at the beginning and go on till you
come to the end: Then stop.

LEWIS CARROLL, *Through the Looking-Glass*

Chapter One

THE TRUTH, THE WHOLE TRUTH, AND NOTHING BUT THE TRUTH

(or something like it)

I Made a Little List

Now, in the frigid and head-clearing morning of the new economy after the New Economy, everyone seems to agree: Time Warner was had by AOL.

That is, at the turn of the new millennium, the world's biggest and arguably most influential media company merged itself with the highflying online giant and central icon of the Internet boom for a 44 percent stake in the combined company. The problem was AOL's business was soon to crater as that boom turned to bust, and its once lofty stock would become almost worthless. In this simplistic scenario, the trade of the century soon became known as the worst deal in history.

This is most certainly the tale that has taken up residence in the stony prison of conventional wisdom: A wheezing and increasingly desperate traditional media company, scared of inevitable death (or, worse still, irrelevance) in the hot swirl of a digital revolution, marries itself off to the young, sexy, and possibly sleazy starlet of the new-media society.

Disaster ensues.

And this merger has most definitely qualified as a disaster of belly flop proportions, by any measure you might care to use, which AOL Time Warner's own magazine, *Fortune,* dubbed "one of the greatest train wrecks in corporate history." The stock's 75 percent drop within two years of the deal's completion, the vicious purge of the top executives responsible for the merger, the investigations into dicey accounting practices, the poisonous atmosphere—all this has resulted in a constant barrage of ugly news headlines and poor morale at the company.

As I sit here in 2003 surveying the carnage, it is hard not to feel a bit queasy about the whole sorry mess. I had been following AOL's history—and the course of the whole commercial Web revolution—from early on, so it felt a bit like I was watching someone fall down a flight of stairs in slow motion, and every bump and thump made me wince. It made me reassess old ideas and wonder what had gone wrong. And it left me deeply confused as to what had happened and, more important, what was coming next.

That was certainly how one of the company's largest and most vocal shareholders, Ted Turner, seemed to be feeling, too. Turner, the legendary media entrepreneur who'd gained as much fame for his headline-grabbing antics as for founding CNN, had begun ranting regularly about AOL Time Warner CEO Gerald Levin not long after the January 2000 merger announcement. In meetings, according to many sources, he'd call Levin a "liar and a thief"—when, of course, he wasn't discussing his separation and pending divorce from Holly-wood star Jane Fonda, which the couple had revealed just a few days before the merger announcement.

Things got only worse after Turner had lost $7 billion in stock value by the end of 2002. "I'm poor, but I'm proud," he'd say loudly and often. And he took to showing up at the offices of various Time

Warner executives, where he'd turn his pants pockets inside out and cry out to anyone who would listen: "I was robbed."

Turner was perplexed. Perplexed at what had happened in the deal, and perplexed at how he'd managed to lose more money in two years than almost anyone in the world had ever possessed. In December 2002, on the fifth anniversary of his $1 billion pledge to the United Nations, he announced to reporters, "I went from no money to a pile of money, just as big as the World Trade Center." Unable to stop himself despite the crassness of the comparison, he went on: "Then—just like the World Trade Center—Poof! It was gone."

Possibly the most vexing part for Turner—though he never seemed to admit it in all his angry outbursts—was the knowledge that he'd done this to himself. Not only had he voted for the deal as a major stockholder; he'd also publicly declared, without any prompting, that he "did it with as much or more excitement and enthusiasm as I did on that night when I first made love some forty-two years ago." As much, okay. *But more?* No wonder he was suffering such postcoital pique.

Turner's transformation—from sex-crazed teen to ranting, grumpy old man—got me thinking about the whole deal. So I made a little list, titled: Questions to Ask Ted Turner, If He Ever Agrees to Talk to Me.

1. Were you really robbed?
2. If not, why are you saying you were?
3. What did Gerald Levin lie and cheat about?
4. Why did you and Jane Fonda break up?

(That last one was just for me personally.)

This led to another list, titled: Questions to Ask Gerald Levin.

1. Do you think you robbed Ted Turner?
2. If so, where is his $7 billion?
3. Are you a liar and a cheat?
4. Why do you think he broke up with Jane Fonda?

I went, to tell the truth, a bit list-crazy, making them for everyone involved—Steve Case, other executives, the investment bankers, the

Wall Street analysts, major institutional investors, and on down the line to the smallest schmoo at the companies.

It seemed like an easy job then. I'd just take my many lists and get some answers. Then I'd be able to explain what had happened—which would then go a long way toward explaining what had happened in the whole Internet boom and bust. Yes, this should be easy.

Or so I thought. But the mood in the business world as I began doing interviews in the fall of 2002 was very ugly, and the AOL Time Warner deal was being held up as the biggest and stupidest moment in the whole era. What I would soon learn was that this was a story in which everyone was to blame, but no one was at fault. And only a few would go on the record about what happened, although everyone would tell you in detail why someone else screwed up. Worst of all, so heavy is the stench of the fetid merger itself, it's been nearly impossible to determine if the main idea of the merger—the virtuous combination of old and new media to face the inevitable digital future together—was ever a worthy one.

This was, in short, a bad deal in search of a big scapegoat.

Nobody Still Knows

As I started writing this book, the multiplicity of competing agendas and few truly honest players quickly made it hard to sort things out. Soon enough, I felt a bit like a spun top—which was, as it turned out, an oddly familiar feeling. It was the same one I'd had when I first started writing about the Internet many years ago.

"The truth is: Nobody knows" was the opening line of my first book, *aol.com: How Steve Case Beat Bill Gates, Nailed the Netheads, and Made Millions in the War for the Web,* which chronicled the rise of an unlikely group of entrepreneurs on the edge of disaster to the heights of status, power, and money. The line was meant to show how few people understood the power of this entirely new and highly disruptive online medium. And, more to the point, how fewer still thought America Online, which had been left for dead many times on its rocky journey, could ever amount to much at all.

That book was a story of the losers winning it all. With crazy characters and huge hype, big-time moguls and risky deals, and piles upon piles of money, the AOL story was a primer on the dot-com revolution that electrified the country at the end of the 20th century. As the biggest player of them all, AOL sat at the very top of this world when I completed the book in 1997.

And then, AOL somehow rose even higher, capping its lofty position at the dawn of the new millennium with the announcement that it would buy the world's most important media company, Time Warner, rather than the other way around. The losers now stood ready to transform the combined company into a place that would control much of what Americans read, listened to, and watched, as well as how they communicated.

Today, it's easy to forget how bullish the world was on the merger news in January of 2000, because the context of that once hopeful and perpetually frenzied time had vanished almost completely by 2003. The Web-will-change-the-world-and-make-us-filthy-rich cheer had morphed rather abruptly into an It-was-all-a-Ponzi-scheme-wasn't-it? shriek. But let us try to remember anyway: When the merger was announced, it was hailed as the new paradigm and few questioned its wisdom. Its key executives—Steve Case, Jerry Levin, Bob Pittman, and, yes, Ted Turner, too—were seen by many as rock star–like icons of the future. The new sages of the business world, they were admired and envied for their immense wealth, power, and seeming ability to influence the future direction of the world. Mere mortals had become accidental gods, as one Wall Street analyst had told me soon after the deal was announced.

But now the losers are losers once again, having fallen Icarus-like to earth after arrogance and hubris had brought them too close to the sun. The merger of the century is seen as an abject failure. Instead of high fives and dreams of perfect synergy, AOL Time Warner has become a place of vicious boardroom infighting, management coups, shaky morale, and a general feeling that the whole effort to merge the old and new economies has been a farce. There are, of course, lawsuits on top of lawsuits, as the molten anger hardened into a much colder and more urgent need for revenge and retribution.

As things started to teeter and then topple at the company, I, too, found myself weirdly upset. First of all, there was an element of self-interest in my discomfort. The column I wrote about the tech sector for the *Wall Street Journal* was called "Boom Town." "Been watching the NASDAQ. Think we should change the name to 'Bust-town'?" *Journal* deputy managing editor Dan Hertzberg had written me in an email on November 30, 2000, as the Net royalty started to show major signs of wilting. When your boss starts making little "jokes" like that, you know it's time to start looking for answers.

But it wasn't just that. There was also the dirty little secret I have continued to hold in these antidigital times: I am still a believer. Maybe not in the AOL Time Warner merger anymore, but in the essential idea at the heart of it—that someday the distinction of old and new media will no longer exist. Despite the grave dancing everyone's been doing about AOL Time Warner's fate, I still believe we're at the very start of realizing the promise of the many technical innovations that burst on the scene at the end of the last century. Borrowing from Winston Churchill, I call it the end of the beginning of the digital revolution.

By that, I mean that it is from the ashes of this bust that the really important companies of the next era will emerge. And that evolution will, I believe, be shaped by what happened—and what is happening now—at AOL Time Warner. Because the moment the deal was struck has become a kind of Internet Rubicon: It stopped the boom that needed stopping and ushered the nascent industry into maturity with a rough shove.

In the wake of the crash, true faith in the eventual dominance of the Internet is not an easy thing to admit to. In fact, largely because of this one disastrous deal, saying you believe in the Internet as a revolutionary medium is now a bit like admitting to a capital crime. It may even be one, if you also happen to express confidence in convergence—that longed-for mix of technology and media that will someday enable consumers to get any kind of information anytime and anywhere. And I won't even begin to imagine how pilloried someone who also touts synergy—the fabled ability to make a company worth more than the sum of its parts—would be.

But I still believe. And in order to find out what would happen next, I needed to find the real story behind the failed merger, and how we got here from there. That, and the answer to another question:

Who really robbed Ted Turner?

Whodunit?

But figuring out who is responsible for the flameout of the AOL Time Warner merger is not such an easy thing, because the list of potential perpetrators is long. It's also convoluted, since the suspects and the victims are often one and the same. And they're all so in denial (and, more important, so financially burned) that it's hard to get a rational answer out of anyone.

Was it AOL? Cynical observers think Steve Case and his AOL crew fully expected the coming dot-com bust, and that they bought Time Warner at the peak of the Internet bubble with a little bit of aggressive—and possibly illegal—accounting to help the deal along. In this scenario, AOL simply snookered Levin into selling his jewels for fake currency.

Was it Time Warner? Some see the company as a desperate curmudgeon, unwilling to cooperate because of its rank jealousy of AOL. An old-style company accustomed to enjoying lavish perks and exhibiting little shareholder regard, Time Warner was, some suggest, unable to see the vast problems and opportunities the digital revolution was bringing their way.

Was it Wall Street and its handmaidens in greed, the venture capitalists? After all, it was the fee-seeking investment banks and their cheerleading analysts, along with the venture capitalists, who ginned up the huge valuations for Internet companies like AOL. These players clearly had a hand in pushing for such a massive deal to go forward without any cogent analysis or due diligence. They all got their cut, of course—and will again if the whole sorry mess is unwound.

Was it the investors? They're the ones who agreed to play by these frothy rules, whipping up stock prices to new heights and celebrating every uptick without question. Both individual shareholders and huge institutional investors played an important role in the game, buying into the deal and its elevated promises without the slightest hesitation. Then, at the first sign of trouble, they turned on it without a backward glance.

And what about the media? The rah-rah press praised the deal to the skies when it was announced—and then did a complete about-face, damning it without a trace of irony. Or how culpable are once-lax regulators, who failed to rein in the excesses of the dot-com era in real time and then swooped in with subpoenas when the climate changed? Or perhaps it was simply the shift in times—from insane euphoria to total depression—that is part and parcel of the American business cycle. Digitalization was in? Well, so sorry, now it's out.

Or possibly it was just the classic reason for so many merger failures: It was way too much, too soon, and it became an unmanageable entity that overpromised and underdelivered quite spectacularly.

Perhaps it was all these suspects, suddenly converging to create what one of AOL's top executives, Myer Berlow, dubbed "the perfect storm." As the economy tanked, all the factors combined to upend an already overburdened ship. The result: The AOL Time Warner merger has become the *Titanic* of business deals—except without Leonardo DiCaprio around to pretty it up a bit.

Making sense of this miasma was going to be a challenge. Worse still, the overwhelming deluge of details—from critical moments to pointless gossip and everything in between—made it hard to discern what was truly important in the story and what was not. Was the key to understanding this debacle, its aftermath, and the future of the industry too buried in minutiae to paint a true portrait of what happened? (How many of Ted Turner's fist-banging outbursts, for example, really mattered, as entertaining as they might be to write about?)

With that in mind, I put together one last list of the questions I really wanted to answer, this one for myself:

1. So, who really robbed Ted Turner?
2. Should he (and everyone, really) have seen this coming?
3. Will the demise of this merger be the final and inevitable chapter of the dot-com debacle?
4. And how did the person who first made love to Ted Turner "some forty-two years ago" like being compared to a mega-merger?

That last one was, of course, just for me personally.

> The will to grow was everywhere written large and
> to grow at no matter what or whose expense.
>
> HENRY JAMES

Chapter Two

THE PERILS OF PAULINE

Pardon My French

I'm not sure exactly when Steve Case developed his King of France walk.

I first saw the transformation as the new century dawned with the AOL Time Warner merger. Case rapidly assumed an unusual statesmanlike gait, perhaps due to his newfound importance in the world. Apparently, he was thinking such great thoughts and carrying around such weighty visions in his newly expanded head that getting around now required a bearing that was slow, deliberate, self-important. Aloof and possibly rude. Above it all and imperial. Always accompanied by a look of slight displeasure.

At a big cable television event in Silicon Valley on February 27, 2000, a little more than a month after the merger was announced, I got my most potent whiff of Case's new air of royalty. He and a cluster of other big Internet gurus, such as Yahoo's cofounder Jerry Yang, were appearing on MSNBC's grandly named "Summit in Silicon Valley," hosted by NBC anchor Tom Brokaw. Case was now important enough *not* to attend, and appeared instead on a giant screen suspended above the crowd at Stanford University. I was there, too, as a kind of living prop—one of a group of reporters brought in to ask these Web gods "tough" questions.

Naturally, I was assigned to ask questions of Case, since I'd written a book on his company before he had hit the big time. So, from my little seat near the stage, I peered at his big head looming over me and asked him if he thought perhaps AOL Time Warner was just too big a company now to operate properly. Case said he did not think bigger was better, in a tone that suggested I was clearly not illuminated. "Better is better."

I was flummoxed. Was this a New Economy haiku? A Zen insight? Or, as I suspected, was it just another of the kind of meaningless declarations he'd suddenly taken to spouting of late? I asked the obvious follow-up question: "What does that mean?" But the sound to my mike had been cut, as Brokaw took over and nodded in serious agreement with Case's pearls of wisdom.

The NBC anchorman was not alone in his deference to Case. So many people seemed to agree with him in that golden time after the merger with Time Warner was announced that it was easy to see how Case had developed this new, preening posture. For one shining moment, at least, Steve Case was the Sun King of the New World Order. Young yet wise, entrepreneurial yet solid, wonderfully wealthy yet understated—he personified a new kind of American Dream. And his brand of khaki capitalism was apparently capable of transforming everything.

Most people involved in the deal seem to be suffering from a peculiar amnesia now, so it's easy to forget that kind of hype and optimism. Today, almost everyone near to this toxic merger runs screaming from it in an attempt to avoid any culpability. The denials come fast and furious: Not me. I wasn't involved. I thought it was wrong from the very beginning. And—most of all—Steve Case is a big, fat idiot.

This was more familiar territory for me, since that was exactly how most of the world had regarded Case throughout his career. For most of it, he had always and forever been a loser. I lost count of the many times over the years that Case was disdained, insulted, and considered a bit of a fool by both the powerful New York kingpins of media and Silicon Valley's technology czars.

And why shouldn't he have been pilloried? For much of its short life, his rinky-dink little company was in serious distress; it bled cash, lost customers as fast as it got them, was derided for its clunky technology, and lived under constant attack from major competitors, including giant Microsoft. AOL's path has been one of the bumpiest ones possible—a dramatic journey that has at times seemed like a mix of the Keystone Kops with Indiana Jones and the *Perils of Pauline* thrown in.

From the beginning, in fact, the history of AOL has been, to put it politely, a disaster waiting to happen. The company had veered from one crisis to the other in a way that has terrified and fascinated its longtime observers. Stewart Alsop, the venture capitalist and AOL supporter, once noted quite correctly, "AOL has turned being in trouble into a corporate culture."

During its journey, the company acquired a plethora of nicknames—"The Online Kmart," "America On Hold," "The Giant Sucking Sound." But the one from its earliest days, "The Cockroach of Cyberspace," was the one that turned out to be most true. No matter what happened, AOL survived, through constant reinvention and an astonishing ability to leave behind any baggage so it could move on to the next thing.

That's why, over the many years I covered AOL, I always kept on the wall above my desk a little clip from an old issue of *Wired* magazine. Titled "Demise of AOL," it read, in part: "Someday, the history of cyberspace will be written as a chronicle of the predictions of AOL's demise. From claims that America Online would fail because it wasn't 'open,' to charges that it was inherently unreliable, the service has been the canary in the coalmine for all of cyberspace."

This was true. No matter how big its business got, no matter how high its stock went, it was still the most ridiculed company around. Even though it completely dominated its competition throughout the late 1990s, no one could ever quite believe AOL was succeeding. After the CompuServe purchase in 1997, *Fortune* magazine pictured Steve Case on the cover under the headline "Surprise! AOL Wins!" How could this be happening? Didn't AOL suck?

Well, yes, AOL did suck a lot of the time. But it also offered the easiest way for people who didn't know (and didn't want to know) anything about computers to get online. The genius of Steve Case lay not in developing the most sophisticated, versatile product he could, but in realizing that most people wanted the exact opposite of that. Most average users simply longed for a convenient way to be part of this great new communications medium without doing a lot of heavy lifting.

In these times of tearing down AOL, it's impossible not to credit it with almost single-handedly popularizing the online medium and bringing it to the mainstream. This was due in large part to Case, who was also the most unlikely suspect to lead one of the greatest communications revolutions of all time.

In fact, he's about the last person one would pick as the great communicator. It's not for nothing that Case garnered the nickname "The Wall" among his staff. He's difficult to read and more difficult to know—he's even uncomfortable with those he should be comfortable with, from Wall Street analysts to his own executives. It's rare to meet a person Case has encountered, even among those closest to him, who doesn't have some story of his inability to make a connection and his pervasive social awkwardness.

I've actually been collecting such stories over the years. My recent favorite was a Time Warner executive's painful tale of having to introduce the stiff Case to Lil' Kim, the bodacious rap singer of Time Warner's Atlantic label, at the Grammy Awards show in Hollywood in 2002. It's hard to imagine two more disparate personalities trying to find something to talk about. "It hurt my eyes to watch the encounter," moaned the executive.

One reason Case is hard to know is that he's a mass of contradictions. He professes not to care (and shows no indication that he does) when waves of critics deride AOL and even Case himself. Yet every once in a while, he has expressed deep hurt and bewilderment in emotional emails whipped out after a minor slight. He has been lauded for his ability to delegate, as well as for his willingness to listen and amend his views. Yet he can be astonishingly pig-headed when he thinks he's right.

Case is usually modest and soft-spoken about what he's achieved, yet, as one major investor who's dealt with him describes it, "He's got Tourette's syndrome of arrogance. He acts humble . . . but then he bursts out with these arrogant comments." This odd combination of superciliousness and standoffishness would prove to be critically damaging to his ability to lead at AOL Time Warner later.

I have probably spent more time interviewing him than any other reporter. Yet even now, when people ask me what he's like, I pause, realizing I can't really describe him. Usually, I rely on the crutch of anecdotes, such as those resulting from my attempts to get him to do interviews for my first book, which focused on AOL's early days.

Despite promises to the contrary to be open and accessible, Case had reneged on his vow and suddenly proved reluctant to talk. I spent four long, frustrating months trying to convince him to submit to an interview. I'd tangled with obstructive PR people, sent insistent emails, cajoled and pleaded to be seen, and even resorted to bringing fresh pies to entice cooperation. Basically, I stalked him.

He'd already talked to me several times before, for stories I'd written for the *Washington Post*. But now that I had a book to write, he kept fending me off in that wary, sarcastic way I would come to know so well. This was partly due to a lot of things, including a divorce he was going through and concern over how his family would be addressed in the book. But partly, I think, it was because Steve Case didn't feel the need to explain himself. And he didn't care what anyone thought of him until pressed by advisers to do so.

Then, one day, he finally agreed to an interview, many months after he had promised to cooperate. We set the date: December 11, 1996. It happened to be my birthday. That morning, I drove out to Dulles in freezing rain and sleet, hunched over the steering wheel and squinting through the windshield. I pulled into the AOL parking lot and ran inside the headquarters building, drenched. When I walked into Case's fifth-floor office, escorted by a public relations person, I found him peering out his window at the downpour.

"I was just looking out at this rain," he said in a dreamy tone, "and thinking, 'If she gets in a fiery wreck on the way out here, I won't have to do the interview!'" He then turned to face me, a half-smile on the placid mask of his face. "Oh," he added cheerily. "Happy birthday!"

The PR person stuttered out some feeble attempt to smooth over this horrid remark. And yet, it actually made me like him a lot more. I sat down and opened my notebook.

Island Boy Wonder

Stephen McConnell Case was born to be an entrepreneur.

By now, the story of the boy-wonder salesman Steve Case has passed into AOL mythology. Born in Hawaii to a lawyer father and schoolteacher mother, he was raised in an upper-middle-class family of comfort and privilege. Steve was always close to his brother Dan, who was just 13 months older. The brothers were outwardly different—Steve was shy and intense, while Dan was outgoing, glib, and charming—but they shared a precocious entrepreneurial streak. Adopting the name "Case Enterprises," and calling their bedrooms their "offices," the brothers undertook several fledgling businesses, including selling limeade and magazine subscriptions.

To me, this boyhood focus on making money and doing deals always seemed a bit odd, but it gave the Case brothers a kind of all-American geek patina and a raft of stories they could recount over and over as the pair got more famous. It certainly makes for a good tale, with all sorts of premonitions of greatness. In reality, it was a lot less elaborate.

But in the first part of this story, Dan was the clear star of the family, forcing Steve to differentiate himself to stand out. One way Steve did that was by choosing hobbies that Dan had shown no interest in, such as photography and journalism. Another was the music business, which Steve discovered in his teens. He began writing typically positive music reviews for the student paper, *Ka Punahou,* at Honolulu's exclusive Punahou School, and he entered into a happy cycle of getting free tickets and albums as well as backstage access at concerts when he told promoters he wrote for the largest student paper in Hawaii. Dan Case later joked to me that this was Steve's "first pyramid scheme."

After graduation, Case enrolled at Williams College in Massachusetts, his father's alma mater, shunning Princeton University because Dan was a student there. He expanded his efforts in the music business, promoting concerts and arranging events at the college. He even fronted his own bands, called The The and The Vans. Despite, or perhaps because of, his involvement in extracurricular activities, Case was mostly a B student. Ironically enough, the course he hated most of all was computer programming.

Yet even in that era of clunky computers, dot-matrix printers, and 300-baud modems, he was already fascinated with the idea of how interactive technology might change the way people live. In 1980, when he began applying for postcollege jobs, he wrote a remarkably forward-thinking essay to include with his applications. "I firmly believe," Case wrote, "that technological advances in communications (especially two-way cable systems) will result in our television sets (big-screen, of course!) becoming an information line, newspaper, school, computer, referendum machine, and catalog."

It sounded like a blueprint for the Full Service Network, Time Warner's experimental interactive cable service that would launch in the early 1990s. And, in fact, the 21-year-old Case applied for a job at HBO in 1980—the division of Time Inc. that Gerald Levin had headed. In one of history's delicious near misses, Case didn't get the job and the two men didn't meet. Instead, Case took a job in Ohio with Procter & Gamble, where he would learn marketing by developing campaigns for hopelessly mundane products. P&G was the training ground where Case learned the marketing skills he would later bring to AOL. But not surprisingly, he was soon bored with this job. He hated the constraints of big-company life, so when Pizza Hut offered him a position as "manager of new development," he jumped.

His work at Pizza Hut was only marginally sexier, providing yet another good tale for the storybook rise of Steve Case. For Pizza Hut, he traveled all over the country, sampling regional specialties and considering how they might fare atop pizzas (in a nod to his roots in Hawaii, he soon suggested pineapple chunks). But, once again, this position felt like a lead weight to the ambitious young marketing man.

One reason for his boredom was that Pizza Hut had sent him to live in the American Siberia of Wichita, Kansas. Years later, when I asked him what was the best thing to do in Wichita, since I planned to stop there on a cross-country trip, he told me, "See it in your rearview mirror." Wichita was clearly no place for a lonely, single young man stuck in a post he felt was beneath his talents. But soon enough, Case discovered a unique outlet for his restless feelings.

Case bought a boxy Kaypro computer and painstakingly configured it to log on to The Source, a fledgling online service. With that, he was suddenly able to tap into a whole new world, communicating with dozens of other users in far-flung places. Years later, he would paint the same lonely picture for almost every story written about those early days, a genius in exile miraculously touched by digital lightning.

But for the shy and awkward Case, the ability to reach out online from the darkness of his lonely life in Kansas must have been a powerful influence. So it was perhaps inevitable that he would find a way to get a job in this new, exciting medium. He was helped in this endeavor by his brother, Dan, who by that time—after earning Phi Beta Kappa honors at Princeton and winning a Rhodes scholarship—had become a rising star at the investment firm Hambrecht & Quist in San Francisco.

In 1983, Dan introduced Steve to one of his clients, a colorful and eccentric entrepreneur named Bill Von Meister who lived in the Virginia suburbs just outside of Washington, D.C. It was here that Von Meister—not Steve Case, despite what most people think now—had planted the seed that would later grow into AOL.

They Shoot Founders, Don't They?

Bill Von Meister was a classic serial entrepreneur. He loved to start businesses, and he was terrible at seeing them through to maturity. He was a thrill addict, a man who loved fast cars and expensive wines, and whose free-spirited nature made him both endearing and maddening to those who worked with him. He died before I could ever meet him, but his personality came alive in the vivid memories of those who knew him well. Von Meister was the kind of character reporters tend to love, and interviewing people about him always made me smile. Even dead, the man was highly entertaining.

Silicon Valley venture capitalist Frank Caufield, who invested $100,000 in one of Von Meister's early schemes, described him as "like that cartoon character in *Who Framed Roger Rabbit?*—he wasn't bad; he was just drawn that way." Indeed, everything about Von Meister was extreme, from his gold jewelry to his endless chain of cigarettes, his huge appetite for food, and his beefy facial features.

His ideas were also excessive. Unconstrained by any kind of self-censorship, he spewed forth schemes both visionary and absurd. Some of his more marketable ideas included Light Alert, a device that allowed night watchmen to turn on store lights by shining a flashlight through the windows; and the Home Music Store, a way of delivering music into homes via satellites and cable that he hoped to launch with investments from the 1970s icons, the Osmond family.

More important for the early history of the commercial Internet, he was also the founder of The Source—the online service that had so captivated Steve Case in his Wichita apartment. But as with so many of his ventures, Von Meister lost control of that business after spending too much money and exhausting the patience of his investors.

Still, Von Meister—whose ideas often blended practicality and whimsy, generally with some kind of online component thrown in—was always on the lookout for the Next Big Thing. "Let's take another run around the rosebush!" he'd bark at investors, usually with a glass of Chivas Regal held high. As former Imagic vice president Brian Dougherty, one of Von Meister's many investors, described him, he was the perfect combination of "P. T. Barnum and a technologist in the same body."

When Steve Case walked into his life, Von Meister was busy launching his latest product, called the GameLine Master Module, at his new company, Control Video Corporation (CVC). The idea was to create a device that would allow users of the Atari 2600 video game machine to download games over telephone lines. Despite the fact that the product itself didn't yet exist, Von Meister had arranged for a splashy debut for the concept at the Consumer Electronics Show in 1983. With characteristic ebullience, he rented a room at the Tropicana, enlisted a few showgirls to spice things up, raffled off a gold bar, and loudly trumpeted GameLine as the newest video game sensation. Inspired by Malcolm Forbes, he also used precious marketing dollars to fly a hot air balloon with GameLine's logo on it outside the hotel. Von Meister—referencing the hot cable channel made popular by AOL's future president Bob Pittman—bragged that it would soon be the "MTV of video games."

Watching from the back of the room as Von Meister laid out his GameLine vision, 24-year-old Steve Case was entranced. Dan Case had invited his younger brother to the show just for fun, but Steve ended up deep in conversation later at a dinner with Von Meister, who in turn was impressed with the young marketing man's insights. A bit drunk and always spontaneous, Von Meister approached Dan in the men's room and asked if it would be all right to hire Steve as a consultant for CVC. "Go ahead," said Dan. "But since I'm his brother, just leave me out of it." Giving a job to the brother of a major investor was not a bad move, so Steve Case began his career with the company he'd one day turn into the behemoth of the media and entertainment world.

In those early days, however, in its small headquarters in northern Virginia, it seemed more likely that tiny CVC would simply go bust. Despite all the hype and excitement in Las Vegas, GameLine soon proved to be an expensive dud when the Atari comet flamed out as the video games market peaked. By the time Case made plans to go full-time with the company, GameLine sales were abysmal and CVC was burning cash at an unsustainable rate. The venture sold only 2,400 modules out of the 75,000 manufactured—and had spent $9 million doing so. "You'd think [customers] would have shoplifted more," grumbled Caufield.

The increasingly dire situation at CVC made Case's jump from his traditional company job look like a poor choice. Both his father and his brother advised him not to take a full-time position at CVC. "Job hoppers don't wind up anywhere," his father warned him, "and this new job seems a little crazy." But Case, who had a stubborn streak, was adamant. He joined the company full-time in August of 1983—just in time for the meltdown.

Over that winter, the CVC investors took a hard look at where the company was headed. Turnaround executive Bob Cross, brought in to assess the company's chances, quickly dubbed it "Out-of-Control Video" after getting a look at the numbers. Trying to get spending under control, the company laid off all but a dozen employees. Case was kept simply because he was paid the least among the marketing team and he worked hard. Soon enough, the profligate Von Meister would also lose his job. He was effectively sacked after ordering himself a brand-new luxury car, then having it delivered to the office parking lot at the same time angry creditors were due to arrive for negotiations.

Over the next decade, as his protégé Steve Case transformed himself from green young marketer to an online icon, Bill Von Meister took a few more "runs around the rosebush" with various new products. But after the CVC debacle, he always had trouble getting sizable investments, and he never managed to hit the big time with any of his ideas. In the mid-1990s, he was diagnosed with an aggressive cancer. Irrepressible even in illness, he suggested new business ideas to his doctors in the middle of his treatment.

Bill Von Meister died in May of 1995, practically broke and all but forgotten. His brief obituary in the *Washington Post* made no mention of his having founded the company that became AOL. And when Steve Case spoke at his funeral, saying that without Von Meister, there would have been no AOL, even Von Meister's children had no idea what he was talking about.

Looking back at Von Meister's life, no one could have blamed him if he'd watched the ascent of AOL and Steve Case with some bitterness. But one of his business collaborators, John Kerr, later told me the opposite was true.

"He left behind a series of miserable SOBs who benefited from his ideas," Kerr said. "And yet he was always looking forward to tomorrow's sunshine in the middle of a monsoon."

Backing the Wrong Horse

If Von Meister found sunshine everywhere, Jim Kimsey, the man who replaced him at CVC's helm, saw something darker. To him, the company had no clear product and no apparent market. Creditors hovered, its backers were tapped out, and the dispirited employees questioned its very viability.

But Kimsey liked a good fight. A West Point graduate and Vietnam veteran who'd started a second career as a successful bar owner, Kimsey was a man of a certain breed. Handsome and self-confident, he was at home in power-lunch steak houses. His deep voice was resonant of the tawny timbre of expensive cigars and cognac, and his reputation as a ladies' man was well established. In fact, he was usually the one who talked that up, often in the highly ribald terms he used to describe pretty much everything about himself.

Kimsey was, in short, a throwback—a classic man's man. And in 1984, he was determined not to have his good reputation sullied by the crash and burn of this little business he'd been talked into trying to save. Kimsey had gotten involved with CVC at the request of his fellow West Point grad and close friend Frank Caufield, a venture capitalist who thought the company needed a sterner hand. But with the company teetering on the brink of bankruptcy, Kimsey realized what a mess he'd gotten into. CVC was like "Br'er Rabbit and the Tar Baby," he said. And now that he'd gotten his hands sticky, he couldn't see a way to get free of it.

There were not many options, although the team tried to put up a good front in a corporate outline in July 1984 that described a broader new service to push to the consumer entertainment, education, home productivity, and interactive home services. It was still GameLine, but dressed up into a new set of costumes and redubbed MasterLine.

What followed was a series of just-in-time deals that barely kept CVC solvent. As it would end up doing so often in its history, the company tried desperately to leap from one teetering ice floe to another to save itself from sinking. In one deal, CVC burned through $5 million of Bell South's money in a failed bid to create an at-home subscription service. The next deal was to help create a private-label online service for Commodore International Ltd., maker of the Commodore 64 computer. More important, Commodore was also the largest manufacturer of modems, which would be critical to any MasterLine rollout.

Both deals allowed CVC to keep hanging in there, but the company continued to be dogged by its less-than-stellar reputation and massive debts. So Bob Cross quietly arranged to phase out CVC, which would in turn be replaced by a new company untainted by the failures of the past. Quantum Computer Services Inc. was incorporated in May of 1985, and over the coming months, CVC was allowed simply to wither as its business was transferred to Quantum. "We put it in a drawer and it just disappeared, *poof,*" Kimsey confided to me in 1997 in a conspiratorial whisper that made him seem like a Mafia don who had ordered a hit.

In homage to the company's new name, the online service developed for Commodore was dubbed Q-Link. It would cost $9.95 a month (plus 6 cents a minute in premium areas), and would offer news, games, and even a rudimentary chat area called People Connection. The service would run only at night, so programmers could fix ever-present glitches during the day.

On November 1, 1985, at 6 P.M., Q-Link went live. That night, 24 users got online—a rousing success that the staff toasted with cheap champagne. But soon after that, Q-Link suffered its first service outage, on a night when 60 users logged on simultaneously. The outage marked the beginning of the long battle for scalability, a techie term for getting a service to work without problems as the numbers of users increase. That struggle would continue long after Quantum's successor company—America Online—had millions more customers than anyone would ever have dreamed.

Q-Link continued to add members, reaching 10,000 by January of 1986, but its growth was too slow to satisfy Commodore. Worried that Quantum's fate was too closely linked to Commodore's whims, Case insisted that the company explore new partnerships. He wanted to start with Apple Computer. The problem was that Apple already had a deal with General Electric Information Services (GEIS) for its dealer network online service. It also had its own Apple II areas on the granddaddy of all online services, CompuServe, which had been founded as a computer time-sharing company in 1969.

Nonetheless, in late 1986, Case moved to Cupertino, California, where Apple was headquartered, so he could harass the company in person every day. He approached several divisions simultaneously, figuring if he could get in good with one, he'd have the foothold he needed. He even somehow finagled himself a desk in the Apple head-quarters, then posted a sign above it that read, "Steve Held Hostage." For three months, he parked himself at Apple, trying to beg, cajole, annoy, or charm his way into a deal.

Apple's customer service division finally gave in, offering Quantum the opportunity to build AppleLink Personal Edition, a private consumer online service for its Apple II computer. With that, Case had landed the biggest deal of his life. He then rushed straight to rival computer maker Tandy, using the Commodore and Apple deals to convince them to take on Quantum as well.

Quantum's success was short-lived. Within less than two years, the partnership with Apple soured, because the two companies had vastly different ideas about how to develop and market the service. Apple executives, for example, were aghast at AOL's suggestion that the soft-ware be distributed for free to get people on the service. And Quantum was unable to afford the kind of fancy features and elegant marketing that Apple envisioned as being important to maintaining its brand.

Case felt he had to put up with the problems, since his aim had always been to win the ultimate prize of becoming the partner for the online service that would be linked to Apple's new flagship Macintosh computer. But given the friction and the middling results from AppleLink, it soon became clear that Quantum wouldn't be getting the Macintosh deal. And when results were unimpressive for the Tandy and Commodore platforms as well, things began to look very grim once again.

The failure of these partnerships prompted a few Quantum board members to push Kimsey to fire Steve Case. He'd taken the company out on this limb, they argued, and now everyone was paying for it. But Kimsey refused. He'd developed a kind of paternal feeling toward Case. Later, they would tangle for control—with Kimsey carping as Case rose higher and higher, and Case chafing over Kimsey's tendency to take too much credit for AOL's success. But at the time, Kimsey rightly understood that he and Case had complementary skills, and he knew the company would need both of them in order to succeed.

So he convinced the investors to give Case another chance. In characteristically colorful terms, he told them, "You don't take a twenty-five-pound turkey out of the oven and throw it away before it's done."

It was clear that Quantum's partnership with Apple was ending. But in an unusual stroke of luck, a paragraph buried in the original agreement gave Quantum the rights to use the Apple logo for its online service. If Apple wanted to create another online service with another partner, it could do so—but Quantum could legally stop the company from using its own Apple logo.

Naturally, Apple wanted its precious logo back. So Kimsey offered it to them—for $2.5 million. Apple was forced to pay up, and with this cash infusion, Quantum was once again barely saved from the ash heap of history.

Such middling muddling was far away from the power canyons of New York and Time Inc., where Jerry Levin had enjoyed huge success at popularizing a new pay cable station called Home Box Office, or HBO, which went live in November of 1972. He was now busy trying to push the staid media company to even greater heights, by involving it in fledgling online efforts such as an interactive news delivery product called teletext. He'd also begun noodling on the idea of how to create a massive "entertainment-oriented communications company." Tiny Quantum was nowhere on his radar screen.

A-O-Hell

In fact, by the end of the 1980s, it was a minor miracle that Quantum was still alive. But what would the company do? It had made hash of its partnerships, its ability to use the AppleLink name was coming to an end, and it still had no real identity of its own. The company was like a starving parasite, latching on to bigger companies and hoping to fill up before being flicked rudely away.

But the end of the Apple partnership also offered the perfect opportunity to establish a new business direction. Quantum would continue running the online service it had built—but it would no longer carry the AppleLink name. So in October 1989, Case announced a company contest: What should Quantum rename its online service? The suggestions that came in—Crossroads, Explore, and Infinity—sounded like drug-treatment programs or new car brands. Dismissing them all, Case offered a bland creation of his own: America Online. Other staffers understandably derided it as hokey, but Case voted his suggestion the winner anyway.

Case also wanted to add a friendly, more personalized touch to the service. "We wanted people to think they were members and not customers," he explained. "That was important, because we needed to be different than big, faceless services."

He also hit on the idea of attaching voice files to the software with cheery little sound bites that would make the service feel homey. The team settled on four phrases: "Welcome," "You've got mail," "File's done," and "Good-bye." A customer service representative named Karen Edwards had mentioned that her husband, Elwood, was a professional broadcaster, so for testing purposes, Case asked if Elwood might read those four phrases into a cassette tape. The test tape was put into use, and now Elwood Edwards, quite by chance, has one of the most listened-to voices on the planet.

By the beginning of 1990, Case had, in effect, been running the company for several years. But it wasn't until January of 1991, nearly eight years after he'd joined the company, that Case was officially named its president. Now in his early thirties, he was maturing into a confident young executive, and America Online, having recently broken the 100,000-user mark, was maturing as well. Quantum had also recently signed a lucrative deal with IBM to run their private online service. It seemed that the growing little company had managed to right itself.

Not surprisingly, suitors soon came calling. Jim Kimsey had already fielded a few queries from potential buyers, including Prodigy and AT&T. But now, in the late winter of 1991, he received a more serious offer from the then-Goliath of the online world: CompuServe. For $50 million, CompuServe said it would take the Tar Baby off Kimsey's hands. By just about any standard, CompuServe's offer was generous; with fewer than 150,000 users, revenues of only about $20 million, and negligible profits, Quantum couldn't reasonably expect a bigger price tag. Kimsey was leaning toward accepting the offer, a sensible move that would achieve decent, though not spectacular, returns for the investors.

But Steve Case had no interest in cashing out and going merrily on to whatever the next project might be, because he had turned from a quiet worker bee into an online evangelist. Online services and AOL in particular, he believed, could change the very nature of how people communicated. Case thought selling out at the very beginning of this revolution would be more than just a missed opportunity—it would be a travesty. He told Kimsey that he'd quit if the company was sold to CompuServe. Many of the staffers, now loyal acolytes to Case and his lofty dream, threatened to do the same.

Kimsey still wanted to sell, but he knew the $50 million offer—as generous as it was—was simply not enough to beat Case's arguments with the board. At that amount, the investors would get some money back, but not very much. Reluctantly, he turned down the offer. "We stayed open for business this long," he said he thought to himself. "So, why not go just a little further?" If CompuServe had upped its offer to $60 million, Kimsey would tell me in 1996, the deal would have been done. Instead, Quantum would now push on toward the next level independently.

But it wouldn't get there as Quantum. At trade shows, Quantum's executives kept finding that no one had heard of the company, until they mentioned they were the ones who ran America Online. Pretty soon, it made more sense to introduce themselves as being from AOL rather than Quantum. So in October of 1991, the company officially changed its name to America Online Inc. It was a critical juncture in the company's history—finally deciding to go it alone and create a new brand name.

The company would use its new name when it went public in March of 1992, a time when there was no World Wide Web, no "Internet economy," and no hint of the market madness soon to come. So it's perhaps not surprising that AOL had trouble finding an investment firm willing to take it on. While only a few years later a youthful face and an ability to lose money hand over fist was the formula for success, Steve Case had to contend with a market that frowned on concept companies like AOL.

And Case's youth was a real problem for AOL's public offering. To boost the company's chances, the board decided AOL needed to present a more "mature" face to the firms. So even though Case had been made CEO in late 1991, the board decided to strip his title and install the suave and graying Kimsey in his place. Kimsey was tasked with breaking the news, which he did over lunch at a restaurant called Clyde's.

"Steve had an Elmer Fudd expression on his face," Kimsey recalled, in a demeaning quote he delighted in repeating frequently over the years. "He could have quit over it, but he handled it perfectly." It was a classic example of a trait Case has always shown in abundance: His uncanny ability to ignore the slights, unpleasantness, and criticism of the moment by keeping his focus on the ultimate goal. Though others in the company, angry at the demotion, urged him to fight or even quit, Case refused and simply swallowed the insult.

After initially taking a pass, investment firm Alex. Brown & Sons eventually agreed to take AOL public. On March 19, 1992, the company offered two million shares on the NASDAQ stock market, at $11.50 a share. By the close of the market, nearly all of AOL's 116 employees were rich. Jim Kimsey's shares alone were worth more than $3.2 million, and Steve Case's stock was worth $2 million. With that, the wild ride of AOL stock had begun. Over the next seven years, the share price would soar as the stock split multiple times.

For Jerry Levin and Time Inc., which had just completed its rocky merger with Warner Communications, the entertainment giant, the opposite would be true. Despite predictions of greatness, the company limped along due to severe corporate culture clashes and an inability to make the two businesses mesh as promised. The situation was made worse given that the stock of Time Warner would essentially flat-line until almost the end of the 1990s. The contrast in the behavior of the two companies' stock prices would play a huge role later on when AOL and Time Warner came together. AOL's soaring stock would allow it to have the upper hand in the deal, fueling a sense of resentment on the part of Time Warner employees—and ripping open again a nasty wound left by the Warner deal that had never really healed in the first place.

The Battle of the Billionaires

In the six months following its IPO, AOL enjoyed a string of attention and successes. Its membership climbed above 200,000, influential *Wall Street Journal* columnist Walt Mossberg dubbed it "the sophisticated wave of the future" among online services, and major investors began pouring big money into the company.

One of those investors was Paul G. Allen, cofounder of Microsoft. "Paul thought those guys were on to something," Bill Savoy, his right-hand man, told me in 1997. "It was the early stages of a hockey-stick kind of growth—it seemed as if they might be headed upward fast." At first, Case welcomed the attention, which he considered flattering.

Allen seemed like the perfect kind of investor for a long-term dreamer like Case. A burly, shy mogul with a bushy beard and deep-set eyes, Allen had transformed himself into a kind of "Johnny Apple-seed" of emerging technologies. He was obsessed with the coming boom in computer-based communications, and he spent his time and considerable finances on seeking out cutting-edge companies, even if they never made any money. AOL had caught his attention early, and he'd bought 50,000 shares at the IPO.

Over the next year, Allen continued to add to his holdings, with the aim of having a major influence at the company. But AOL, increasingly wary of Allen's ties to Microsoft and his intentions, wanted to limit his influence. So Case suggested a "standstill" agreement, whereby Allen would not increase his stake beyond 20 percent. Allen, one of the world's richest people, was not pleased to be dictated to by a dinky company like AOL. "We wanted AOL to play, and we were perplexed as to why we were not welcomed with open arms," Savoy said. "Paul considered it personally rude to him . . . so we just thought, 'Let's just go and buy the company.'"

When Allen began quickly increasing his stake, Case went into a panic. "It suddenly took on the tone of the Cuban Missile Crisis," he recalled in 1997. So on April 22, 1993, the board met and set a "poison pill"—an antitakeover defense that floods the market with new shares and makes it extraordinarily expensive to acquire control of a company—to keep Allen from buying more than 20 percent. Thinking the company was now safe, the board adjourned. But Allen had already blown past that threshold prior to the meeting, making the protective measure moot. The board needed to act immediately.

But Jim Kimsey and Frank Caufield had zipped off to New Orleans with a pair of dates for a weekend of partying at a jazz music festival. Getting them onboard for a new vote would prove difficult—and offer a comical moment at a crucial time. Because their cell phones got poor reception at the festival, Kimsey and Caufield were forced to race around a nearby low-income neighborhood trying to find a pay phone. When they found one, they commandeered it for the next half hour or so, mumbling "Yea . . . nay . . . yea," into the phone in response to board votes.

In his inimitable way, Kimsey described the reaction of the people waiting to use the phone: "There was a line of black people . . . behind us," he laughingly explained to me, "saying, 'I've got to call my mother and here are these two white boys talking about money!'" It was a typically tasteless comment from Kimsey, but one that would be added to the odd and evolving legend of AOL as a freewheeling corporation.

The board managed to set a new pill, and the crisis was averted just in time. Shortly afterward, Case, Kimsey, AOL's outside counsel Ken Novack, and Lazard Freres investment banker Steve Rattner traveled from Washington, D.C., to Washington state to meet with Allen. No offense, Case told him, but they just didn't want him, or any major investor, playing such a major role in the company. Allen, piqued, muttered, "This is America and I should be able to invest in AOL if I want to." But the company had successfully stymied him.

One victory won, Case and his team then traveled about a dozen miles down the road to meet with their second aggressive billionaire of the day: Bill Gates, the king of Microsoft. Gates, who had become the most powerful man in the computer industry with his ubiquitous software, was now belatedly turning his attention to the fast-growing new world of online services. He was a bit late, a full five years after Q-Link had launched and after AOL had already gained 250,000 members.

Nonetheless, he opened the meeting in his customarily logical, get-to-the-point way. "I can buy twenty percent of you or I can buy all of you," he told Case in his nasal whine. "Or I can go into this business myself and bury you." It was not a threat; it was a simple statement of what Bill Gates believed was a fact, uttered in a logical style he'd used many times before with other small companies like AOL. Interestingly, however, although many in the room that day remember Gates making this statement, Gates himself has since denied making it. But Microsoft was clearly prepared to enter the online business in a big way.

Gates's behavior put Case immediately on the defensive, and the discussions made little progress. "We didn't trust Microsoft's motives," Case said, "because we knew they could emerge as a major competitor." When the Microsoft side suggested a 50-50 merger, Case thought he knew what would follow. "It was, 'Okay, we'll help build it, teach you all about it, then just when it gets interesting, you'll shoot us.'" After about an hour, the meeting ended.

Though both sides gave lip service to the idea of continuing to explore options, it would never happen. The AOL board voted down the idea, even as Microsoft was pursuing another strategy that would spell big trouble for AOL. Out at its Redmond headquarters, Microsoft was starting to build its own online service, code-named Marvel and later renamed the Microsoft Network, or MSN.

At the same time, big media companies, notably Disney and Time Warner, were gearing up their own strategies to get in on this new game. As little AOL fended off Bill Gates in the spring of 1993, Time Warner was preparing to plunge into the interactive space with its Full Service Network (FSN) cable TV system—a project that would, executives hoped, push the company to the top of the emerging digital heap. Yet Time Warner's hopes for FSN would be dashed and the company would spend the next several years watching jealously as AOL stumbled upward to ever-greater heights in the new online world.

The Race Goes to the Swift

In the summer of 1993, AOL launched the controversial strategy that would propel it to the head of the pack among online services: The relentless, irritating—but hugely successful—mass marketing of AOL diskettes. Starting in the mid-1990s, you couldn't go anywhere without finding an AOL diskette on your seat, in your mailbox, in your box of flash-frozen steaks, at checkout counters.

Blame that on a smart, aggressive marketer named Jan Brandt. A Brooklyn native and career marketer, she got the idea for the mass distribution from a previous job, when she'd overseen the mailing of a free children's book to potential customers. Because so few people really knew or understood what online services were, she figured they wouldn't be willing to buy the software. So AOL would need to put it right in their hands.

In July 1993, Brandt asked Steve Case for permission to spend $250,000 on a direct-mail campaign. She recalls him telling her it wouldn't work. But she got permission, and thus began the very low-tech marketing blitz of hundreds of millions of disks that would make AOL a household name.

Between 1993 and 1994, the marketing worked too well and AOL saw a huge spike in the number of new users. It was so big that it threatened to kill the company, because the influx led to pervasive slowdowns in AOL's service. Everyone now knew who AOL was, all right—but they were calling it America On Hold rather than America Online. These types of slowdowns would happen with worrisome frequency at AOL, leading many to question the ethics of marketing a service it couldn't actually provide. It also led to another of AOL's many paradoxes: Everyone was complaining about the service, but people just kept signing on.

I did the same. I had had little experience online, save for the lame internal computer-based electronic mail system at the *Washington Post*. But when a friend moved to Russia in the summer of 1994, I signed up for AOL, because it was hard to find a cheaper way to communicate. AOL was a crude and simple service then, mostly looking like it was put together with a dot-matrix printer and a bad graphics team. I cannot say I was immediately overwhelmed by its virtues, although I did soon use it on a daily basis.

In fact, when my editor first approached me about reporting on AOL, my response was, "You mean the email company?" Still, I'd been covering workplace issues for the business section, a topic that had left me bored, so I jumped at the chance to switch to covering this small, local story at the end of 1994.

It was a lot more interesting right from the start, since AOL was a dubious proposition. The *Wall Street Journal* had already openly pondered its possible demise in a March 1994 piece that compared AOL to a fad like CB radios. And well-known research firms like Forrester were releasing reports showing that its high growth would soon slow to a crawl. There was one piece of good news that had little to do with AOL's talent: Its two main rivals, Prodigy and CompuServe, both turned out to be amazingly incompetent competitors.

Owned by the giant Missouri-based tax-preparation service H&R Block, CompuServe moved slowly and deliberately in a world that required brash, nimble leadership. The company made numerous mistakes. It refused to adapt itself to the vast potential market that was looking for a simple, fun way to get online. It positioned its product as "the information service you won't outgrow" and promoted it as a productive business tool rather than an exciting new way of communicating. It persisted in assigning cumbersome numbers as email addresses ("4956724@compuserve.com"), even as other services let users pick names. It was, in short, geek central.

And, even as AOL proved that simple and friendly was the way to go, CompuServe waited until the game was nearly over in early 1996 before it finally offered a non-business-oriented service—the oddly named Wow! That spring, a Wow! executive visited me at the *Washington Post* to show off the new service. It was easy to use, he raved, and consumer friendly. "Why don't you just make CompuServe easy to use and friendly?" I asked him.

Prodigy—the product of a joint venture between IBM and Sears—also suffered from a lack of vision and leadership. My favorite line about the service: It was everything IBM knew about retail and everything Sears knew about computing. Its executives knew even less—Prodigy CEO Ross Glatzer, for example, had an antiquated computer that ran on the DOS operating system and didn't even have a mouse. The company didn't offer a Windows version of its service until December 1993, because Microsoft was an archrival of parent company IBM. And its email system was so inferior that Scott Kurnit, an online industry executive brought in to help run the service, announced he would use his AOL account until Prodigy could come up with something as good.

The company did have some pioneering schemes, such as an online grocery delivery service. But it was an idea well before its time and it proved unsustainable. More important, Prodigy joined CompuServe in underestimating AOL, which was much better attuned to what average users wanted from their online experience. Perhaps the biggest problem Prodigy had was its reluctance to give users one of the main services they wanted: Chat. Because its parent companies were so stodgy, Prodigy wasn't allowed to offer chat—the engine driving AOL's growth—until 1994. As Kurnit said, "A corporate guy thought, 'Wow, someone could type the word 'fuck.'"

And it was mostly chat that was beginning to drive AOL's membership numbers into the stratosphere. The reason users came to and stayed with AOL was simple: The service made it possible to chat about anything at all, in near-total privacy. As Steve Case later put it, "Our bias was on creating tools, empowering people, and letting them use them in any way they thought appropriate—sort of 'Let a thousand flowers bloom.'" Not to mention "Let a few million more dollars into the coffers." Because AOL charged by the hour, the time users spent in chat rooms was terrifically lucrative for the company. It also created intense loyalty to AOL.

I saw an example of this on a visit to AOL in April of 1995, and it has stayed with me ever since. Desperate for any press for the company, AOL's Jean Villanueva, the head of communications for AOL and one of its highest ranking female executives, had invited me out to see Case meet with a group of quilters who had met through an online quilting chat group. Without ever having met one another, they had decided to make a quilt for Case. They designed it all online, placing a big AOL logo in the middle, and then parceled out duties to assemble it. Now they had come in person to northern Virginia to present it to Case.

When Villanueva pitched the story to me, I cringed. I had no intention of writing anything about this Norman-Rockwell-in-cyberspace moment. Between Case's delusions of grandeur and Villanueva's earnest efforts to paint the company as a "community," I was beginning to wonder if I'd stumbled into a cult. But when I walked into AOL's conference room and saw this group of older women—not one of whom I would have imagined could even turn on a computer—I was struck by their obvious enthusiasm for the medium and their bizarre familiarity with Steve Case.

Forcing cookies on him and pinching his cheeks, these digital quilters were the first indication to me that perhaps there might really be something to this online thing. These were not geeks, not techies, not the computer elite. They were simply like-minded people reaching out to make connections in a whole new way, much as a very young Steve Case had done years before in his little apartment in Wichita. They had never met one another, nor did they know Case. And yet they did—the direct result of this powerful new way to communicate.

Despite the heartwarming quilting scene, of course, it's true that most chatters weren't trading quilting tips. AOL soon became a hub for sex chat of every stripe—or, as I called it in *aol.com,* "The House That Sex Chat Built." AOL's anonymous screen names, unmonitored chat rooms, and easy attachment of graphical files also made it ideal for trading pornographic photos. Soon enough, the nightly list of "member-created" rooms on AOL began to resemble the personal ads in a sex magazine: "married M4M," "girls4men," and "submissive4you" were a few of the rooms that might be available on any given night.

Though they would increasingly try to position it as a family-friendly service, AOL knew full well the power of sex and had even once considered creating a separate gated adult service. AOLers were aware that its live-and-let-live attitude in its chat rooms set it apart from the other online services. Because of it, over the next two years, the company would quickly outdistance all its competitors. As one former Prodigy executive told me in 1996, AOL's privacy policy in chat rooms was "[the reason] why AOL has eight million members and Prodigy had faded to a shadow of its former self." In other words, precisely because on AOL someone could type the word *fuck.*

The Beast from Redmond

Despite the company's ability to press on through hard times, a new threat loomed just ahead: Microsoft's planned launch of a new online service, MSN, in 1995.

For one thing, it was a safe bet that MSN wouldn't make the same errors of Prodigy and CompuServe. For another, even if it did, it would have enough money to keep coming at AOL indefinitely. For AOL, the threat from the Microsoft monster was born of these simple truths—but defeating it required a bit of fantasy-making, too. So, like in any good fairy tale, AOL had a happy, clever hero who declared he could slay the beast. His name was Ted Leonsis.

Leonsis, born into a working-class Greek Orthodox family, had climbed his way up from being a shoe salesman to becoming an early marketing database entrepreneur. He'd also built a successful consulting career, and had landed at AOL in the summer of 1994 when it acquired his company, Redgate Communications. Ebullient, good-natured, and rotund, Leonsis was the kind of guy who caused faces to light up when he trundled down the hallway, bellowing greetings left and right. His drive to succeed was matched only by his overwhelming desire to be liked.

But his most important characteristic was that he was precisely the person AOL needed at this moment in time, despite the fact that the service had soared to 1.25 million members. As soon as Leonsis walked in the door, he became the company's chief anti-MSN cheerleader, whipping the AOL troops into a warlike frenzy. It was a job for which staid, unemotional Steve Case was spectacularly unsuited.

Leonsis began stirring things up immediately, leading the now legendary "dinosaur rally" at the Sheraton Premiere ballroom in Tysons Corner, Virginia, in November of 1994. First, he referenced a *Wired* magazine quote that declared that AOL was on the "scrap heap of history," "a dinosaur," and "obsolete." As hundreds of AOL employees roared their approval, Leonsis prowled the stage, shouting, "Someday, your children will ask you what you did in the war!" He declared finally that the online battle would be "Microsoft's Vietnam."

He noted that the rich, aggressive Gates was someone people loved to hate and he zeroed in on AOL's sympathetic role as underdog. For the 97 million U.S. citizens who were not online, AOL was the natural choice! "If not us, who?" Leonsis bellowed. "If not now, when?" He wound up the rally by declaring MSN the true dinosaur and exhorting the employees to come forward and sign their names to a cheap dinosaur wooden cutout he suddenly brandished. A crush of people surged forward, many with tears in their eyes.

AOL would also use less showy—but more underhanded—tactics, including pushing the Justice Department to stop Microsoft's online foray, pointing to the potentially monopolistic integration of MSN with its ubiquitous operating system. There was no proof this would give Microsoft any real advantage, but Steve Case, quite cleverly, warned against the dangers of letting the software giant own the "digital dial tone."

To further scare people and put Microsoft on the defensive by creating overblown expectations, Case and others made up massive estimates for MSN, claiming it was likely to sign up nine million subscribers in just one year. An exasperated Microsoft marketing executive called me during this time and sighed, "We don't have one customer yet and now we have to get nine million or look like losers." Case snickered quietly when I told him this later.

Still, AOL was genuinely scared. When MSN launched in August of 1995, AOL employees nervously rushed to check out the competition. Jean Villanueva had been using MSN's beta version for a few months, and it was so bad she was convinced that Microsoft was pulling a ruse. "We kept thinking some secret switch would be flipped, and the real service would come online," she remembered. But there was no secret switch: MSN was simply not very well designed. To begin, it was without a vibrant community element, its email was glitchy, and its interface was simplistic instead of simple. In addition, it was available only for those with the new Windows 95 software, which limited its audience drastically at the start. This kind of weak and underwhelming product launch was typical for Microsoft, which often took several iterations before getting it right.

Despite its reputation for getting it wrong in initial versions of its software and then improving it by the third cycle, MSN looked like it might take a while before it could even begin to compete with AOL. It was so bad, in fact, that the *Wall Street Journal*'s Walt Mossberg ranked it "dead last" in a column he wrote comparing the major services. Customers agreed, staying away in droves. In the first year, MSN drew only 375,000 members in its first three months. By comparison, AOL was then drawing 250,000 new members per month.

But even though AOL was widening the gap with every passing month, it didn't take long before the chorus of doomsayers began chirping again. If the canary of cyberspace wasn't going to be killed by CompuServe, Prodigy, or MSN, AOL would, the critics carped, be put out of business by the Internet itself. A new goofy technology term, *disaggregation,* had taken hold of the digerati, which posited that no one wanted bundled services when the Web was so full of free stuff.

AOL had always offered its own proprietary content, as well as chat rooms. But, as of late summer of 1995, it still didn't offer access to the nascent commercial Internet. By then, scores of critics were again predicting the company's demise. "The Internet is an ocean, and these online services are isolated ponds," declared James Gleick, a writer and founder of an early online service called Pipeline. "Their days arc numbered."

Others were even more definite about the fate of AOL. "Every day the Net gets closer to filling its ambitious promise, their clock ticks closer to midnight," wrote *Newsweek*'s Steven Levy. "They look a lot like dead men walking." This attitude was most pervasive in Silicon Valley, where everyone derided AOL as the "Internet on training wheels." And yet, I often wondered, if you want to ride a bicycle but have never done it before, wouldn't you want training wheels? The snooty attitude of the Net elite pointed up a pervasive problem among those who design computer products: Why was their presumption that complicated always equals better?

For his part, Steve Case was ready to prove that AOL could be all things to all people. If customers wanted Internet access, they'd get it. And at the same time, they'd have the homey, safe environment of the walled-in AOL content to fall back on. First, the marketer in him decided to use the simple trick of adding the word *Internet* to AOL's moniker as the "world's largest online company." And, to back it up in reality, he had undertaken a round of deals and acquisitions using AOL's overpriced stock. None of these deals ever amounted to much, but they were critical at the time to give AOL a Web image.

In a yearlong spree, AOL purchased BookLink Technologies Inc. (for its browser), NaviSoft Inc. (for its high-end Web publishing and development tools), and Advanced Network & Services (to build out its own network). Case also attempted to buy then-tiny Yahoo for $2 million, but he was rebuffed. And he tried to buy a substantial stake in Netscape Communications, the owner of the hottest Internet browser, as well, but CEO James Barksdale demurred.

Barksdale would soon feel the heat from AOL, though, as the company unveiled what would become another of its defining strategies: A hardball and even questionable negotiating style. This strategy became especially apparent during the "browser wars" of early 1996, when AOL negotiated with both Microsoft and Netscape to use their browsers, then stunned the online world with its decision.

Executives at Time Warner would have done well to pay attention to the browser fight. Five years later, following the AOL Time Warner merger, they would complain bitterly about two elements of AOL: The arrogance of its deal makers and their cutthroat negotiating style. Both were in plain view during this time, for anyone who cared to notice.

The Cowboy Culture

AOL's lead negotiator in the browser wars was a stubble-bearded, nasal-voiced tough guy named David Colburn. Despite the cowboy boots he always wore, Colburn had actually grown up in a tame Midwest suburb. But he had acquired a troubling swashbuckling reputation—one that would later cause a lot of trouble for AOL.

There was no question that Colburn, who'd come to AOL in the mid-1990s, was a savvy, smart deal maker, and a talented lawyer. Unfortunately, he also had become known as someone who took particular delight in tormenting whoever happened to be across the table from him. Getting a deal signed wasn't enough—Colburn had to extract the maximum amount of blood from the other side, many observed. And even that wasn't really enough. If he could get maximum blood and leave the other guy feeling frustrated and humiliated, his growing myth posited, that was a truly excellent deal.

When I first interviewed him in 1996, Colburn smiled craftily as he teasingly tortured the PR person who accompanied me. "Can I say 'fucking asshole' when I refer to him?" he queried her, referring to one of his competitors, trying to get a rise out of her. "Or just 'asshole'?" He kibitzed about whom I had interviewed before I saw him, providing me with a ribald running commentary about exactly what he thought of each of them, which was actually pretty accurate. "You've heard I'm a real jerk, a real big jerk," he needled me with a sly grin.

I didn't find him so, but others would consider him extremely difficult. That included Netscape, which was relying on AOL to keep their market share dominant. Despite having bought BookLink for its browser, AOL sought to make a deal to get one of the two best-known browsers—either Microsoft's Explorer or Netscape's Navigator. The choice was an important one for the industry, since AOL was fast becoming the way most average people jumped onto the Internet.

Netscape was the obvious choice. It had become the first wunderkind of the Internet age following its astonishingly successful IPO on August 5, 1995. On that date, which most mark as the beginning of the Internet economy mania, Netscape offered five million shares at $28 each, then saw its stock price double by day's end. The tiny company was suddenly worth billions.

Microsoft was, of course, AOL's sworn enemy, and some simply couldn't fathom the idea of a Microsoft-AOL alliance. "After what we had just been through with MSN," Ted Leonsis recalled, "the idea of doing a deal with Microsoft was just out of the question."

Yet David Colburn felt differently. "I didn't care what the hell Silicon Valley thought, or that Microsoft was the anti-Christ, or that Netscape was so cool," he told me in 1997. "I only thought, 'Who's got what we need?'" At the time and as usual, Colburn was looking for the best deal for AOL.

Negotiations went on through the first few months of 1996. There were numerous points of discussion, and on many of them Microsoft was coming out ahead. Netscape wouldn't alter its browser to suit AOL's needs, for example—and Microsoft would. Netscape wanted AOL to pay for its browser on a per-user basis—and Microsoft offered Explorer for free. Microsoft even offered the ultimate come-on: A folder on the Windows 95 desktop with an AOL icon inside.

These were all significant factors, but the one that might have pushed it over the edge for a guy like Colburn was Netscape's arrogance. "Netscape thought we had nowhere else to go," Colburn told me. "It was like, 'AOL has to do a deal with us.'" By comparison, Microsoft was downright humble. Bill Gates himself even called Steve Case to try to move the deal along.

Even so, on March 11, 1996, AOL announced it had reached a deal with Netscape. Wall Street reacted with excitement, sending Netscape's stock up 16 percent that day. Gleeful Netscape executives spun the deal as a slap at Microsoft. But they only got a day of glory. On March 12, AOL made the announcement that stunned the online world. In a conference call he conducted with Bill Gates, Steve Case announced, "Microsoft will become our primary technology partner in this Internet space."

Colburn and his team had negotiated a nonexclusive arrangement with the Netscape team, which had apparently never considered the notion that AOL might make deals with both companies. Colburn, many Netscape executives insisted to me later, had point-blank denied he would ever do a Microsoft deal when they asked directly. Colburn, in turn, told me he never said that, and that Netscape officials had only assumed AOL would not. Whatever the truth was, prior to the announcement, Steve Case had called Netscape's Jim Barksdale to break the news. Though Barksdale, the consummate southern gentleman, responded politely, he told me later he'd felt totally sandbagged.

AOL, as exemplified by David Colburn, had played this deal as close to the edge as it would go. It hadn't done anything illegal or, some would argue, even unethical in the browser wars. But it had turned and stung a friendly partner for their own gain. Was this a sleazy tactic—or simply a smart business move? Whatever it was, Wall Street loved it, sending AOL's stock up another 15 percent to $55.50. And that—in a pattern that would become way too familiar—was too soon all that AOL cared about.

Colburn's role in the AOL Time Warner merger, as well as other AOL deal makers, would involve similar borderline behavior. In retrospect, the Netscape browser debacle foreshadowed a deal-making style that would raise serious questions later. At the time, though, it would be glossed over, seen more as an overly aggressive move made by a fast-growing company. By the end of 1995, AOL was nearing the five million member mark, doubling its size in less than one year. Its stock was climbing, its brand recognition was expanding, and the executive team was working together smoothly.

But as usual at AOL, things never seemed to go well for very long before some new worry set in.

Online Soap Opera

In the first week of March 1996, Steve Case and Jean Villanueva informed the company's board that they were embarking on a personal relationship. This was trouble for several reasons. For one thing, both Case and Villanueva were still married to others (though separated from their respective spouses). For another, Villanueva—who was AOL's powerful head of communications—planned to continue working at the company. Yet how could she, when Case would obviously not be able to manage her objectively? And how would the other executives react to this strange new balance of power?

Gossip about the relationship flew through the halls at AOL. And the situation was made even more volatile because of the personalities involved. Villanueva, a sometimes-prickly and tough-minded executive, had long served as a kind of lightning rod for Case, deflecting criticism and taking on many of the tasks that might make him look bad. "It was a damn difficult issue, which went right to the question of Steve's judgment," one board member told me at the time, comparing it to a popular soap opera drama on television. "I thought I had walked into the middle of *Melrose Place.*"

Both Case and Villanueva were extremely sensitive about how their new relationship would be perceived. Villanueva chose to break the story by telling me about it in the spring of 1996, at a lunch where I thought we were going to talk about an upcoming deal to bundle AOL with a new AT&T online access service. I figured she and Case had decided to tell me to better control the news. Perplexed at what to do with this unusual development, since I was a business reporter, I passed it to the *Washington Post*'s gossip columnist, who broke the story under the headline "AOL's Love Connection." The romance would garner coverage in *People* magazine and even in a cover story on the rise of AOL and Case in *Business Week*. The items irked Case, as did most reporting about his personal life.

To calm him down, Dan Case teased his brother that he had bigger worries, observing that, "The joke is that once you're on the cover of *Business Week,* that's just when your stock is about to drop." Unfortunately, his teasing would prove prophetic. Though AOL's stock was soaring and the numbers were good, new signs of trouble were arising. Membership growth was slowing again, the result of an industry phenomenon called churn. In increasing numbers, new customers would try AOL, then dump it in favor of another service.

AOL's strategy for the past three years had been growth at any cost. Case had always seen these early years of the online industry as a land grab, believing it would never be easier or cheaper to get new members. "We want more audience," he would tell the *Wall Street Journal* in August of 1996. "We're willing to sacrifice short-term profitability to long-term leadership." Yet the company was now having trouble holding on to those very members they had fought to sign up. According to one top executive, the monthly churn rate was 6 percent—meaning the annual turnover rate of members was an astonishing 72 percent.

There were several possible reasons for this, but one loomed above all others: The ticking clock. Unlike some other Internet service providers, which had begun to offer unlimited Internet access for a flat monthly fee, AOL continued to charge hourly rates for time spent on the service. Many people were willing to pay, either to use the chat rooms or to keep their email addresses, among other reasons. But, increasingly, many more were not. And AOL would— sooner or later—have to find a way to compete with those flat-fee services. The problem was that either way AOL turned, it would lose. If the company went to flat-fee pricing, it would lose the lucrative hourly fees that kept its revenues high. If it didn't, it would lose customers.

There simply was no middle ground. Fears turned ugly after Microsoft started to ready a flat-fee plan and revamped service with a TV-like style, and AOL's president of only four months, former FedEx executive Bill Razzouk, left the company. He had been brought in to bring discipline to AOL, and now it seemed that he had left under uncertain circumstances. He had actually been let go by Case after repeatedly clashing with others in the freewheeling culture, but it looked very bad at the time.

AOL's stock dove from a high of $71 in May to $24 by the end of the summer. *Wall Street Journal* columnist Chris Byron wrote what a lot of more conservative number crunchers had long been grumbling about as they watched the rise of AOL's market value. This was the moment, Byron hoped, "when the last great investment zit of the 20th century gets popped."

While AOL was trying to put a better spin on things—by launching a pricey new marketing campaign, announcing it was going to go into the business of creating private intranets for companies, and even shifting itself to the more stable New York Stock Exchange from the wilder NASDAQ—the company was still fighting a perception that it was simply a flash in the pan. The *Washington Post's* David Hilzenrath said it best in a front-page article in September of 1996. Noting that AOL was a company on the brink, he wrote: "The brink of greatness. Or the brink of irrelevance."

AOL had managed to come this far—but was it doomed to fail anyway?

The Night the Lights Went Out in Virginia

By this time, I'd been covering AOL for less than two years, but I'd already been witness to several cycles of dizzying ascents and sickening drops. I remember wondering if there was ever a dull moment at this company and thinking it would make a great book, since it was the best example of the pains and triumphs in the birth of a new medium.

To me, it seemed as if writing about AOL was like being in the front seat at the start of the television industry. AOL represented the best and the worst at the same time—sometimes ugly, sometimes comic, sometimes tragic, sometimes a bit sleazy, and always riveting. And it was the place where I thought the online world was about to move from being a fad to a necessity.

In fact, I can trace that realization to a precise date: August 19, 1996. That was the day AOL suffered its epic blackout. It was an event that at first seemed devastating to the company, but that later seemed like a strange sort of blessing.

Short outages weren't uncommon for AOL, and the service had been scheduled for routine maintenance that day, so no one on the tech team seemed too worried when it didn't immediately come back up. As the morning hours ticked by and no one could figure out what was wrong, however, panic set in quickly. All over the country, people at home and at work were unable to get their email, check their stock quotes, or send important documents online. And they were getting plenty angry about it.

Throughout the day, CNN covered the outage, and promos for the local evening news shows kept viewers apprised of AOL's status. At the company's new headquarters—an antiseptic concrete-and-glass office building perched in a field in rural Dulles, Virginia—Villanueva and the public relations staff struggled to field calls from reporters. It was a media nightmare, of course. No one had any idea why the blackout had happened or when the service might be up and running again. The only piece of good news was that AOL had been able to determine that the outage was not the work of hackers.

When the problem was finally discovered and fixed—19 hours after the blackout began—it would turn out to be relatively prosaic. A routing error went undetected because the diagnostic systems had been down for the routine upgrade. The national response to it, on the other hand, was anything but commonplace.

"America Online Goes Offline" blared the *Washington Post* in a front-page headline. "CHAOS@AOL.COM!" trumpeted the *New York Post,* which over the years relished any problem at AOL it could find. And all the major networks led their evening newscasts with the story—even ahead of the news that a scientific report released that same day had suggested there might be life on Mars.

But it also indicated that AOL was needed. Steve Case echoed that sentiment in a letter to users apologizing for the blackout.

"Without making light of yesterday's outage, an additional interesting theme did emerge that's noteworthy," he wrote. "The disruption caused by the temporary unavailability of AOL illustrates more clearly than ever before how important AOL has become in the daily lives of our members. From a high-tech gimmick, AOL has evolved over the past several years into a critical part of real people's lifestyles and it is missed when it's not available."

AOL users were not impressed by Case's spin on the situation, considering it appalling to turn a disaster for consumers into a compliment of AOL. But this was classic Case, of course—he was as incapable as ever of delivering any kind of empathetic response. It was exactly this kind of tone-deaf commentary that would drive Time Warner to distraction following the merger. And once again—as with David Colburn and his team's hardball negotiating tactics—it was on plain view for anyone who cared to notice.

But to Case and others at AOL, the blackout was a turning point. Up until that point, AOL had seemed more like a frivolous service than a tool. But now, for the first time, it was clear that people didn't just want AOL; they actually required it.

But did they need it enough to keep paying $2.95 an hour, when the other major services were switching to flat-rate pricing? When MSN announced on October 10 that it, too, would offer unlimited usage for $19.95 a month, the AOL hierarchy decided the answer was no. It was time to make the leap. The company planned to make the announcement on the pricing shift on October 29.

That same day, they'd also make two other important announcements. One would bring glamour, glitz, and a sense of renewal to the company. The other would lead some to think it was doomed. And both developments would later play big roles in AOL's disastrous merger with Time Warner.

Enter Bob Pitchman

Compared to "Vanilla Man" Steve Case, Robert W. Pittman was a multiflavored sensation when he arrived at AOL in the fall of 1996 as the president of AOL Networks.

The cofounder of MTV, Pittman was a smooth-talking Southerner with a mane of thick, dark hair and a taste for the high life.
Born and raised in Brookhaven, Mississippi, the son of a Methodist
minister, he'd taken his first job as a radio deejay in his teens in nearby
Jackson so he could pay for flying lessons. Within a few years, with
stops in Milwaukee, Detroit, Pittsburgh, and Chicago, he'd made his
way to New York City's WNBC, where he soon became one of the
hottest young radio programmers in the country.

While he never did get around to graduating from college, Pittman
was typical of the kind of hardscrabble overachievers whose burning
ambitions and ability to morph into whatever is needed often vault
them ever upward. When his radio career took off, he bought himself a
plane (which he apparently had no trouble flying, despite having a glass
eye as the result of a horse-riding accident when he was a boy) and a
Harley-Davidson motorcycle. This well-constructed image of the businessman maverick was one that would carry Pittman far.

In the late 1970s, Pittman took at job at Warner Amex Satellite
Entertainment Company (WASEC). It was there, in 1981, that he
took an already existing idea for a televised music show first floated by
his boss John Lack and turned it into Music Television. The first all-
music cable channel, MTV not only became a hot new brand, but
also changed American culture and the cable business with its memo-
rable "I Want My MTV" marketing mantra. More than two decades
after MTV was founded, the quick-cut, visually arresting style of its
videos has permeated ads, television shows, and movies. It took marketing and music to a whole new level and introduced the idea of attitude and not plot as a selling point in entertainment. And while
many competitors—including even Ted Turner—tried to emulate
MTV, it was impossible to beat Pittman's head start.

And, through the early 1980s, Pittman did, in fact, seem impossible to beat. While he basked in his MTV success, which many thought
he took too much credit for, he married socialite and fellow adventure
seeker Sandy Hill, made routine appearances in the gossip pages, and
cultivated glamorous friends like *Rolling Stone*'s Jann Wenner and
NBC's Tom Brokaw. He was a runner-up for *Time* magazine's Man of
the Year in 1984. But when MTV was sold off to Viacom—after
Pittman tried unsuccessfully to buy it with the help of Forstmann

Little & Co.—Pittman was left with only a few million dollars in stock options and a scary possibility that he would never replicate his boy-wonder success.

He tried to recapture the glory by forming an investment company called (ironically enough) Quantum Media Inc., backed by $15 million entertainment giant MCA, to make media acquisitions and create new properties. But it was hard to succeed in the difficult late-1980s economic climate. Quantum had one short-lived hit with *The Morton Downey Jr. Show,* but overall its efforts were mostly lackluster, including a failed attempt to take over the J. Walter Thompson ad agency.

Soon enough, Pittman returned to Time Warner, brought back by his old mentor Steve Ross to run Time Warner Enterprises, a business development arm of the company. There his biggest job involved his turnaround of the Six Flags theme park chain. Time Warner bought the chain for $600 million in 1991, and Pittman spent the next few years goosing its revenues and profits. By 1995, he sold it off to Boston Venture Partners for more than $1 billion, earning himself a $40 million payout as part of the sale.

In the process, though, Pittman lost his job when the purchasers didn't want to take him or his demands with the parks. And despite his success with the Six Flags turnaround, there was no room for him at Time Warner. Because there was jealousy over his longtime, close relationship to Ross, who seemed to delight in Pittman's brash style, Pittman was especially vulnerable after the great showman died in 1992.

He had also developed a reputation as an impossibly ambitious executive with a proclivity for flash over substance. While many thought Pittman's potential and talent were huge, he was also branded as someone more interested in short-term fixes than long-term solutions. It was a reputation that would continue to dog Pittman when he later returned to Time Warner after the AOL merger. In yet another portent of things to come, Time Warner CEO Levin dispatched his number two, Dick Parsons, to deliver the bad news to Pittman.

But Pittman was not down for long. He already had an offer of a job working for another longtime mentor of his, Henry Silverman, as CEO of the Century 21 real estate chain. This seemed a bizarre choice for a man with his finger forever on the pulse of everything hip. But Silverman offered Pittman an enticingly lucrative contract that included a $1 million bonus as well as 8 percent of Century 21.

As soon as he'd parked himself out in the pasture of real estate, however, Pittman knew he needed to find another way to stay current. So in 1995, curious about the company at the vanguard of the online revolution, he'd called Steve Case. He had put a Century 21 site on AOL and was impressed by its ability to generate leads, the heart of the real estate business.

At their invitation, he joined Case and Ted Leonsis for lunch at a modest café in the soulless office sprawl of northern Virginia, and Case immediately began needling Pittman about his most recent career move. Case had quickly made up his mind: He wanted Pittman to join the board of AOL, with the ultimate goal of getting him to come on as a top executive. And so Case wasted no time going for the jugular in convincing Pittman to do so.

"Woooo, love those yellow jackets, Bob," Case taunted, referring to Century 21's trademark apparel which Pittman had actually purged. "Very fashionable." Then he pushed further. He asked Pittman: "Is this really your purpose in life? To work with a real estate company?"

For someone like Bob Pittman, there really was only one possible answer to that question. Still, although he was intrigued by the possibilities at AOL, in 1995 the timing was wrong—he'd just started with Century 21 and had promised Silverman two years. But by 1996, he and Case began talking again. In August, Ted Leonsis rented a yacht and took Pittman on a Mediterranean cruise to close the deal. By the beginning of the fall, Pittman was ready to ditch Century 21 and come on board at AOL, part of a new life that included divorce and a new marriage to a woman named Veronique Choa.

"I've seen this movie before," Pittman declared incessantly, comparing AOL to all his past successes in radio, theme parks, and cable, specifically at MTV. But the movie turned out to be more of a thriller than he ever expected. On October 29, 1996, the same day AOL announced Pittman's hire and its move to flat-fee pricing, the company made one other announcement as well—one that would tarnish the company for a long time to come.

In reporting results for the quarter, AOL told Wall Street what it should already have known if it had carefully read the company's last few financial statements. Not only were there no profits, there actually never had been in the entire history of the company. Instead, there was a single, devastating number that wiped them all out: $353.7 million.

This was the amount that AOL had lost in the quarter, the result of a massive $385 million write-off of something it had long called deferred subscriber acquisition costs. This was the very hefty price of all that heady past growth, overspending on acquiring subscribers, and relentless churn. For the past few years, AOL had been spreading out its marketing expenses—largely due to the disk blitz—over two years, rather than charging them to each quarter. It was a practice that made the company's financial results look better.

It was good enough to maintain the appearance of profits that allowed AOL to continue to raise hundreds of millions of dollars in capital and investments and use its fast-rising stock for acquisitions. It also allowed AOL executives—first and foremost Case—to regularly cash in their hefty options and become extremely wealthy. All this, as many observers of AOL's accounting tricks would note, simply because the company had pushed the accounting pencil in a slightly more aggressive direction.

Although it had been disclosed in the company's filings and it was well known among analysts, this type of accounting had increasingly incurred the wrath of purists, who saw it as a sleazy trick to prop up the numbers. When the buzz of disapproval over the tactic had grown to a din, Case realized he'd have to change it. The result: A massive loss and a public relations black eye.

Still, Case continued to insist that AOL's past behavior was standard, though he was abandoning it for a new model. He also added that accounting in the nascent online industry was still evolving, trying to position its businesses as radically different from other media. The change, he summarized, was made only because he wanted to "address the needs of Main Street and the concerns of Wall Street." Case largely glossed over the implications of what AOL had done and gotten away with.

The architect of AOL's accounting practices, CFO Len Leader, also angrily denied that the company had done anything wrong. "We take strong exception to any notion that we are playing games," he told the *Wall Street Journal.*

Others knew better. The master of the scatological metaphor, Jim Kimsey, even had taken to calling the accounting issue "the big turd," since it "sat in the middle of the company and smelled up the place." And critics outside the company were even less kind. Abraham J. Briloff, a university professor and well-known critic of unorthodox accounting practices, called it "in-your-face arrogance." In an interview with me, short-seller David Rocker blustered, "They are morally bankrupt! For them, every revenue is ordinary, and every expense is extraordinary." And respected *Newsweek* columnist Allan Sloan wrote, "I'm intrigued by AOL's ever-changing accounting and by the way it manages to keep telling Wall Street whatever it wants to hear."

As Sloan pointed out, AOL actually hid few of these practices—making it another lesson Time Warner should have been paying attention to. But caught up in their own failures to generate any growth in their digital efforts and blinded by the immense growth of companies like AOL, few at Time Warner would remember this incident. The stench of the big turd would not reach there for years to come.

Money, Money Everywhere

After they vaulted over that hurdle, AOL added insult to injury. On December 1, 1996, AOL switched to a flat-fee pricing structure. For $19.95 a month, users could spend as much time as they wanted online. The result, operations head Matt Korn had joked in an earlier meeting, might be like "drinking from a fire hose." Once again, to AOL's detriment, a joke would prove prophetic.

Right out of the gate, the leap in usage was phenomenal. On average, AOL members had been logging about 1.6 million hours online per day. On December 1, they logged more than 2.5 million hours, leading to widespread slowdowns in service. It was only the first day, but Korn and his team were already in danger of drowning. By the end of December, 500,000 new members would sign on and old users would not log off for fear of not getting on again.

Going to flat-fee pricing was, in the words of David Rocker, "like inviting busloads of fat people to an all-you-can-eat buffet." People were obviously going to take advantage of unlimited use, and AOL was never going to be able to keep up with demand. So in January 1997, Steve Case issued an extraordinary plea in his monthly letter to users.

There is, he wrote, "something you can do to help, and that is to moderate your own use of AOL a bit during our peak evening periods. . . . Just as you would be sensitive about using a public phone booth if others were waiting in line to use it (although you are entitled to use it as long as you want, most people are considerate of the people waiting to get a turn), it would be helpful if you could be considerate of the needs of other members of the AOL community." He advised "restraint." Given that he was taking money from the people for a service they expected to be delivered, the request naturally appalled users. In the two days after the email letter went out, Case received 17,000 emails in response, crashing his mailbox.

Though AOL had always had its share of detractors, with sites like aolsucks.com sprouting all over the Web, this marked the beginning of a new level of ire. Now, according to many critics, AOL didn't simply suck: It was greedy, unethical, and possibly even criminal. Three dozen state attorneys general went after the company, eager to bolster their reputations by winning concessions for their constituents, who had already become inflamed earlier in the year by a billing practice that rounded up minutes. And as the face of AOL, Steve Case found himself the target for vitriolic attacks, both in the press and from users.

As 1997 began, things started getting out of hand. In a *Mad* magazine parody, a character warned the fictional Steve Nutcase to be careful: "No offense, Steve, but I hope you have a bodyguard with all the enemies you make." But it was no joke. Case received enough threatening emails that he was persuaded to take a defensive driving course in case someone tried to run him off the road. Internet polls asked whether Case should be sacked. Late-night comics spoofed his bland demeanor in the face of endless busy signals. And editorial writers chastised him for misleading customers. In an online poll on whether to ax Case due to the near-daily blunders, they dubbed it "Dumb, Dumber and AOL." And Case was further embarrassed when he was called up to the stage to give a presentation at a tony tech conference to the sound of busy signals.

CompuServe, which had fallen far behind AOL in member numbers, gleefully skewered the company in an ad played during the Super Bowl. Against the backdrop of a blank screen, the ad played the sound of a modem repeatedly trying to dial up. Silence fell, then a tagline appeared: "Looking for dependable Internet access? CompuServe. Get on with it." The number to call: 1-888-NOTBUSY.

Though AOL promised to spend $350 million on new servers and modems to solve the problem and reluctantly agreed to cut back on marketing and not accept any new members, many thought it was too little too late. The *Wall Street Journal*'s Thomas Petzinger blasted Case in his "Front Lines" column: "The service breakdown at AOL is an ethical issue," he wrote. "Today's topsy-turvy business world does not excuse a company from offering a product it knows it cannot reliably deliver." At the end of the column, he offered one more slap, publicly dumping his AOL account: "Please note my new email address, tompetz@msn.com."

Case was incensed. In an interview that winter, he told me, "To attack someone's character without knowing the facts is terribly unfair. [The column] said I was immoral, and I'm not. We went to unlimited, and we had problems. The motive was to do the right thing for members and our profits even took a hit."

But I was not feeling very sorry for Steve Case, who appeared not to realize that he might be at fault in any way. The lingering accounting issues and the disastrous move to flat-rate pricing once again raised troubling issues about AOL's willingness to stretch rules to their breaking point. That tone pervaded AOL's culture and few people expressed any embarrassment over the issue.

That's because Case still had the stubborn righteousness of an entrepreneur with a big vision and seemed unwilling to see that others should not pay the price for his miscalculations. In fact, Case and others at AOL actually had the audacity to compare the situation to when my newspaper, the *Washington Post,* failed to deliver the paper because of a winter storm. What they conveniently left out was that AOL had created the bad weather that had left everyone stranded deep in the snow.

Milk That Cow

Incredibly, members did not leave and regulators did not hinder AOL's progress in attracting millions of subscribers. Now, as many AOLers told me, it was time to milk the cow, a critical strategy once the lucrative hourly rates were history. Until then, AOL had been singularly focused on building membership at all costs. The benefits of this approach were obvious: More users meant more fees coming in. But it was clear that bigger numbers would yield even more benefits and AOL's dominant position would open up other lucrative revenue streams.

It was a many-pronged strategy, including focusing on original content, a push led by Ted Leonsis. He had already made AOL more like TV by adding channels and frequently extended that metaphor by claiming that the service's true competition was the NBC comedy hit *Seinfeld.* I found that dubious given that one episode of a sitcom could draw 30 million viewers at once. And while its user base was growing, AOL subscribers quickly fanned out over the whole service. That made it not much of a mass medium, but a niche medium with masses of people. Users also did not seem to like being programmed at from the top down, the way it worked in television, as Time Warner was then finding out with its own failed Internet efforts.

In fact, Time Warner and AOL had a long history in the content area. While *Time* magazine defected from AOL after getting a pricier offer from CompuServe, the pair had begun to cooperate on joint programming ventures, such as on a health site called Thrive and an entertainment offering called The Hub.

Leonsis had long pushed for more and more programming, having earlier initiated a "Greenhouse" project that tried to seed new

Web properties that AOL would own a piece of and also promote. He pulled in television luminaries such as legendary programmer Brandon Tartikoff to create for AOL, in hopes of launching money-spinning television and publishing franchises from content born online. He opened a Hollywood online studio called Entertainment Asylum.

But Leonsis's energetic efforts—and Leonsis himself—were losing favor at AOL when it became clear that such asset building was costly and took a long time. AOL needed a much quicker fix to get it off its addiction to hourly subscriber fees. That would only come by plunging deeply into the potentially profitable advertising market, which then only accounted for 10 percent of AOL's revenues.

The man who would first lead this new charge was Myer Berlow. An Armani-clad, slick-haired advertising man who dubbed himself the "Darth Vader of AOL," Berlow had joined the company in 1995, after spending 25 years in the advertising business in New York, Los Angeles, and Mexico City. His mission was to sell the AOL service as an advertising medium, despite the fact that its ability to help sell products was completely unproven.

Within AOL, the advertising idea was anathema at first. The "community" feel of AOL was not just an online phenomenon. For many of the young men and women who worked at company headquarters in the rolling fields of Dulles, Virginia, AOL felt like a safe community where the goal was both simple and idealistic: Help people get online and explore a whole new world. "I think every antibody in the company reacted when I got here," Berlow told me in early 1996. "The idea of selling the service to advertisers had not been something very ingrained in the company ethos."

It was initially a hard sell outside of AOL, too. Most potential traditional advertisers with the big bucks wanted to create their own sites rather than buy ads on AOL. Berlow caustically warned them such money was wasted with the snarky retort: "Build it and they won't come." He pressed them to see how important the AOL audience would become. While he got some traction, it was still an uphill battle to get much cash in AOL's coffers.

But soon enough, under the guidance of Bob Pittman, AOL would be all about making money through its ad deals. So much money, in fact, that eventually everyone—even those who paid lip service to AOL's homey roots, most especially Steve Case—would get on board.

The ride began on February 25, 1997, when Pittman announced a deal with New Jersey–based Tel-Save Holdings, Inc., a dinky, then-unknown reseller of long-distance phone service. In exchange for being able to market its discount telephone offerings to AOL users, Tel-Save had agreed to pay the astonishing sum of $100 million as an advance on future commissions, a percentage of profits, and warrants to buy shares in the company.

With this immense check in hand, AOL had another new lease on life that promised more riches and acclaim than ever. It had been a long and wearying journey to get there and now it appeared they had made it to the big time and were ready to fly higher than ever before. They had no idea then how high they'd get—capturing Time Warner within three years' time. On the way, they'd continue to skirt the boundaries of propriety, amass enormous personal wealth, and gain a reputation for arrogance and hubris that would one day help bring down the unusual structure they'd built from nothing in only a decade.

To Case and his band of misfits, it finally looked like AOL was winning. But they had no idea how much they all still had left to lose.

> It might look as if my hands were empty. Actually, I was sure of myself, sure about everything, far surer than he; sure of my present life and of the death that was coming. That, no doubt, was all I had; but at least that certainty was something I could get my teeth into—just as it had got its teeth into me.
>
> ALBERT CAMUS, *The Stranger*

Chapter Three

NOTHING LEFT TO LOSE EXCEPT EVERYTHING

Good-Bye to All That

Gerald Levin was in love.

"Profound love," he told me, saying it a second time, and then a third. I wrote it down in my notebook, underlined it, and then wrote it again.

It was January of 2003, and I was sitting with Levin in his second-floor office at Time Warner headquarters at Rockefeller Center. I was interviewing him for the third time about the merger and its collapse, when he began telling me about the new woman in his life—a clinical psychologist and former Hollywood agent he'd met recently named Laurie Perlman. She had first approached him regarding business guidance for a plan to open a chain of holistic mental health centers. Later, they'd kindled a romantic relationship in a series of marathon phone conversations—she calling from Southern California, he from New York.

The next month, the *New York Times* had gotten a bit giddy over this development, printing an article with a photo of Levin on the beach, looking uncharacteristically laid back as the sun set behind him over the Pacific. And the news had, of course, sent New York's tabloids into their usual frenzy—especially the *New York Post,* which pondered openly whether Levin had gone crazy.

Some of his friends wondered the same thing. Levin had been calling many of them from Hawaii, where he had gone with Perlman to get to know her better in person and where he'd quickly decided to marry her. In what many would describe to me as awkward conversations, Levin had waxed on about how his life was now perfect, offering personal details and unburdening himself emotionally. "I was very unhappy," he said to one friend. "I had no idea how unhappy." To his mostly dumbfounded listeners, this kind of opening up was unimaginable for a man who had kept mostly to himself for his entire career.

The change was certainly dramatic. Levin was, after all, leaving his wife of more than three decades—who was apparently just as shocked as everyone else was by the news ("You're the last person Jerry could fire," Barbara Levin had been told by one friend). Even more surprising, Levin also declared that he was departing the powerful environs of Manhattan, planning to move across the country to the sunny shores of Marina del Rey to live the rest of his life in peace. "I used to hate California," he told me. "Now, I can't wait to get there." For Levin it was like the title of an essay that Joan Didion wrote about leaving the soured life in New York for the jasmine scents of the West Coast: "Goodbye to All That."

This recent shift in Levin's life was—there was no other word for it—transformational. But I didn't want to suggest that word to Levin, because "transforming transaction" was precisely the millstone of a concept that had dragged his career from the pinnacle of power to the depths of ignominy.

Perhaps, as one person close to him suggested, Levin's newfound candor was born of the fact that he had nothing left to lose. Unlike Steve Case, who'd transformed himself from goat to genius in the years leading up to the deal, Levin had toppled from being the most powerful man in media to a virtual untouchable. The metaphorical fall he took was just as dramatic: Levin had been shunted from his aerie in the power corridors on the twenty-ninth floor to an outpost on the second floor, near the information technology staff. It looked like the same office—"It's kind of a replication of my old one," he told me on a short tour, as he pointed out photos and other mementos from his glory days. But it was clear he had been exiled here.

And yet it appeared as if Levin could not care less. At a time when all had been lost in the deal he had personally architected, Levin seemed as if the weight of the world had been lifted off his perpetually hunched shoulders. Yes, he still looked a bit like a mortician, which had been my impression when I first met him in 1999, but the difference now was that he appeared to be a very happy one. In the margins of my notebook, near "profound love," I scribbled, "fun-loving funeral director."

Gloomy metaphors had always seemed appropriate for describing Gerald Levin. Friends, foes, and the press universally described his manner in severe, vaguely mystical terms—rabbinical, monkish, inscrutable, cryptic—as if Levin occupied a different plane of existence. Levin himself had cultivated this persona, offering up obscure quotes and frequently referring to his love of French existentialism—particularly philosopher Albert Camus, whose greatest work was titled *The Stranger.*

Not surprisingly in the backbiting world of media, Levin's detractors had long thought of him as a poseur, a man who created a faux-philosopher façade to mask his true Machiavellian tendencies. But others believed his airy, visionary gazes were genuine, and that Levin was much more than your standard quarter-by-quarter CEO. In any case, he'd cultivated this professorial air and hangdog visage for so long that it was now the image that everyone thought of when they thought of Jerry Levin. And the persona was further etched in stone after the violent murder of Levin's son in 1997, which lowered over him a perpetual shroud of grief that made him seem even more remote.

This darker, more somber Levin was the man I encountered soon after the AOL Time Warner merger. In the spring of 2000, just as Levin was perched at the very peak of the media world, I'd met him in person for the first time at an event celebrating the debut of a new Time Warner magazine called *eCompany Now.*

These were the last heady moments before the dot-com sector would begin to crumble, and the magazine had put together an opening party that befit the times, renting out San Francisco's newly built Pacific Bell baseball stadium, offering free ballpark food and giveaways, and bringing in the Warner Music pop band Barenaked Ladies (as evidence of synergy, no doubt) as entertainment. On a sun-drenched San Francisco Bay boat ride that preceded the festivities, I stood chatting with Levin—or trying to, anyway, as it was hard to get him talking about anything much. Unlike the razor wit of entertainment mogul Barry Diller or the obstreperous opinionating of Disney's Michael Eisner or the bossy imperiousness of Sumner Redstone of Viacom, Levin was almost comatose for a media mogul. In desperation, I brought up the issue of cable systems, since I'd heard this was his passion.

It was only then that Levin dropped his distant affect and started talking in an animated way about how quickly high-speed Internet access would catch on with mainstream consumers. While he wasn't awe-inspiring in his arguments, it was clear he was thinking many years down the line, to a future far beyond the next earnings announcement. The next time I saw him was at a conference, and once again, cable and its ability to jumpstart the next Internet age was his main topic.

But the next time I saw him, in the fall of 2002, he had recently left AOL Time Warner under a cloud of scorn. He was considerably less remote then—but his mood was shot through with a bitterness that would eventually lead to what he called "opening up and finding my voice." And as I discovered during my interviews with him then and later, it was a voice that would prove to be pretty direct.

"I have no respect for them at all," Levin told me in that meeting, when I asked how he felt about those who turned on him after his fall from power. At least you can say this about the man who described himself as "the personification of the stock decline": He agreed to speak on the record. Most others who had similar responsibility for the merger mess did not.

"I am not into self-justification and legacies," he insisted, calling himself a "student of anthropology." "I know how we got punished with the Time and Warner merger, and then with the Turner merger . . . [the AOL Time Warner merger] is a large transaction and it doesn't matter how smart or well intentioned you are, it is always off the mark.

"Until," he added, "it shakes out into something right, which it will."

And, later, in the interview where he told me about his new love, he remained as defiant, despite even more bad news piling up about the merger. "I know what occurred over the last thirty years, and I'm not interested in setting the record straight for anyone," he said.

He was actually smiling quite pleasantly as he made this declaration of stubborn certainty against a chorus of detractors, part of Levin's strong need to play the contrarian. Perhaps this was due to that "profound love" that was now allowing him to be even more philosophical than he'd ever been. Whether anyone thinks it's merited or not, Levin's attitude about the merger is clearly a good thing for him personally. Because no matter how he could look at the situation, Levin has had a very steep slide.

Or, as he must have known from studying Camus's *The Stranger,* "He seemed so certain about everything, didn't he? And yet none of his certainties was worth one hair of a woman's head."

Stumbling Upward

Gerald Levin was an unlikely corporate climber. Growing up in Philadelphia, he studied Hebrew and loved to read books. His mother, who was of Romanian origin, was a piano teacher, and his father, whose parents were from Russia, ran a mom-and-pop store. Never a rebel, Levin studied hard and did well in school, eventually enrolling in Haverford College, a small liberal arts school founded by Quakers just outside Philadelphia.

Levin enjoyed writing and planned to major in religion and minor in English. He loved the intellectual freedom and challenge of college, and he excelled in his studies, eventually being selected for membership in Phi Beta Kappa.

He was an intense, idealistic young man, even going so far as to burn his papers after graduation in deference to the poet Virgil. "Since I had studied all kinds of philosophy, I had come to the conclusion that keeping papers was an assertion of ego that I had to rid myself of," he explained to me, before adding, "Of course, I wish I had those papers now."

His dream for his life's work was equally passionate—he wanted to write novels. But one doesn't simply become a successful novelist, he knew, so he decided he needed to establish a career that would allow him to write on the side. With that in mind, he enrolled in University of Pennsylvania Law School in 1960. But his dream of writing soon took a backseat to the corporate life.

Levin started his career as a lawyer with the white-shoe firm Simpson Thacher & Bartlett in Manhattan, but he spent only a few years there before moving on. He never intended to practice law for long, he said, because he wanted to involve himself in the world more. Soon enough, he'd wrangled himself a post working in a firm in New York run by the legendary David E. Lilienthal, who had chaired the Tennessee Valley Authority and later served as the first head of the Atomic Energy Commission. He was inspired by Lilienthal, especially by his 1967 book, *Management: A Humanist Art.* Levin told me he liked the idea of being able "to do something socially significant through economic development, while also making money." When I visibly raised my eyebrows at this statement, Levin insisted his motives started off with some measure of idealism.

In his job, Levin traveled to southern Iran to represent the Development and Resources Corporation on a dam project. It was there that he formulated his ideas on the importance of distribution, no matter the product. "In my mind, the transmission of water and power and later electrons were all the same thing," he said, "You just had to be in a position of controlling the conduit."

He returned to New York in 1972 and took a job at the company where he would stay for 30 years: Time Inc. Levin found the company intriguing in part because he felt it was all about distribution. And he also liked the idea of working near journalists—"though you might not believe that today," he added, referring to the media flaying he would get frequently over the course of his career. His first job at Time Inc. was working on the business plan for the company's new cable channel, Home Box Office.

There was no doubt in Levin's mind that television was changing the way Americans spent their leisure time. Levin felt there were even bigger opportunities, including the novelty of pay television via cable. Time's offering was HBO, test-launched on November 8, 1972. Levin himself introduced the first two programs—a Paul Newman movie called *Sometimes a Great Notion* and a New York Rangers hockey game. About 350 subscribers in the coal country town of Wilkes-Barre, Pennsylvania, tuned in.

While HBO was at the forefront of the new cable industry, it still wasn't clear whether Americans would be willing to pay for programming when they'd been watching free TV for years. And though the technology was cutting edge—very basically, coaxial cable wires transmitting content—something better would soon become available to take the idea nationwide, a necessity for the true success of the endeavor. But it was something no one at Time Inc. except Jerry Levin and a handful of others seemed to think was worth investing in.

In 1975, for the first time, commercial enterprises were offered the chance to rent space on a communications satellite about to be sent into orbit. Levin, intrigued by the possibilities, had spent some time talking with various satellite entrepreneurs. "I had satellite in my head from that moment on," he recalled.

Levin proposed that Time rent satellite time in order to beam HBO to cable providers across the country. This would, he argued, make HBO a truly national service—at a cost to the company of more than $6 million. Was this space-age genius, or madness? More than a few of Levin's colleagues thought the latter, but he eventually pushed the idea through. "Making it a national service, I thought, would also be good for psychological reasons," said Levin. "It would get a lot more respect around the company." The satellite move did in fact turn around the HBO division, and it would later be hailed as Levin's first brilliant technological gamble.

This pattern of making risky technological bets, followed by derision, followed by success, would increasingly be part of the Levin playbook, and it fueled an ever-growing ego. It was a characteristic he would share with another high-tech dreamer—Steve Case, who was still a teenager when Levin was making his satellite bet. And it was a quality that would eventually cause both great problems when they united their companies.

But, back in the mid-1970s, by rescuing then-struggling HBO with this move, Levin solidified his position at Time Inc. and began his rise. Despite his reticent, sometimes awkward manner, he displayed a potent combination of ambition and managerial skill that some would later perceive as conniving.

Emboldened by his successful satellite gamble, in the late 1970s and early 1980s, Levin began urging Time to explore new means of interactivity with its subscribers. Earlier than most other American media executives, he foresaw the approaching boom in what would come to be called the Information Superhighway. But these moves would fritter away the gains he had made at HBO. Most damning were a new subscription television project he spearheaded as well as a groundbreaking teletext service—both of which lost tens of millions of dollars. But Levin was unbowed. He hadn't found the secret recipe yet, but he was sure it was out there.

Others at the company were not so sure, and Levin's career would take a hit as a result. His failed forays into new technology and other deals led to his removal from overseeing Time Inc.'s video business in the mid-1980s. Nicholas Nicholas, a longtime rival of Levin's, replaced him. By 1986, Nicholas had been elevated to president of Time Inc., and Levin, his satellite victory a distant memory, had been stuck with the mushy title "chief strategist" of the company.

Some thought Levin might leave, having been outmaneuvered by Nicholas. But he stayed and threw himself into creating a forward-looking plan for the company. Only now, instead of pushing the latest technological gambit, he focused on something new—a blockbuster merger. Or two.

In 1987, Levin wrote a memo that would chart the future for Time Inc., in a way few in the company could have foreseen. Based in part on notes taken during a conversation with Nick Nicholas (the pair would later disagree vehemently on who was the strategic genius),

the memo urged the company to pursue two mergers: one with entertainment behemoth Warner Communications; and one with Ted
Turner's upstart radio, television, and cable empire, Turner Broadcasting System (TBS).

Merging with these companies would, Levin posited, create an
"entertainment-oriented communications company"—a brand-new
kind of entity that would be able to tell stories in all possible forms.
"News is a form of storytelling, and I thought we should get even
broader to become a truly creative company," Levin explained. "And
the growth level in the entertainment industry was also important for
a publishing company that did not have that."

Levin knew this would be a tough sell to the conservative Time
Inc. board. But as he later told Connie Bruck, author of the superb
Master of the Game, the biography of legendary Warner CEO Steve
Ross, "I had thought for a long time that we needed what I always
referred to as a 'transforming transaction,' because I didn't think we
could build ourselves into this new world."

A decade later, this exact same phrase and sentiment—which he
would repeat to me and many others—would lead Jerry Levin into
the biggest business blunder of his life.

Revenge of the Nerd

It's the late 20th century. A group of powerful executives has just
announced a megamerger between America's most influential media
company and another, more fast-moving and sexy company, one in a
completely different kind of business.

There's some initial confusion over who has acquired whom, and
many observers find themselves surprised at who's in charge in the
new management structure. Employees in the media company end up
losing scads of money due to the structure of the deal, and they look
enviously upon their counterparts in the flashy company, who'd
cashed out handsomely.

Sound like the AOL Time Warner deal? It's not. It's the merger between Time and Warner that closed in early January—exactly a decade before the AOL Time Warner merger announcement. By all accounts, many considered it one of the worst mergers ever consummated. Before the AOL Time Warner merger, Time and Warner would play out a dress rehearsal of sorts for that deal.

It was certainly a lively one, even in the wrangling leading up to it. Initially, the deal was proposed as a basic merger and was announced in 1989. Both the Time and Warner sides would be in seemingly equal control of the company in a complex power-sharing management structure. But before the deal could be done, Paramount Communications mogul Martin Davis offered a hostile $200-a-share bid for Time Inc. itself. This was a huge premium over its share price, which hovered in the $125 range.

But rather than taking the money and running, Time executives were horrified over Davis's unsolicited bid, mostly because the upstart billionaire was not the kind of owner they envisioned for their conservative and respectable selves. Instead, they initiated a costly takeover struggle to thwart Davis by making a counterproposal to buy Warner in cash. The problem was that the move added onerous debt to the deal, turning the merger into an outright purchase of Warner.

Despite its cost, the Time-Warner marriage did produce the raw material for a powerhouse. The $14 billion deal created the world's biggest media and entertainment behemoth, putting Time's vast array of magazine and television properties under the same roof as Warner's music and film divisions. From HBO to *Sports Illustrated* to Warner Brothers Studios to Atlantic Records, the merged Time Warner now ruled the entertainment world like a king.

Warner executives certainly got a royal payout in the deal, since they were able to cash out their shares immediately. Time Inc. executives, on the other hand, could not. Worse still, they did not have full control over the company either and were forced to share power with those they considered somewhat vulgar. "From the standpoint of the Time executives—who, even decades after [Time Inc. founder Henry] Luce, still inhabited a remarkably genteel, upper-class kind of world—it was one thing to have to merge for compelling business reasons with people whom they found rather déclassé," wrote Connie Bruck in

Master of the Game. "But it was quite another to recognize that those people—after having been acquired, at full price—had the upper hand in terms of both money and power. It was the kind of recognition that tended to inflame already existing prejudices."

The differences were immediately highlighted at the management's first off-site meeting after the merger, at Lyford Cay in the Bahamas, an event that would morph over the years into a potent symbol of the dreadful mismatch. "Here was Time with those Oxford shirts and blue blazers, high-WASP and Manhattan," one high-ranking Warner executive in attendance recalled. "And there was us in pedal pushers and colorful shirts, very Hollywood, very Jewish—even if not every one of us was."

Or, as another former Warner exec told me, "The Time guys were all interested in lineage—what school did you go to, where were you from? And the Warner guys all wanted to know, what deals have you done? And how much did you make on them?"

The problems were, in fact, much deeper than that and longer lasting. A decade later, as I interviewed them about the AOL Time Warner deal, many Time Warner executives spoke of the difficulty of that earlier merger as if it had just happened. They sounded as if the pain of it would never be assuaged—with Time executives still angry at being fleeced, and Warner executives much annoyed at having been painted as gauche and money grubbing.

Perhaps that is because, as many noted, there was never a basic agreement on the culture and attitude of the company from the start. "At Warner, if you didn't make mistakes, you'd be fired because you weren't taking enough chances," another executive said. "At Time, the attitude was, don't make mistakes."

It was definitely a rocky beginning, made even worse by the lack of clarity about who was really in charge. While there were all sorts of agreements in place, in practice, the arrangement proved impossible. Jerry Levin was named vice chairman of the new company, while his old rival Nick Nicholas was named co-CEO with Warner's Steve Ross, a gregarious, energetic businessman who'd transformed himself from a funeral director to the head of one of the country's biggest entertainment companies in just 15 years.

Unlike Levin, whose blood ran hot at the thought of cables, satellites, and set-top boxes, Ross loved the glitter and gloss of the entertainment world. He counted Hollywood royalty among his friends—including Steven Spielberg and Barbra Streisand, with whom he had very close relationships. He'd invited opera diva Beverly Sills to serve on Warner's board and moved easily in circles of wealth and glamour.

Ross also was a boss everyone seemed to love, with his junior executives—including the young Bob Pittman—becoming lifelong acolytes. "Steve Ross was my hero," Pittman has told me many times over the years. Pittman was a Ross favorite, but his sentiment was one repeated by almost everyone who ever worked for Ross, who would often grab different executives and fly off to some glamorous destination for the weekend. He set a tone of a freewheeling culture, where the fun never seemed to stop.

Levin acknowledged Ross's iconic status, his charisma, and his considerable business talents, but he clearly didn't worship at the altar of Steve Ross the way others did. "He was someone who had that 'big man' syndrome of needing to be bigger than life and wanting to be loved by all," Levin told me. "Still, as different as we were, I think we understood each other." Despite their differences, Ross and Levin, the schmoozer and the loner, would end up forming an unlikely bond. It was one that Nick Nicholas apparently didn't notice until it was far too late.

As the two companies struggled to digest the merger, Levin quickly angled his way into the position of chief operating officer. Over the course of 1991 and 1992, he worked behind the scenes, setting a strategic course for the company and quietly continuing to woo Ross and also his closest adviser and personal friend Oded "Ed" Aboodi. Luckily for Levin, Ross would also soon become disenchanted with co-CEO Nicholas and, according to many sources, would engineer his ouster—from his hospital bed where he was attempting to recover from prostate cancer in the early winter of 1992.

While many believe Levin was the principal driver of that corporate move, most agree that Ross and his lieutenants were behind Nicholas's ouster for a number of reasons. They felt that Nicholas was attempting to grab power when Ross was ill and cringed at his suggestions to cut costs and also sell off pieces of the company, particularly the music division. Warner was a growth culture, inspired by Ross's serial deal making and not interested in using cost-cutting and strict management to force change. But Levin helped them actively, lobbying many important figures on the Time side and being the main instigator of what amounted to a palace coup. Soon enough, with board power on the Warner side, Nicholas had angered enough of the power structure that he was pushed aside. (Interestingly, Nicholas's interest in selling the music business, for example, would have in hindsight been an excellent move at the time.)

Levin—who sounded more amenable to Warner's dreams and had the support of its powerful division heads—was quickly pushed to the forefront, soon to be named Ross's new co-CEO. It was from this incident that the quiet Levin emerged with a reputation as a corporate opportunist. Today, Levin readily acknowledges his own ambition in the matter, although in a less vicious light. "I realized I could really run this company, and that something was going to give if Nicholas was running it," he said.

Two decades after he'd started working at Time Inc., Jerry Levin had made it to the top. And though he was sharing the pinnacle of power with Ross, he would soon have it to himself. By November of 1992, Ross was undergoing chemotherapy treatment and was expected to recover sufficiently to come back to work on a part-time basis in 1993. Yet it was not to be.

At around the same time, Levin had launched an effort to restructure the Time Warner board. As it stood, there were 12 board members from the Warner side, and just nine from Time. With deft maneuvering, Levin managed in just a few months to force through a new, more equal board. It was an impressive display of political power. But quite by chance, it would become public at a high price.

The crucial vote on the new board came on December 19, 1992. Unfortunately for Levin, Steve Ross died unexpectedly the very next day. Levin was forced to release the company's statement about the board reshuffling—essentially, what appeared to be a minicoup against Ross—on the same day news of Ross's death hit the wires. Levin insisted to me that Ross knew of his efforts and supported them, although it is not clear Ross had an ability to fight back by then. Levin admitted the move made him look bad nonetheless. "It was unfortunate," he said.

To some, the timing of the board reshuffling was another callous, nakedly aggressive move on Levin's part—just the latest feint-and-strike of a corporate shark. But no matter what people thought of his ethics, they had to acknowledge one thing: Jerry Levin, who at first had seemed like little more than a technogeek strategist, was a master of corporate political manipulation.

Or, perhaps, as some think, it may have just been due to a little bit of luck. "If Steve Ross hadn't died, Jerry would have been gone," Joe Ripp, who served as controller and later chief financial officer of Time Warner, told me in 2003. Others close to Ross concur, noting that Levin and Ross would inevitably have had a falling out, and that it was likely Ross would have won any battle between them.

But Ross died, and Levin became the leader of Time Warner. While he would never gain strong control over the company, he was its leader and was ready to resume the march to the future he'd been dreaming of ever since his first satellite victory back in 1975. He'd have to fight off one last incursion into his power—beating back a potential takeover attempt by Seagram's in 1993 and 1994—but this time Levin had no one to stop him.

And as he soon demonstrated, he was ready to move forward quickly with his own agenda—one that would, he hoped, put Time Warner at the forefront of the coming revolution in interactive communications. With AOL, Prodigy, and CompuServe jockeying for position and MSN not yet a gleam in Bill Gates's eye, the online playing field was wide open. While it had gone public, AOL was still struggling to attract consumers and stay afloat—which might have been a perfect moment for a powerhouse like Time Warner to step in and buy it. But Levin, who never seriously considered AOL as an acquisition target, chose at first to go in another direction.

Full Splat Network

One month after Ross's death, in his first major presentation as Time Warner's sole CEO, Levin described the future as he saw it. Time

Warner was, he announced, planning a product that would "change the way people use television." What sounded like a radical idea stood in stark contrast to its desperately dull name: The Full Service Network, or FSN.

FSN was an experimental two-way cable system scheduled for testing in Orlando, Florida, at the end of 1993 (though its launch ended up being postponed a year, to December of 1994). With a specially designed cable box and a subscription, FSN users would be able to shop, get movies on demand, and play interactive games on their TV sets. And this, Levin believed, was only the beginning. To him, it was the start of Time Warner's transformation from staid old-guard company into the vanguard of the future. He established an online committee to help guide the company through the FSN launch, other online opportunities in cable, and also the launch of Pathfinder, which would become the most-visited site on the new World Wide Web.

The future appeared to sprawl ahead of him like a limitless plain and Levin finally had the means to make his dreams come true. "He staked out his vision rather boldly," observed Walter Isaacson, who would lead many of Time Warner's early online efforts. "I think he was always looking for new ways to deliver information . . . and he had a real sense that the future lay in giving people control of their information."

Henry Luce III, the son of *Time*'s cofounder, told me such dreaming took its toll. "Levin put a lot of energy and commitment into the automation of the media and of advances through technology, as well as company money," said Luce, who served on the Time Warner board until the mid-1990s. "It was almost always a big miss, but he always believed in it."

Thus, Levin made sure that he'd have the ability—meaning, the cash—to do what he wished by inking a huge deal with the telecom and cable company U.S. West in the summer of 1993. For $2.5 billion, U.S. West acquired a 25 percent stake in Time Warner Entertainment, a division formed earlier from pieces of various Time Warner assets, including its cable and entertainment assets. Announced in May of 1993, the deal was greeted optimistically by Wall Street, boosting Time Warner's stock by 4 percent.

"The partnership between U.S. West and Time Warner Entertainment," Levin told the *Wall Street Journal,* "means the future is here now." And he even took it an unusual step further. "I've staked my career on it," Levin said about FSN. With plans to invest $1 billion of U.S. West's money and up to $5 billion of Time Warner's, FSN would be the biggest risk Levin had ever taken.

On December 14, 1994, at a Sheraton hotel near Orlando, Levin launched his vision of the future. In front of a crowd of hundreds, he and an accountant named Karl Willard played a hand of virtual gin rummy via FSN, as reported by the *Orlando Sentinel.* As Levin went on to demonstrate the other games and features of FSN, he insisted to the assembled reporters, "This is not a hollow demonstration. This is not hype."

And it wasn't really, despite all the scorn FSN would endure over the years. In retrospect, FSN was a groundbreaking system that offered a whole catalog of useful services—the same kinds that would soon spawn countless Internet companies and help create the greatest economic frenzy the country had ever seen. With FSN, customers could read *Time* magazine, shop at Winn-Dixie, buy music CDs, look up local restaurants, print maps, download movies, and play interactive games, all through their television sets.

Years after FSN's flameout, Levin defended the idea behind it but admitted he promised too much. FSN was, after all, an unproven consumer product with no immediately executable business. "I probably should not have hyped it quite so much," he told me. "We should have positioned it from the start as an experiment."

A failed one, as it turned out. By the summer of 1995, only six months after FSN's launch, the service was already struggling. There were fewer than 50 subscribers, and the cost of the set-top box still hovered around $5,000 (a number Levin now recalls as possibly even too low). In any case, it was far too high for any kind of serious rollout, especially since some key technological glitches still needed to be worked out.

An even more serious problem loomed, one that was inherent in FSN's basic concept. Even if FSN worked perfectly, and even if the costs could be brought down, would people really want this kind of interactive TV-based service? On June 19, 1995, the *Wall Street Jour-*

nal offered its answer to that question in a lengthy article titled "The Myth of Multimedia."

"Time Warner's vision of the future is a chimera," the newspaper opined. "Interactive multimedia technology is invading the home, but in a way that revolves around the personal computer rather than the television." The article went on to correctly predict that the real boom would be in Web development, quoting research studies indicating that about 14 million consumers would be buying products and services via personal computers by the turn of the century. (That estimate, as high as it seemed at the time, would actually turn out to be woefully low—by 2000, almost 100 million users were making online purchases of some sort.)

The *Journal*'s prediction was dead on: Interactivity would soon be the province almost exclusively of the personal computer, not on the television as Levin had wagered. As Time Warner's Joe Ripp told me in a 2003 interview, "Jerry was always a little ahead of himself. With FSN, he had it right, but he had the wrong device. . . . The whole world was rushing toward the Internet."

Levin was going down the wrong path entirely with FSN—but luckily, he'd had the foresight to place another bet on the fledgling commercial Internet as well. Or, at least it had seemed lucky at the time. With $10 million in initial funding from the FSN project fund, Time Warner leapt into the Internet with a Web site of its own. It would be headed by up-and-coming Time Inc. editor Walter Isaacson and Curt Viebranz for the business side, and run by a core team that included Time Warner executives Bruce Judson, Paul Sagan, Linda McCutcheon, Oliver Knowlton, and Jim Kinsella.

The choice of Isaacson was a clear signal of the venture's importance, since he was one of the fairest-haired boys at a company filled with them. A respected writer and the assistant managing editor of *Time,* Isaacson had a honeyed accent redolent of his home state of Louisiana. But his level of ambition was pure New York, and he displayed an impressive ability to link himself up with even more impressive people. To the politically attuned denizens of the Time Warner empire, the involvement of Isaacson was a signal that the Internet was hot.

Isaacson firmly believed it was more than just a political game for Time Warner, especially since the future was digital and that would eventually have an impact on every aspect of the company. In a March 1994 document entitled "Proposal for a Time Inc. Electronic Network and World Wide Web Site," Isaacson wrote, "In targeting an audience, we will follow Russell Long's advice about shooting a duck: Aim ahead of the duck. We would aim for a mass market audience of people who have not been early adapters to the online world: Ordinary folks rather than 17-year-old get-a-life geeks who want to download software." Case and AOL had already started to do this, though AOL's own efforts were just getting traction.

Isaacson also listed the goals for the service, which, in true Time Warner blue-blood fashion, had been code-named Calliope after the muse of epic poetry. But the service's aims were more pedestrian than its code name: To provide "online access to the content of Time Inc.'s publications and databanks, to new products and services based on Time Inc.'s titles and journalism, and to relevant material licensed or acquired by Time Inc."; "a place to communicate, interact and form 'virtual communities'"; "an environment for interactive advertising, shopping and transactional services"; "an easy way for average consumers to get onto the Internet"; "a front-end for cable systems that want to sell to computer users a high-bandwidth link to online networks, the Internet, shopping venues, email and other electronic services."

Because Time Warner had acquired a number of cable systems (a strategy that later became a key part of the eventual AOL Time Warner merger), cable was an important element of the first plans for Calliope. These plans included regional high-speed versions of Calliope for cable systems, which would link to things like school lunch menus. It was all part of a stated aim to eventually put dial-up online companies such as AOL out of business, and replace them with supercharged cable connections instead. While AOL struggled with phone costs and getting modems out to the masses at the time, Time Warner was hoping that it already had the right lines in place—cable lines, that is—that jacked more directly into the consumer.

"In the next few years, high-speed Internet connection via cable may become commercially available," noted one internal memo from the summer of 1994. "It will transform the online experience and could make dial-up services such as CompuServe and AOL, which pretend to be content services but are mainly connectivity services, vulnerable." It was, in fact, the right idea, although way too early both technologically and creatively.

But with such lofty goals, the new service would need a suitably fancy name. One internal memo listed about a dozen suggestions, including Cavalcade, Gateway, Avatar, Arena, Tempo, Jamboree, The Time Machine, Orion, Tidings, and the unfortunate Twin: The Time Warner Information Network.

The eventual winner was Pathfinder, which was, as Isaacson wrote on the opening screen of Pathfinder on its debut day, "a tribute to a great character trapped in a dreadful novel: Natty Bumppo, the uncorrupted natural man who follows the wilderness westward in the James Fenimore Cooper novel that threatened to turn us off to reading when we were in high school. As he meanders his way through Cooper's works, he picks up a bunch of other names, but most of us agreed that Pathfinder was a better name for an Internet service than Leatherstocking or Deerslayer."

In the same note to users, Isaacson linked the service to Time Inc.'s history. "When Henry Luce and Britton Hadden founded our company 72 years ago," he wrote, "they spoke about how the glut of information in our daily lives created the need for a guide to what was important and interesting. We like to think that if they were alive today, among the things they would do is build a website."

With that perceived historical blessing and overly classy pedigree, Pathfinder was launched in October of 1994. Levin presented the service at an annual meeting in Manhattan, intending to show it off by instantly bringing up online photos of the World Series. Worried the technology might fail, the team had devised a plan: As Levin got into this part of the presentation, Isaacson sat poised nearby, a pen in his hand. If it seemed the photos weren't going to appear, he was to drop the pen as a signal, and Levin was to move on quickly in his talk.

No pen was dropped. But, despite that small victory and despite all the planning, Pathfinder ended up quickly becoming little more than a sprawling, badly organized patchwork of thousands of Web pages.

Though it resembled an explosion at a Time Warner magazine factory, the company nonetheless dubbed it "The World's Best Web Site."

And supposedly, it would be a profitable one. In a series of memos, executives outlined a plan to make money from a number of different revenue streams. These included "licensing fees paid by cable operators for the opening screens, software and package of basic services; selling advertising and transaction services that are featured on the initial screens; and creating a broad market for its own premium Time Inc. service, which will have a competitive advantage over existing services in a high-bandwidth environment."

In fact, the team was so certain that Pathfinder would make lots of money that it noted in another memo in December of 1994, "It is pointless to fight over how to divvy up the proceeds before we've finished robbing the stagecoach."

One stagecoach the team planned to rob was AOL, through the licensing of its powerful content brands. In fact, Time Warner had already signed a couple of deals with AOL in the spring of 1994, about a half-year before Pathfinder and FSN were launched.

Isaacson and his team had briefly considered pushing Levin to buy AOL, but those efforts were never serious. Instead, Time Warner opted for a deal. In what was a typical transaction at the time, AOL paid an annual fee of several hundred thousand dollars in exchange for being allowed to offer *Time* magazine exclusively to its customers. The payment formula would shift, as AOL grew stronger, because content providers would eventually pay AOL rather than the other way around to reach its growing subscriber base. But these first Time Warner deals were vital to AOL in its early days, lending the fledgling service the legitimacy of Time Warner. And Time Warner, much to its delight, got cash.

AOL was only one of dozens of Internet companies looking to make deals—either for content or investments—with the mighty Time Warner. Like tadpoles zipping around in search of a sustaining bit of algae, fledgling companies with quirky names like Netscape and Yahoo kept swimming up, offering percentages of their businesses in a variety of deals. But Time Warner turned down most of them, deciding it was not in the venture business. It was early in the game, executives believed, and no one knew whether any of these companies would last until the next year. In any case, the mighty Time Warner believed it could develop a major Internet business on its own.

Levin was thrilled with Pathfinder and showed it off at every opportunity, especially to important visitors he could lure to the new media room at Time Warner headquarters. He'd push buttons and display instant Web pages to the inevitable oohs and ahhs of visitors. "I really thought we were on our way," he would later recall about that time.

But even though Time Warner shied away from deeper involvement with AOL, Yahoo, or Netscape, the company would soon leap headlong into a merger with another, more volatile partner. And this one would have a major role in the eventual marriage of AOL and Time Warner a few years down the road.

Jerry and Ted's Not So Excellent Adventure

"I am being clitorized by Time Warner," boomed Ted Turner in front of dozens of journalists at Washington's National Press Club in September of 1994. Robert E. "Ted" Turner III was perhaps the only major American executive who could utter such a bizarre and desperately offensive statement without anyone really being surprised.

It was typical Turner, I would learn—the ranting of the company's resident "madman." His outbursts—by turns amusing, embarrassing, and sometimes horrifying—were often greeted with eyes rolling and sighs by managers and fellow board members at the company. "That was Ted," said more than one high-ranking Time Warner executive to me, in what appeared to be the generic explanation for Turner's tantrum role at the company. His flashes of brilliance, most agreed, more than made up for the trouble, which often required someone dispatched from headquarters to calm him down, much as one would a small child.

By that time, Turner was already a legend. His list of accomplishments was as eclectic as it was impressive: He'd won the America's Cup sailing trophy in 1977, founded the Cable News Network

(CNN) in 1980, and started the Goodwill Games in 1986. He'd even been named *Time* magazine's Man of the Year for 1991. A person whose extremes of personality made him at once magnetic and repellent, he had a knack for business success that was matched only by his well-known appetite for the pleasures of female company.

Born on November 19, 1938, in Cincinnati, Ohio, Turner grew up seeking (and rarely receiving) approval from his father, Ed Turner, who struggled with alcoholism and depression for much of his life. His father sent him to boarding school, where Ted worked harder at pulling successful pranks than at making good grades, eventually developing into a cocksure young man. But when he was a teenager, his younger sister, Mary Jane, suffered an agonizing death from a form of lupus—an event that seems to have pierced Turner to the core. As the *New Yorker*'s Ken Auletta wrote in a 2001 profile, "The experience transformed Turner. 'I decided I wanted to become a success,' he says."

Yet Turner's ambition wouldn't become apparent just yet. After being expelled from Brown University in his junior year (for a host of infractions, including having women in his dorm room), Turner began working for his father's billboard company, Turner Advertising. He married his girlfriend, Julia Nye, began sailing in earnest, and seemed to have his life on a fairly typical upper-middle-class track. But on March 5, 1963, when he was just 24, that all changed abruptly. On that day, his father shot himself to death at home with a handgun.

It's impossible to fully gauge the emotional effect of a parent's suicide on the child who is left behind. This is especially true when the relationship was as volatile and complex as that between Ted Turner and his father. But what is certain is that, following his father's death, Turner took over the family business, and with a combustible blend of skill, desire, and chutzpah, he turned it into a major media empire.

In the late 1960s and early 1970s, Turner began acquiring radio and television stations, soon venturing into the new phenomenon of cable TV. His programming tastes were part practical (whatever he could get for cheap) and part personal whim (mostly sports and movies). In 1976, he bought the Atlanta Braves baseball team, turning them into "America's team" by broadcasting their games over his

WTCG channel nationwide, a step that was both controversial and bold. By 1980, Turner was already a notable personality in the American business and sports landscape. But that year, he went a step further, making the move that would ensure his place in history. He launched CNN.

The first 24-hour news station, CNN was Turner's most passionate gamble. He believed, of course, that the station would eventually make money, but more than that, he believed it could change the world. Over and over, people who have worked closely with Turner have testified to his desire to truly make a difference. And while it's true that Turner exhibited all the hubris and love of success one would expect from a prosperous entrepreneur, he was arguably the most idealistic soul in the pantheon of major American executives.

He was also one of the most bedeviled. Even as he burned up the yacht-racing circuit and expanded his business domain, Turner often startled friends and associates alike with his widely reported erratic behavior. According to Porter Bibb's 1993 biography of Turner, *It Ain't As Easy As It Looks,* it was not unusual for Turner to suddenly strip naked, tell baldly racist jokes, or spew egregious insults at colleagues, his wife, or his children. The patina of success surrounding Ted Turner was always dimmed by a sense of gloom that hovered just below the surface.

Turner suffered from violent and unpredictable mood changes, and he often talked about suicide. He even, according to Bibb, kept in his desk drawer the loaded pistol his father had used to kill himself. Then, in 1985, a doctor at last gave a name to his demons: Turner was diagnosed as suffering from bipolar illness, or manic depression. Characterized by wild emotional swings, bipolar disease can often be successfully treated with lithium. Turner began taking the drug, and soon his peaks and valleys began to smooth out.

They would smooth out even further when Turner began dating actress Jane Fonda in 1989. The two began seeing each other following Turner's divorce from his second wife, Jane Smith. It seemed almost impossible that two such enormous personalities could be in the same room together, much less in a relationship. But Fonda, who'd gained fame as an actress, antiwar demonstrator, and workout guru, seemed to have completely captivated the restless Turner. The couple married at Turner's sprawling Florida estate in December of 1991.

Turner now seemed to have it all. He was rich, handsome, and physically fit. He was married to a beautiful, famous actress, and the sheer star power of their union turned heads in Hollywood as well as New York. But as always, he still wasn't satisfied.

Turner had long wanted to own one of the "big three" television networks—and, in fact, had tried unsuccessfully in the 1980s to purchase CBS. Then, he'd been outmaneuvered by the network itself, which reportedly didn't want to be owned by the maverick newsman from the South. Despite the success of CNN—which had become a respected news organization, after initially being derided as the "Chicken Noodle Network"—Turner was a loose cannon and was not welcome in the staid world of network news. In the 1990s, when he shifted his attention to buying NBC, he was thwarted by an enemy on his own board. It was an enemy he'd come to despise even more in a few years' time: Jerry Levin.

Levin had the upper hand, because Turner had sold off sizable stakes in TBS in the previous few years in order to pay down crushing debt and raise cash for his often-precarious empire. After the sales, one group of cable companies run by cable mogul John Malone owned 21 percent of TBS, and Levin's Time Warner held 19 percent. That gave Time Warner a board seat and a strong influence on Turner's fate.

When Turner announced his desire to make a bid for NBC, Levin and others used their voting power to block the move. Turner was outraged, believing Levin was acting not in the best interests of TBS, but because he wanted Time Warner to buy the network. While it was a fair enough reason to be angry, the way Turner expressed it, in his speech at the National Press Club, was downright bizarre. Despite his medication and newly contented lifestyle, the "Mouth of the South" was clearly still capable of uttering things that were both deeply shocking and patently offensive.

During his 1994 National Press Club speech, Turner had begun talking about the "barbaric mutilation" of clitorectomies—a custom, practiced in many parts of the world, in which young girls have parts of their genitals removed to prevent them from enjoying sex. Turner was, he declared, outraged by the practice. Then he made a peculiar segue, comparing the practice to his own business experience. "I'm being clitorized by Time Warner and the women are being clitorized by—that's exactly right," he said. "And I don't like it any more than they do."

Nearly a decade after Turner uttered these words, Levin told me his opinion of it. "To compare a brutal practice like that to his business life," he said, "was just beyond the pale of even Ted." He later added that it was the only one of Turner's tirades that still made him furious.

And Levin had many such harangues to choose from, as Turner was soon habitually aiming them at him. Turner began calling Levin "The Administrator," deriding him as someone who stayed holed up in his office, reading papers and exerting influence via information control rather than talent. It was meant as an insult, but, in fact, Levin often described himself in pretty much the same terms. "I was an information junkie," he told me. "I always thought the guy who owns the information is the guy on the way up."

Turner's name-calling would get much, much worse. But despite their differences, he and Levin papered over their feud less than a year after the notorious Press Club appearance, when Turner agreed to sell the rest of TBS to Time Warner. The acquisition of TBS, which Levin had won partly because Turner didn't want to have to sell to News Corp.'s Rupert Murdoch, was the second deal that "chief strategist" Levin had advised for Time Inc. back in the late 1980s. And now it was coming to fruition.

Where a year before there had been acrimony and talk of mutilation, now there was nothing but love between Jerry Levin and Ted Turner. In fact, at the August 25, 1995, announcement of the deal, Levin proudly introduced Turner by calling him "my colleague, best friend, and new partner, Ted Turner!"

"Best friends" definitely seemed like a stretch; it's amusing to imagine these two men having anything to talk about beyond stock deals and cable television. Nonetheless, after raising his eyebrows in surprised amusement, Turner flashed his trademark gap-toothed grin, stepped to the podium, and proclaimed himself pleased at this turn of events.

As was typical for Turner, he would later express irritation and say he'd felt forced to do the deal. He'd also, in the midst of the AOL Time Warner fallout, poke sarcastic fun at Levin's friendship remark.

But at the time, he was all smiles. The $7.5 billion stock deal, approved in 1996, further solidified Time Warner's position as the world's largest multimedia company and it made Turner the company's biggest shareholder with holdings of about 10 percent. He was also named vice chairman of the company. With that, Jerry and Ted's not-so-excellent adventure had truly begun—with the pair presiding over an ever-growing media powerhouse that had limitless possibilities.

Meanwhile, Steve Case was struggling through the summer of 1996 with subscriber churn, a dubious Wall Street, and consumer anger over technological snafus. Incredibly, it would be less than four years before he would determine the fates of both Levin and Turner.

Pathloser

By 1995, the year Time Warner announced it was buying TBS, the company had had nearly five years to digest its first "transforming transaction"—the Warner merger. Not surprisingly, things had been very bumpy for the first few years. But after that, the company had settled comfortably into the structure that would become its defining trait.

Rather than pushing to fully integrate Time and Warner, Levin presided over executives who ran the divisions almost as separate entities. Each was responsible for hitting its own numbers and, to a large extent, charting its own course. Within Time Warner there existed independent "fiefdoms," and for the most part, nobody messed with anybody else's turf.

Mostly, it was because Levin had little choice over the matter—unable to truly influence his divisions without taking drastic measures such as firings. While he was adept at that—dumping HBO's Michael Fuchs and a raft of other top executives over the years—the power of Time Warner was dispersed. That contrasted sharply to the command-and-control structure that would soon characterize AOL under Bob

Pittman, when he arrived at the online company in 1996, after years at big media companies like Time Warner.

Indeed, this has long been the standard cliché about Time Warner, where the company is more about the power of its warlords than about pulling together as a whole. While some have criticized this structure, many of the division heads—both past and present—liked it. "We were allowed to operate and we did very well between us, when it was right," one former division head told me. "No one had to or didn't have to cooperate—which was a good thing, I think, for the individual businesses." At times, however, this "fiefdom" structure resulted in absurd intracompany fights. Divisions tended to keep to themselves and were loath to get involved in each other's business. And not only did they not work together, much of the time they continued to negotiate and battle each other as competitors.

The most famous example of this was the fight between the company's online and studio divisions over the use of the Road Runner name. The online team wanted to name its new high-speed Internet service (which was originally dubbed Excalibur) after the sprightly cartoon character. Isaacson and his team had picked out the name, thinking it would be easy to get since it was from a sister division. The difficulties of getting this seemingly simple deal done have gone down in legend, often being pointed to as the perfect example of the internecine nature of Time Warner.

As in most things, the real story was a lot more complex and much less dramatic. "I thought, 'Hey, great, we own [the Road Runner name],'" remembered Isaacson, who wanted the name immediately for the cable service. But since the Warner Bros. studio was the real owner of the cartoon icon, it naturally wanted hefty licensing fees for the use of the character. On the surface at least, the studio's reasons seemed like good ones. The cable service had other partners outside of Time Warner, for example, who had no right to share in the Road Runner copyright for free.

To the fast-moving Internet division, such niceties seemed ridiculous given a successful high-speed service would, in turn, help the movie studio, which was known for its internal hardball tactics. In any case, getting the deal done required plenty of footwork, starting with a trip Isaacson and Time Warner president Dick Parsons took to Los Angeles to convince Warner Bros. coheads Terry Semel and Bob Daly of the value of the cable service. This was the beginning of multiple negotiations at the top of the company that would be required before the Road Runner name finally was set free.

But cooperation was not a celebrated idea within the core of Time Warner. When the magazine division tried a spate of cross-marketing strategies, for example, they resulted in little more than discounted ad prices. And forcing the various units to do business together was often financially onerous to each division, since better deals were often struck with outside partners. If they worked independently, the divisions could often do better, even if the whole company suffered. Synergy, that mystical goal of both the Warner and Turner mergers, was elusive.

This was most apparent at Time Warner New Media, the online ventures division, which would need support from the whole company to truly succeed. But instead of support, it was, by late 1995, getting little more than resentment (for the money and public attention it got), and skepticism (for its results) from most parts of Time Warner. And, within the online unit itself, executives began to war with each other. Walter Isaacson, the head of new media and the presumed leader of Time Warner's charge to the future, fled back to the "dead-tree" side of the company, becoming the editor of *Time* magazine in 1996. So much for the future being digital.

Before he left, Isaacson sent his replacement, Paul Sagan, a strategy memo. "It now seems to me less likely that [customers] will pay one flat fee for a disparate conglomeration rather than pay for their particular interests," he wrote. "Especially when there is neither a clear coherence about what is in the conglomeration nor an established sense that various elements of that conglomeration might have a fee of their own." Good luck, he might as well have added, and see you later!

So, how could Pathfinder make money? Isaacson had a parting idea: "For us to make money in new media," he wrote, "we have to develop a few core, branded services we can charge for. I think these services should be based on core brands and content that Time Inc.

owns." This would lead to Pathfinder Personal Edition, a "premium" service costing $4.95 per month.

But Personal Edition fell flat from the outset. And Pathfinder continued to struggle, with no realistic plan on the horizon of how to make any real money, despite the fact that its page views grew at one point to number more than one billion per month. Those kinds of traffic numbers would soon put multibillion-dollar valuations on a spate of independent Internet companies—including AOL, Netscape, and Yahoo—but Pathfinder was trapped inside Time Warner and unable to escape.

In these times, numerous Web companies were celebrated despite their inability to make money. Not so Pathfinder, however, which made it into the Internet Hall of Shame in November of 1995, in a now-famous comment by Time Inc. Chairman and CEO Don Logan. A Southerner with an advanced mathematics degree and a reputation for speaking his mind, Logan responded to a reporter's query about Pathfinder's financial performance by snapping, "It gives new meaning to the term 'black hole.'"

Those who know Logan say his comment has been unfairly interpreted to mean that he hated the Web. "I think he was realistically ambivalent—disgusted with the hype, but very interested in the Internet's potential," said Linda McCutcheon, who became Pathfinder's last top executive. "I mean, he was a mathematician, and it didn't add up for him yet."

Unfortunately, nothing about Time Warner's technological forays was adding up. Down in Orlando, the Full Service Network was all but dead. In a half-hearted attempt at spin, the company finally began characterizing the venture as an "experiment" and as a lesson-learning experience. That was true enough; FSN had yielded some interesting data and technology that the company would later use in digitizing its cable unit. But it was a terribly expensive tutorial.

By the beginning of 1997, it was clear Time Warner would have to shut down FSN. The announcement in April drew caustic press comments. The most stinging came from one of the company's own publications. FSN, *Time* magazine declared, "might have been the most expensive pizza-delivery system ever invented." With FSN losses estimated at more than $100 million and Pathfinder flailing toward its own death throes (it would sputter its last breath in the summer of 1999, after eating up tens of millions more), Time Warner's early and ambitious foray into cyberspace looked like a bust, despite the massive effort put into it.

Writer and entrepreneur Michael Wolff, who had been brought on as a consultant to Time Warner's online efforts, would later recall that he had seen it coming all along. Wolff was an acid-tongued iconoclast with a prickly wit, a keen eye for detail, and a biting writing talent—all of which he'd unleash on Time Warner (and AOL, too) in his 1998 book, *Burn Rate,* about the early days of the commercial Internet. I would often find myself wrangling with him about the true meaning of the Internet and its prospects—he thought the Web was a complete scam and I did not—but he was spot on about Time Warner being woefully out of sync with the Internet wave.

"Even with my scant knowledge, I knew that a mess of plans were being made on the basis of assumptions about technology that were comically haphazard," Wolff wrote in *Burn Rate.* "It was often a cascade of misunderstandings or knowledge synapses: A wonderful, patrician, 1950s-style *Time* editor having a weighty discussion with the salesman from WAIS, the search software company, and throughout the discussion helplessly confusing the client-server relationship; a determined Isaacson acolyte insisting to a programmer that while something may not be possible now, it would surely be possible in the next 12 months or so ('Wouldn't it?'). They treated technology like a service arm of what they were trying to do."

In fairness, as I always argued with Wolff, Time Warner might have been clueless, but just about everyone else was, too. At the birth of the commercial Internet, it really didn't matter what you didn't know; everyone was just making things up as they went along. Not only were there no rules, but also it seemed entirely possible that whoever took the initiative could simply make up the rules themselves, and everyone else would be forced to follow along.

Yet, as so often happens, those who are first are not necessarily the best. That was certainly the case for Time Warner; today, one rarely sees a reference to the company's fledgling online efforts without the accompanying word *fiasco*. FSN and Pathfinder were simply too early for their time, not to mention way too much like old media to satisfy those who were flocking to new media. As services, they were cumbersome, confusing, and spoke down from the top in a medium that thrived on bubbling up from the bottom.

Pages referred to other pages in Time Warner, rather than out to the Web, just as users were embracing the idea of limitless choice. It was graphics heavy, making it slow to download, more like a magazine paradigm than the less fussy Web. And it disdained community, a critical element of all successful Internet sites. Like all traditional media companies, it talked while consumers were supposed to listen. That was problematic, since on the Web everybody talked. Finally and perhaps most damning, the site was too costly for a company that Wall Street counted on to make dependable profits (and was punished when it did not).

Many other media companies made similar mistakes—including News Corp., Walt Disney, and Viacom—but Pathfinder still remains the model of how little the old media companies understood the Web at its commercial infancy. Worse, it gave Time Warner the reputation of being a digital loser. It was an image that would stick with the company and have a major impact on its later decision to merge with AOL.

By 1997, it appeared as if Jerry Levin was clueless about the one thing he seemed to care most about. In just three years, he'd gone from being at the leading edge of new technology and a visionary among the lumbering media pack to potentially falling out of the race altogether. AOL, on the other hand, had begun an amazing upward trajectory, aided by a new push by Pittman to goose AOL's revenues by focusing in on ad deals by taking advantage of the massive amounts of capital about to be pumped into Silicon Valley dot-com startups.

It was a frustrating position to be in, but as Levin watched the Internet whirlwind start spinning even faster, he was still determined to get in the center of it. At high-level executive management meetings, he became what one division head described to me as "increasingly desperate and obsessed with the Internet killing Time Warner."

His fervor grew, the executive said, as a spate of startup companies—including a number that Time Warner had turned down as investment opportunities—went public at astonishing valuations and rose even further.

More important, he fretted that as those market valuations rose, they would give enormous power over the future development of media and entertainment to companies that he had ignored to his peril. According to many, Levin was worried that companies, especially AOL as the largest online player, could easily contemplate a takeover of his company if their stock rose even further. "I think he, like a lot of us, could not quite believe it," said cable pioneer John Malone, who was also a large Time Warner shareholder. "And it scared him more as it got more and more possible." Levin told me he doubted this would happen, but it made him nervous the possibility existed.

Levin decided then that he needed to double down rather then cut back on Internet plans. But not everyone at Time Warner thought a big bet was needed. Most divisional executives wanted to pursue a longer-term strategy, with limited losses and minimal risk, especially since the prices of Internet firms Time Warner might consider buying were getting steadily higher. Time Inc.'s Don Logan was feeling especially cautious, given that he was the first to get burned in the Internet space with Pathfinder. "We all wanted to dip our toes in the water, especially after we saw what happened to Logan," said one executive. "He stuck a whole leg in and it got bitten off, so we were cautious about losing another one."

But Levin was adamant that the company should think big, since after Pathfinder the media were always asking where Time Warner's Internet strategy was going. "He always said, 'Let's be the leading media company to embrace the Net,'" recalled Warner Bros. cohead Terry Semel, who would later take over the helm at Yahoo. "But after our experience, we found it was too expensive and it put our earnings at risk, so more of the same made us fearful. We wanted to do things more slowly and not lose money at it."

Semel understood the urge to make bold digital moves at Time Warner. But he, like others, wanted to move in a way that wouldn't damage Time Warner's old media assets. Levin, on the other hand, felt that times were changing too fast to act tentatively. "Jerry was frustrated trying to find an interactive opportunity and was reaching a point of no return," said Semel.

Those who know Jerry Levin describe him as a man who, when he believes in something, doesn't hold back. To underscore his digital commitment, he began telling division heads at the phone-centric company that the best way to communicate with him was via email. And he talked incessantly about the Internet at every meeting, reveling in tiny details about the latest new Web trend and pointing out things Time Warner should be doing.

"I think much of his self-esteem was built on how technology would periodically transform the media business," said influential media investor Gordon Crawford. "So everything built to that point."

Later, after he left the company, Levin acknowledged his growing worry, saying to me in early 2003 that he didn't feel there was any talent or innovative spirit within the company that was capable of competing in the interactive space. The FSN and Pathfinder failures, coming as they did when so many others seemed to be succeeding, had seemed to prove this definitively.

"Internet DNA was absolutely essential to me," he said. And if Time Warner couldn't find it internally, it raised some troubling questions. Would other companies, some of which weren't even in existence before 1990, become the true leaders of the next age, as Time Warner withered under the onslaught? Was there anything Time Warner could do to change that unhappy fate? What was the right path, given the many deadends the company had run into? And what should Jerry Levin, who had dedicated his life to finding solutions through technology, do now?

These were the big-picture ideas that began to consume Levin. But any answers to those questions would have to wait until after the events of June 2, 1997, when Levin's personal life took a tragic turn. On that date, the body of his son, Jonathan Levin, was found in his New York apartment, the victim of a brutal murder. His death would further put Gerald Levin into a fervid state of mind that would eventually push him right into the arms of AOL.

Yeah, they say two thousand zero zero party over, oops
out of time. So tonight I'm gonna party like it's 1999.

PRINCE, *"1999"*

Chapter Four

THE $10 MILLION NAPKIN

To Mogul or Not to Mogul?

Not many people have a $10 million napkin, but I do.

It's a hotel's typical cocktail napkin, white, four inches
square, made of medium-quality paper with little to set it
apart from similar ones you might find strewn on any bar.
Except, that is, for the wobbly scrawl on one side, written
by a well-known Silicon Valley venture capitalist, who had
offered $10 million for a 20 percent stake in a new com-
pany. To be technical, it gave my little piece of paper an
instant valuation of $50 million.

You have to love the New Economy. Or, since we're talking now in much less heady times, you had to.

And why not? That there was actually no company made
no difference. That there was no staff made no difference.
That there was no product made no difference. Perhaps
most of all, that I and some other tech reporters had cooked
only the barest whiff of an idea—mostly on a lark—for a
new kind of tech news Web site made absolutely no differ-

ence. I had told the venture capitalist about the concept more as a joke. But it was the summer of 1999 and this is the way it was then on a dulcet night at a frenetic Internet conference at a luxury hotel in a swanky resort town. Hence, my $10 million napkin.

There were, of course, margaritas, and the venture capitalist was a little tipsy, too. He was clearly teasing me, but there was also an unmistakable air of possibility. Swinging a giant, expensive cigar to and fro with one hand and his drink with the other, he painted a picture of untold riches that could come to me if I only junked my risk-averse reporter's nature and joined the all-night dot-com party that had been going on for two years now and showed no signs of abating.

I was intrigued enough, I admit. The last time someone had made me an offer like this, I was flying high above the Atlantic coast on the way to Florida in a small private plane rented by America Online's Ted Leonsis. It was March of 1997, and I was working on a book about the then-struggling company. AOL's prospects seemed, at the time, limited. With a churning user base, a sorry balance sheet, chaotic management, and the disdain of most of Wall Street and the larger business community, its volatile journey looked to be just about over.

But Leonsis dismissed all of that, pressing against me knee-to-knee in the tiny cabin and offering what he clearly thought was my big opportunity. "You should work for me," he said—completely ignoring the fact that I was trying to write an independent journalistic account of his company's history. "I like to have you reporter types around." He liked us so much, in fact, that he was offering me a large dollop of stock and a job with few parameters or any real description. "I'm thinking of doing an area on AOL called Sacred Cows," he opined. "You'd basically pick people to skewer every week and write about that."

This was a time, you must understand, when online executives, such as Leonsis, were just beginning to style themselves as "media" moguls rather than accept the duller reality of their existence as purveyors of email, sex and celebrity chat, and endless pop-up ads for doodads. Leonsis had even taken to declaring that AOL's true competitors were the mandarins of Hollywood rather than the geeks of Silicon Valley. That he had little idea of the true challenges of the media business and even less experience figuring out ways to create alluring content that sells made little difference to him.

I had taken time off from the *Washington Post,* where I had worked as a journalist for a decade, to write *aol.com.* This was a risk in and of itself, since it was questionable whether AOL would survive and, thus, whether the book would sell. But to write a book no one reads is one thing; to work for a company that files for bankruptcy was something else altogether.

So, I uttered the words to him that still make me cringe to repeat: "Why would I ever want to leave a media giant like the *Washington Post* to work for you at AOL?" And with that flip remark, I turned down my alternate future at the company that would, within five years, purchase Time Warner and vault to the top of the media world at the dawn of the new century. My "stock," needless to say, would have been worth millions of dollars.

Fast-forward to June of 1999: Now a reporter for the *Wall Street Journal,* I stared back at the venture capitalist and wondered what I should say. Was he joking? Was he serious? All I knew for sure was that he was definitely drunk. Even still, fending off giant offers from people like him was actually becoming an almost daily occurrence. The rulers of the new economy had begun to flex their newfound power and wealth by going after people who continued to toil in old-economy jobs, seducing them into cool deals that promised the world. Like most tech reporters then, I had a clutch of job offers from every dot-com-of-the-moment, and the stakes were getting financially juicier by the day.

At another press dinner, yet another venture capitalist, Charlie Lax, had told me without a trace of irony that when he met with entrepreneurs, the most important question he asked them was: "Do you want to be a billionaire?" Presumably, he could tell who the idiots were by those who answered no. Since I had already said no once before and appeared to have lost big bucks, was I going to fail again at this obvious second chance at mogulhood? Was I going to turn my back on a life of huge choices and no restrictions at a time of unprecedented wealth creation, the likes of which the world had never seen?

I stared down at my napkin, which was full of figures and percentages and endless possibilities, and wondered what I should do.

I Came, I Saw, I Got in Bed With a Venture Capitalist

As it turned out, I did nothing—my reporter's natural antirisk nature won out once again.

Even deciding to move west in the fall of 1997 to work for the *Wall Street Journal* had been a struggle for me. I came to San Francisco hating the entire idea of California, if not California itself. Here, it seemed to me, was where the seeds of insanity are often planted and where disasters are a daily event.

But writing about AOL—which had survived and even thrived, despite all predictions otherwise—and meeting exciting new companies in the Internet space had gotten me hooked. In researching the book, I had gotten to observe the one-floor operation in a bad Seattle neighborhood from which Amazon founder Jeff Bezos hoped to change the face of modern retailing. I had visited Yahoo's tiny Santa Clara headquarters, where its team of Web "surfers" ruled the Internet roost by selecting good Intenet sites for its growing directory. And the energy that permeated the Netscape campus in Mountain View was practically explosive, as its Navigator browser seemed to threaten even the great software powerhouse Microsoft.

In fact, the Internet boom itself had been sparked by Netscape's legendary IPO only a few years before. Founded in the spring of 1994, Netscape shipped its browser by the end of that year and dominated the market within months. More important, it introduced the "concept" IPO—a big idea, with little revenue, no profit, a compelling management team, and a young and charismatic cofounder named Marc Andreessen. The poster boy for young and bold entrepreneurial heroes, Andreessen would appear on the cover of *Time* magazine barefoot and sitting on a throne, as the king of the Next Big Thing.

Netscape's IPO was a monster, which made all its employees and investors fabulously wealthy almost instantly. The IPO pricing range was doubled before the offering and the stock soared when it debuted in August of 1995, giving the company an astonishing $2.2 billion valuation on its first day as a public company.

Soon enough, even the big players were terrified. Goldman Sachs analyst Rick Sherlund downgraded shares of Microsoft because of Internet threats, and Microsoft quickly shifted its strategy. By December of 1995, Microsoft head Bill Gates announced plans on what was dubbed "Pearl Harbor Day" to become "hard-core about the Internet."

From then on, the idea of disruptive technology—that is, technology as a deeply revolutionary force that could upend anything in its path—was the order of the day in the tech world, popularized by Clayton Christensen's landmark 1997 book, *The Innovator's Dilemma: When New Technologies Cause Great Firms to Fail.* The very idea that so much business tradition could be immediately overthrown was a powerful one, although it was deeply juvenile at its heart. Nonetheless, a rash of other concept IPOs soon followed, all aiming to radically change the way retail, ordering, information retrieval, and pretty much everything else was done. Blown up, too, were the basic rules of startups. The long time frame that included early seed capital and years of investing and likely failure before any hopes of a "liquidation event" was suddenly compressed to a few months.

This new paradigm seemed to be working, helped mightily after venture firms turned the fire hose of capital on the region. In 1996 and 1997, venture capital funding levels would hit close to $10 billion annually, but then leap to $50 billion in 1999. The number of IPOs would soar, too, from a few dozen annually in 1996 through 1998 to more than 200 in 1999. The financial bonanza was further fueled by a surge in online-addled individual investors, huge press, and analyst hype. It also saw the birth of more than a few new tricks by clever investment bankers, such as the practice of "spinning," which is basically bribery, where corporate executives got hot IPO stock in exchange for investment banking business. (It was a questionable practice that would later draw intense regulatory scrutiny.) But armed with huge instant fortunes, the CEOs and founders of exciting new Web companies became leaders of the economy, as their valuations topped those of old-line firms and their clout grew. Something big was surely happening after a massive number of regular consumers discovered the Internet (and vice versa). And with money and talent pouring in, it was clear it would be centered in Silicon Valley.

So, despite my reservations, when this brewing revolution began to really take off in late 1997, it made sense for me to leave the safety of the East Coast to cover what might become a very big story. As I would soon learn, there was nothing about the burgeoning digital world that readers weren't fascinated with. In fact, that was my new job—to produce more "colorful" stories about tech, which had long centered on mostly dull accounts of chip production and complex software programming. *Wired* magazine had pioneered a trendier style of coverage earlier in the 1990s for and about the digerati—focusing on compelling high concepts and big personalities much as a movie magazine would. Now, everyone wanted to know about Web culture. Soon enough, every single facet of the digital culture was about to get its 15 minutes of fame. And I mean every facet, most especially the rash of money being made and its impact on the lives of once-boring techies.

These techies were actually starting to seem sexy, so much so that the *Wall Street Journal* was even contemplating boudoir stories. "You'll have to get in his bed for a good story," joked Greg Hill in one of my first story meetings. As San Francisco bureau chief for the *Wall Street Journal,* it was Hill's job to find tech stories that would pique the interest of editors in New York. "I don't see how you can do it without getting horizontal," he laughed.

Not exactly, but close. It seemed a well-known venture capitalist had a giant sliding skylight ceiling over his bed that opened and closed depending on barometric pressure. I was charged with finding it, trying it out, and writing about it. The self-effacing financier thankfully refused to let me see it. While he was always up for flacking his investments, he turned out to be one of the very few who didn't encourage the chronicling of every aspect of their wild and exciting private lives.

But the invitations from most of the cream of the Internet royalty come pouring in, in an unending stream. I had much less difficulty getting access to them than reporters who chased after executives from more traditional businesses. This young, brash, arrogant generation wanted everyone to know everything about it, mostly because they believed they were changing the world.

The come-ons were enticing and often frivolous. Come ride with me in my new Ferrari Testarossa! Come admire all the many Lava lamps with which I decorate my new company! Come see how we name our conference rooms after snack foods and our computer servers after gross diseases! Come let us show you how someone who just became a billionaire still lives in a crappy rental and wears ratty old Birkenstocks!

To better understand the Web culture, I reluctantly rode down the giant red slide at the headquarters of Yahoo-wannabe portal Excite ("C'mon, it's *fuuuuuuuun!*" urged the public relations person who went down first, ignoring my look of scorn). I chronicled the cheap eating habits of wealthy techies ($4 burritos were very popular). I wrote of their incessant need to make up weird titles for their jobs (*chief cheerleader* was my least favorite). I dissected and defined new terms like *clicks and mortar* and *Internet incubator* (they turned out to be more clever than meaningful). I reported on their $800 Aeron chairs and the complex hierarchy of billboard ads on Silicon Valley's Highway 101 (what can I say?—this was considered extraordinarily relevant at the time). It was a bit of an unusual situation—serious reporters from all the major business publications were covering an industry as if we were writing about the latest fashion trend or hot Hollywood actor.

And there were the parties and high-level conferences, of course, where exotic drinks, fancy food, and massive crowds were the norm. One, for a startup dedicated to startups called Garage.com, was held at a luxury car dealership. Another, for the Inktomi search technology company, featured a giant climbing wall temporarily installed in a San Jose hotel. Yet another dot-com hired an army of fake 1940s-style paparazzi reporters and photographers, who incessantly chased everyone entering the party. At another event, tough-girl rocker Courtney Love appeared to be seriously flirting with newly minted billionaire, Broadcast.com's Mark Cuban—the kind of moment that made you rub your eyes in disbelief. At one conference, I watched a massive fireworks show better than those presented by most major cities. At another private party, the B-52s played into the night. Public relations people were everywhere, of course, so much so that I had taken to calling them "oxygen."

I certainly needed to clear my head after one party thrown by an online conferencing outfit called WebEx, where I ran smack into the statuesque drag performer RuPaul. She had been hired—presumably for an ungodly amount of cash—as spokesperson for the company. It seemed an inexplicable choice, another celebrity with zero tech knowledge paid to help bring glamour and help build the brand name for these unknown outfits. In a churlish mood, I asked RuPaul what kind of computer she used, doubting she even knew how to turn one on. "One with as much power as possible," she shot back. Alrighty then, girlfriend.

The truth is that the giddiness got a bit wearying after a while, as the gushes of money flushed predictably in and out and the level of arrogance grew. I started telling people there weren't enough rat holes in Silicon Valley to shove the cash down. I contemplated murder as one teenaged billionaire after the next would lecture me on the fate of old media and say they were going to put the *Wall Street Journal* out of business. Though these Internet ventures were often their first jobs out of college, I secretly feared they might be able to do so.

Rather quickly, the mercenaries were replacing the missionaries I had loved so much at the start, such as Jerry Yang of Yahoo and Jeff Bezos of Amazon, as well as legions of much smaller players who created the Web for the love of it rather than the cash. IPO valuations kept rising and the quality of the companies kept declining in what I can only explain years later, with some perspective, as an absolute suspension of disbelief in what was a very permissive era. There were several aspects to this disturbing trend: The warping nature of wealth, the explosion of ego, and the abandonment of traditional business rules. It was an old story, I suppose—an industry started in relative innocence was very soon waylaid by greed.

But, not everyone agreed. The wife of one entrepreneur told me I wrote too much about the money and lectured me at a party she hosted on New Year's Day of 1999 that money was not what the Internet was all about. "It's about changing the world, it's about making a difference," she insisted. "It's not at all about making money." I only nodded at her, as we stood in the lovely multimillion-dollar mansion bought with the barrels of cash her spouse had made in Internet IPOs. On a nearby table, she was serving fancy caviar in giant bowls, which doubtless cost more than my first year of college.

Things seemed to reach a particularly frenzied peak at a live charity auction held in July 1999, which pretty much the entire Internet pantheon attended. The purpose of the event was to raise money for a nonprofit outfit called Schools Online and it was held by the pool at the posh Ritz-Carlton seaside resort at Laguna Niguel, California, during *Industry Standard* magazine's first big Internet conference. In very short order, the *Industry Standard* had become the business bible of the Web, selling a record number of ad pages and making barrels of money doing it.

At that particular moment, the Internet was going gangbusters and its leaders handed over more than $350,000 in a few short hours for what was referred to as "unique items of unclear value." That was an understatement: $17,000 for dinner with homemaking guru Martha Stewart; $4,000 for $2,400 worth of toys from online retailer eToys; $89,000 for an executive search; and even $22,000 to sup with AOL's top three deal makers, Myer Berlow, David Colburn, and Miles Gilburne. And there was more. Sunil Paul, founder of a company that helps deflect unsolicited email, paid $53,000 for the singular privilege of pushing eBay CEO Meg Whitman and three other Internet leaders into the pool. Cybercash founder Dan Lynch bid $10,000 to buy the sexy dress—a size 4 Herve Leger—that another entrepreneur had worn in a controversial software ad.

Perhaps most jaw dropping of all to me, Lynch also forked over $12,000 for a navy-and-silver tie belonging to superstar venture capitalist John Doerr. I was sitting at the table with Doerr and his family while a bidding melee broke out. His eight-year-old daughter got excited and wanted to bid, too. Doerr let her raise a hand to the $1,000 mark, but stopped the little girl when it got higher and quietly told her: "To pay that much for a tie is a little crazy." Later at the conference, I ran into that entrepreneur's wife who had chastised me for writing too much about the profligacy of the era—and she started in on me again. Not about the money, *okay*, got it.

Of course, the *Industry Standard* would go out of business within two years of this party, due to the Web economy's implosion, a potent symbol of how quickly Internet time took place. Yet it *was* all about the money back then, but in much more insidious ways than just a tie that costs double the salary I got in my first job. Not surprisingly, the number of companies actually ready to go public—that is, that were fully "baked"—dropped precipitously by late 1999. The reasons were many, including the need to beat competitors out the door, the need for additional funding from a nearly free money market, and the need for public currency to undertake mergers and acquisitions. The VCs were deftly offloading the risk they usually carried for many years to willing public investors, who seemed eager to take a risk immediately. And the bankers seemed interested only in the flood of fees that came to them.

Now, I am not naïve about this. I did not expect much more from the moneymen, who knew the getting was good, so they got. I will never forget when a banker told me that he was thinking of taking a company public that was "prerevenue." I suggested that he just cut to the chase and start mugging the average investor right on the street. He was still laughing at my joke when I hung up.

But even those individual investors—those folks who turned out to be the last suckers in line—did not care at the time. They were going along for the very profitable ride, caught up in a day-trading frenzy that was hard to explain and impossible to stop as stocks soared. That was helped a lot, I must admit, by the media's incessant cheer-leading, as it trotted out one magazine cover after the next celebrating the boom and did fawning interviews with Internet CEOs on the sets of cable stations like CNBC. And even those journalists who were more circumspect also failed by not consistently pointing out that the revenues and profits were terribly out of sync with the valuations.

Many tried, of course. In one instance in 1998, one of the *Journal's* reporters, George Anders, wrote a devastating front-page piece about a medical-practice Web site for doctors called Healtheon, which was backed by such Valley luminaries as Netscape cofounder Jim Clark and the venture firm Kleiner, Perkins, Caufield & Byers. Despite Healtheon being keyed up for an IPO in the fall, Anders correctly reported that doctors in pilot programs found that its complex products were unusable and that its losses were massive. In other words, Healtheon was still a very unproven startup, and possibly a dud.

Healtheon delayed its offering, because of the article and also a temporary deterioration of market conditions. But it was soon out the IPO door again, grabbing tens of millions of dollars by February of 1999. In fact, its share price quadrupled immediately and reached as high as $125 a share that golden year. When Anders emailed Healtheon venture investor Brook Byers about another time soon after the story ran, the reply he got was typical. "George, why did you run the Healtheon story at the beginning of their road show?" wrote Byers. He was irked that Anders had actually dared to raise questions about critical business issues in the middle of this nonstop party and had—if only temporarily—slowed down the fun.

That kind of experience proliferated everywhere on the Internet landscape. It was clear to all that investors didn't seem to care, at least for the moment, about niggling details like earnings, viability, and costs. Thus, company promoters prevailed quite naturally over company builders. The mantra was clear: Think of market share and not revenues, spend more money to get more scale, and don't worry about the past since the future was so much easier to sell. Indeed, anyone who was reticent did lose, by not participating in the constantly upward trajectory of stocks.

David Rocker knew that all too well as a frustrated short seller of stocks—that is, an investor who bet on stock price downturns rather than upticks. I had met the increasingly apoplectic Rocker years earlier, in 1996, as he unsuccessfully battled AOL by harping on its shoddy accounting practices. He had later attempted the same thing with a range of Internet stocks, and kept losing—despite the fact that he was entirely correct about the precarious state of their finances. "It was a mass hysteria and, honestly, if you tried to be a cautious voice, it was not productive, because your caution was drowned out by the cheers," Rocker reflected in 2003. "The thing is, if you got looser and looser in behavior, the more you were rewarded for it." Rocker recalled that he found himself frequently shrugging his shoulders during the Internet fever years, as if to say, "Why fight it?"

At the time, it was nearly impossible to fight it, even though there were moments of absolute clarity to be found in the smallest details. I will never forget, for example, walking out of yet another dot-com party with Jim Barksdale at the height of the mania. The well-known and genial former head of Netscape, Barksdale was by then, like a lot of others, dabbling in the venture capital business. One of his investments was a small online shopping service called Respond.com, and now he had to attend the obligatory party in San Francisco's trendy South of Market neighborhood to celebrate a new round of funding. Packed full of young people whooping it up on free food and exotic drinks in expensively decorated rooms pulsing with loud music, the party was a pretty normal scene for the time. There was a rumor floating around that the party invitations alone had cost the company $30,000.

In another typically extravagant gesture, everyone in the huge crowd was handed a bottle of expensive champagne on the way out. Neither of us took one, but Barksdale, a courtly Southerner who didn't go to many of these parties, was a bit amazed and perplexed by the offer. "Is this normal?" he asked me. In truth, after all I had seen, I expected an even better bottle to be offered.

"Your venture capital money at work," I replied, as we watched thousands of dollars sail out the door to points unknown.

From Ponzi to Powermonger

Actually, for all the decadent spending that made headlines, the real money garnered from both venture investments and public offerings was flowing to one place: Directly into the coffers of America Online. With the biggest audience in cyberspace, AOL was in the catbird's seat to attract the venture funds of Web sites looking to boost their business. More important, an affiliation with AOL had a more lucrative impact than just garnering new customers. A deal with AOL soon became a key factor in creating a supercharged IPO. I may not have known it at the time, but all along AOL was feeding the fires of the Internet frenzy to strengthen itself for their next transformation. It is critical to focus on AOL's machinations in this time, because it is key to understanding how they ended up on top in the merger with Time

Warner. Without the boom, AOL would never have been able to exert its burgeoning power so deftly.

That power wasn't much in evidence after AOL's terrible performance in 1996 and into 1997. The company had faced myriad problems: The day-long service outage; the disastrous shift to flat-rate pricing that attracted such consumer ire and regulatory scrutiny; management turmoil; accounting questions; and a stock free fall caused by its churning membership. Worst of all, there was a growing belief in investor circles that AOL's business might be a lot closer to a Ponzi scheme than anything else.

But under the new leadership of Bob Pittman, the company slowly began a turnaround, helped in large part by that first improbable $100 million check from Tel-Save. Later, both Tel-Save and AOL would be scrutinized for how the deal was accounted for. But when the then-obscure long-distance discounter made its bold move to tap into AOL's eight million customers in February of 1997, it was a watershed moment for AOL and the online industry. It also marked the first appearance of the "halo effect" on Web stocks that would become commonplace after any AOL deal. On the announcement of its AOL deal alone, Tel-Save's shares leaped from $13 to $19. And its stock price would rise to $30 a share within a year, until the onerous cost of the AOL deal would take its toll on the business.

But the Tel-Save coup started to recharge AOL stock and put Pittman in firm control of the business. Top executives, who had once worshipped at the altar of Steve Case, now transferred their loyalty to the charismatic Southerner. On the surface, Pittman could be extremely amiable—one AOL executive described dealing with him as being "sucked into the charm zone"—and also compelling. His deft presentation at a Goldman Sachs investment conference in February of 1997—a variation on the typical Pittman folksy Southern speech that always included the phrase "my momma"—actually made bored investors sit up and listen.

But despite his reputation for affability, Pittman was a hands-on manager who left little room for error. Throughout his career, he had become well known as a bit of a control freak with his focus constantly fixed on meeting the quarterly numbers. This kind of management was a welcome change at AOL, which had a history of behaving like a chaotic startup, where meetings were without agendas and executive decision-making seemed to include almost everyone in endless free-for-alls. Under Pittman, though the bureaucracy did manage to grow even further, it became a command and control organization with a management system called the Matrix in place. Simply put, it meant all power tended to reside at the dead center in a structure where functions of multiple divisions flowed together. Or as one executive said to me, "AOL is a place where five thousand people can say no, but only one person can say yes."

That would be Pittman, who made sure he had total purview over his minions and received little interference from those above him. In practice he struck a kind of hands-off deal with Case, with whom he had little in common. Pittman disliked Case's nagging emails and never-ending agonizing about AOL's business, as well as his poor communications skills, and he tried to limit Case's access to operational executives. The shy and awkward Case was in turn put off by Pittman's glib manner, as well as by his distaste for the kind of endless email debate about almost every move, which Case found so exhilarating.

The fact that neither man particularly liked the other initially created a tense situation at the company and gave rise to warring public relations camps. Even more unsettling was the fact that many Steve Case loyalists didn't trust Pittman's ultimate motives, especially since he had positioned himself in the press as the company's savior. Did that mean Pittman was going to try to take over the company? Or was he there to sell it out from under Case, as the Wall Street rumor mill buzzed?

Even Pittman's office décor came under scrutiny. A typical stroll down the corridors at AOL's staid Dulles headquarters revealed the extent to which Case's low-key, khaki-pants style had permeated the place. Employees were dressed in casual clothes, offices were decorated with goofy toys such as Magic 8-Balls and gumball machines, and the whole place had the feel of a smart-boy college fraternity. Then there was Pittman's office, which many AOL employees would sneak past to get a look at when he wasn't around.

It was a hipster's vision, with a white shag rug, bulbous lamps, and designer furniture—and a bowl filled with perfect green apples. The first time I came to Pittman's office for an interview, I plopped myself down on the creamy soft leather couch to wait for him and grabbed one of those apples. As I raised it to my mouth and bit a big chunk out of it, one of Pittman's assistants gave me a horrified look. It turns out, the apples were for show—an apparently vital design touch from Pittman's decorator that I'd sullied.

Yet Case looked past their differences, knowing that Pittman was precisely the man he needed for the time—much in the same way he had pulled in Leonsis years earlier to transform AOL into a consumer company. The pair soon settled into a working relationship in which Pittman concentrated on the short-term quarterly issues and Case was free to think about the bigger picture. While Case still retained the title of CEO, it was Pittman who was in charge of all operations—a position that was made formal in early 1998 when he was named AOL's president.

The team Pittman assembled was soon dubbed the "hunter-gatherers" of AOL. It was their mission to leverage the vast audience the company had managed to corral and finally make some real money off of them. The core was made up of an unusual band of misfits, who often operated like a highly dysfunctional, though strangely cooperative, family.

It included ad sales head Myer Berlow, with his bomb-throwing demeanor. He played the good cop to bad-cop deal maker David Colburn, who sported *Miami Vice* stubble, a patter of Don Rickles–style insults, and cowboy boots, despite a dullish suburban upbringing. Marketing chief Jan Brandt continued her zealous quest to bring in subscribers, even going as far as ordering up a conference table made of concrete and crushed AOL disks. Gadget-obsessed Barry Schuler ran the service itself. And closest to Pittman was a trio of longtime advisers who had worked with him consistently for years, including pinch-hitting manager Mayo Stuntz, researcher Marshall Cohen and, perhaps most important, Kenny Lerer, the well-known New York public relations guru and strategist.

Case played the more strategic role. He and his most loyal lieutenants—Ken Novack and Miles Gilburne—were the designated "visionaries" at AOL. They thought about the big moves and key trends that were taking shape in the industry at large, and were charged with seeking out alliances. Novack, an affable-seeming Boston-based lawyer, had been around AOL almost since the beginning and played the role of Case's alter ego. Dubbed AOL's *consigliere,* he was also the one charged with doing much of the actual work in getting big initiatives completed. The bearded and cerebral Gilburne, who came to AOL in 1995 after a successful career as a lawyer, entrepreneur, and venture capitalist in Silicon Valley, was the one tasked with thinking up the big ideas, and mapping AOL's many strategic options. Gilburne, who affected a professorial image, relished complexity and bragged about doing deals that were so confusing only he understood their inner workings.

Case, Novack, and Gilburne were the trio who spearheaded the purchase of CompuServe in the fall of 1997 in a three-way transaction with WorldCom and H&R Block. They also took charge of the even more complex acquisition of Netscape a year later. The Pittman forces often derided their world of white-board thinking and endless and frequently perplexing ideas about AOL's next chess move and characterized the trio as the "eggheads." These eggheads, of course, would be responsible for the momentum that carried AOL to the Time Warner deal.

Serving both teams was new chief financial officer Michael Kelly, a burly former telecom executive who specialized in banging heads in order to bring order to the three-alarm fire that had long been AOL's business. Kelly, whose brash demeanor would later wreak havoc within AOL Time Warner, was thought to be just what the AOL business needed to finally garner much-needed credibility on Wall Street after years of growing worry about the quality of the company's accounting. Already, in its short history, AOL had attracted huge notice for writing down its marketing expenses in 1996 and was being watched by many regulators for its aggressive accounting treatments. Given how new the industry was, AOL was able to claim that it was making pioneering accounting decisions and should not be held to the same traditional standards. It was an argument it would try to make later when the online unit accounting was once again called into question after the Time Warner deal.

But accounting debates were shoved into the background, as the online industry began to rapidly change in 1997. Rather than focusing solely on the service and growing the customer base (which had long been AOL's mission), Pittman set out to strengthen two even more critical parts of AOL: Its brand name and its ad base. Pittman, who had been in charge of several well-known brands such as MTV and Century 21, felt that AOL needed to be as well known as Coca-Cola, with a simple message of purpose. He quickly junked trendier ad campaigns and settled on one somewhat hokey idea for the service: "So easy to use, no wonder it's #1."

Pittman knew that being the top dog had its benefits and he knew that he needed to sell the fact that AOL was the place you had to be if you wanted to reach online customers. That was the simple proposition he began to peddle to advertisers, most especially the legions of dot-com companies eager to make a name for themselves by doing a deal with AOL. Publicly, the AOL team sold potential partners on the idea that being on AOL would garner paying customers by pointing its massive subscriber base in their direction. In truth, no one had any real idea whether this would work or not, especially considering the high prices needed to grab those coveted AOL spots. Pittman's team was able to make those deals mostly because while no one had substantial proof online advertising did work, no one had proof it did not. This strategy would have dire consequences later on, as many companies would abandon their expensive AOL deals.

What did work for sure was the huge financial boost every company immediately got after signing a deal with AOL, which turned out to be the main reason many companies flocked to it. AOL was, for all intents and purposes, the dot-com IPO enabler of the highest order, followed by Yahoo and other major traffic sites on the Web. As a key part of allowing companies to go public and giving a giant boost to those already in the markets, the deals to be the exclusive advertiser in every category on AOL soon came in huge numbers.

A constant barrage of press releases was also part of the game, which instantly sent shares of both AOL and its partners upward in the heady market atmosphere. The idea was to convince Wall Street that AOL had a legitimate momentum and that business was flowing to it en masse. The company had largely avoided working with powerful ad-placement agencies, preferring to deal directly with company brass to get deals done. That had slowed the flow of more traditional companies to AOL, since their ad-buying habits changed only glacially.

Luckily, dot-coms were ready, willing, and able to jump in. So, after Tel-Save's bet, by the end of 1997, AOL was in the online real estate business in a series of multiyear deals. Shopping service CUC International agreed to pay $50 million, online auto retailer Autobytel paid $6 million, travel service Preview Travel paid $32 million, and 1-800-Flowers paid $25 million. Sometimes AOL got major competitors to pony up. While Barnes & Noble's online bookseller paid $40 million to be on the main AOL service, Amazon paid $19 million to get the paltry aol.com Web site spot. N2K forked over $18 million, more than twice the online music retailer's annual revenue.

By 1999, it got even more lucrative—Web auctioneer eBay paid $75 million in a four-year deal, while medical site Drkoop.com paid $89 million to provide health information on AOL. As part of that four-year deal, in a move that became increasingly common, AOL also got warrants to purchase shares in many of the companies that became its partners.

This right to buy shares of ad partners became increasingly critical to all AOL transactions, because the stock of dot-com companies was soaring, due in large part to those same AOL ad deals. Drkoop's shares, for example, initially jumped 56 percent on the announcement of its AOL transaction. AOL, in a practice known as round-tripping, or a boomerang, began making more direct investments in dot-coms, which often turned right around and invested that same cash in AOL ads. In addition, AOL pressed its vendors and other business partners to buy ads and also engaged in complex "barter" arrangements, where services were exchanged instead of cash.

These seemingly virtuous circles soon became common practice throughout the industry and had embedded in them the seeds of worrisome conflicts of interest and potential opportunities for abuse, including the inflation of the costs of the deals. Later, even more disturbing issues surrounding the proper accounting of such unusual transactions would become hugely damaging to AOL. While AOL sold huge amounts of legitimate advertising, the mania to book any kind of revenue and dub it "advertising" became like a drug addiction at the company.

The warning signs of this deal-making obsession and its repercussions came soon enough. In August of 1997, just six months after the Tel-Save deal was signed, AOL was forced by the SEC to change the way it accounted for the deal. Regulators determined that AOL had recognized too much of the $100 million deal as revenue in its earnings statements and booked that money well ahead of the introduction of the telephone service itself. The charges related to this SEC-mandated change meant that the only two quarters that had appeared to be profitable following AOL's earlier accounting change (which had eliminated all of AOL's historical profits) were also wiped out. Making identical excuses to those proffered during AOL's earlier accounting woes, Case again blamed the problem on the relative immaturity of Internet industry, insisting that the accounting was subject to debate. He had previously promised "gold-standard accounting" in the marketing-expense accounting mess from 1996.

But, few paid any attention to the Tel-Save snafu or Case's broken vow, since it was hard to hear much of anything over the roar of companies lining up and loudly demanding to do a deal with AOL. But the seeds of the later accounting problems had taken root and were growing quickly into the AOL's corporate culture. It was a pattern of accounting abuse that Time Warner would ignore until it was too late.

If I Had a Hammer

The way AOL conducted itself while doing deals would also come under increasing scrutiny by the industry and its players, given the proclivity of the team to beat up on many of the companies whose wallets they were busy emptying.

Berlow was charged with reeling in the prospects, but Colburn and his team put on the real squeeze. He was aided in this by a passel of mostly narcissistic young men who copied his mannerisms right down to the boots and stubble. Colburn's group, called Business Affairs, was infamous for its aggression against all comers. As AOL's power grew, its potential partners increasingly began to feel that they were being subjected to an AOL shakedown, although AOL sold itself as partner-friendly. As the old saying goes, if you're a hammer, everything looks like a nail. And AOL was a proficient carpenter. Colburn often joked to his colleagues about his rotten reputation: "I'd better make a lot of money at AOL, since I'll never be able to get another job again."

Indeed, Colburn's antics were legend in the industry, especially since they often verged on the absurd, and sometimes got blown out of proportion. And sometimes not, according to many sources. He would splay himself across tables to make a point. He'd stick his boots in the face of someone wanting a deal. He'd rant and call people names, and then just as suddenly compliment them effusively. He was even impertinent to Pittman, sitting next to him in meetings on Pittman's glass-eye side and making faces he knew his boss couldn't see. Others at AOL made similar jokes, but only Colburn was remembered for them.

Some AOL deal-making tactics were less humorous, according to many sources. They included a proclivity to change deal terms at the last minute deep in the complicated wording of contracts; agreeing to a deal with one company and then keeping it off balance by threatening to do a similar deal with its competitors; putting attractive terms on the table, only to quickly remove them; and not honoring a raft of promises about aiding companies in attracting customers for their ad dollars. In addition, some of those who signed deals were later unhappy with the company's follow-through, seeing little payoff from their big payouts to AOL.

"With AOL on the other side, you always thought you were being screwed" was a sentiment I heard repeatedly from many who did deals with them—and yet the line of companies waiting to partner with AOL grew longer and longer. When I asked a few why they did it, most told me they needed to, desperately, for their next round of funding or their upcoming IPO, before asking me like some junkie if I could hook them up with AOL executives I knew well. I demurred, but it was hard after that to feel sorry for those who later complained after the deals went sour for one reason or another, since they had also sought to take advantage of their affiliation with AOL by lining their own pockets as their stocks rose.

Berlow thought such stories were overblown. "It makes for a better story if we are crazy," he said. "And in the context of the times, we were not that different than others."

Yet this was not so, since AOL was so powerful. "If everyone tells you that you walk on water, you usually get what you ask for," said Mike Kelly, who had instituted a more formal system of signoffs to prevent abuses of the system that, in the end, were inevitable because many potential conflicts of interest loomed over most every deal. Even at the height of the boom, there were already worries inside AOL about potential problems. But few questioned a more troublesome aspect of the deal bonanza: The proper way to account for the many flavors of deals, since many of the gains made by AOL were not easy to characterize as traditional revenues. While many of their deals were commonplace throughout the industry, Colburn and his team's aggressive nature only underscored the image of a too-powerful company that was willing to take things to the edge of the edge.

Not everyone believed that all of AOL's hard-hitting behavior was wrong. "I thought it was perfect—you squeeze anyone you can when you are in ascendancy," said John Malone—the legendary cable titan and deal maker, who had watched AOL's rise after passing on making a major investment in the company in the early 1990s—to me in 2003. "The problem, of course, comes when it is all over and you see those people on the way down."

Inside AOL, the celebration of toughness, in Business Affairs especially, was a major concern to some. "It was hard to call anyone on it, because of its success," said Dan Prieto, a director of corporate development who was involved in more strategic acquisitions on the Gilburne team. "But the scorched-earth tactics made some of us worry that we were going to end up like Microsoft, successful but deeply resented by our peers and partners. We worried that if AOL ever found itself in a tough spot, no one would stand up for us and everyone would be against us."

But arrogance is the luxury of success, although many wondered why Pittman allowed such behavior. It would later prove corrosive. While he did frequently chastise his underlings for their more outrageous antics, he never actually stopped them. Neither did Case, who sometimes teased partners who complained. "Are you really scared of Colburn?" he once ribbed a major Internet executive who had told Case he was put off by the rough AOL style.

Scary or not, that tone was encouraged. "The top guys and board of AOL wanted delivery, and they were loyal to their people," said one executive, who noted they also wanted the money to keep rolling in. "We couldn't stand up to Wall Street and say, 'We sold enough,' since we would get shish-kabobed."

In truth, both Pittman and Case needed people like Colburn—however distasteful some tactics might be, especially compared with AOL's lofty corporate mission goals to make it the "most respected company." Said one top executive succinctly, "He marshaled revenues for Bob and a war chest for Steve and that beat back all the complaints." At the moment, when lucrative deals were plentiful, short-term gains made by Colburn beat out long-term concerns.

By pulling in huge sums from the coffers of dot-coms, AOL also created an even bigger set of expectations and the skyrocketing stock soon gave the company an ability to do anything it pleased. Not surprisingly, AOL began a series of acquisitions, easily swallowing a range of online companies in a series of stock-for-stock deals. The biggest fish was the purchase of Internet icon Netscape for $4.2 billion in the late fall of 1998.

This was another achingly complex deal, which included a critical side deal with Sun Microsystems with intricate back-and-forth revenue and operational agreements. Dreamed up by Gilburne, executed by Novack, blessed by Case, and handed over to Pittman to run, the deal was done for a range of reasons. They included a continued fear of Microsoft, a need for a Silicon Valley presence, and a desire to diversify the company's business and increase its distribution ability. And it didn't hurt that it would give the stock a huge lift, too.

It was also a highly symbolic move, given that Netscape had set off the Internet boom in the first place. The idea of scooping up Netscape seemed so unreal that when a source I ran into at the premiere of Pixar's *A Bug's Life* told me about the acquisition talks, I responded immediately and inelegantly: "No way—you are a liar."

When the deal was finally struck, members of the Netscape team called me at home early in the morning—we had been reporting in the *Wall Street Journal* that a deal was imminent—with a new take on the famous AOL mail phrase. "They've got Netscape!" they chimed together. Yes, AOL did, right down to acquiring the Web's golden boy, Marc Andreessen, who was also scooped up by the company as a new executive. CEO Jim Barksdale also joined AOL's board.

The Netscape deal, combined with AOL's continuing ability to squeeze more and more money out of ad deals, gave AOL an air of invincibility. All the analysts' reports from then on out were uniformly positive. In one report, for example, Goldman Sachs's Michael Parekh gushed that AOL was now the "firstest with the mostest." Such sentiments helped AOL stock rise even higher. And it was further turbocharged when AOL joined the Standard & Poor's 500 at the start of 1999, becoming the first Internet company to be added to the benchmark index.

AOL's market cap, which had been hovering around $14 billion in the early spring of 1998, hit almost $65 billion the day it debuted on the S&P. Such gigantic leaps in market cap yielded huge fortunes to the major executives at AOL—and, in fact, to many hundreds of employees throughout the company. As did so many tech executives in this period, the AOL executives took full advantage of the share rise and regularly sold off their stock for ever-larger amounts. Steve Case made about $20 million from 1991 to 1996, but in one transaction in 1998 alone, he netted $61 million by trading in stock options he had gotten for pennies.

Others, including Pittman, Berlow, and Schuler, also cashed out and quickly bought private planes, luxurious homes, and other accoutrements of wealth. Ted Leonsis used his gains to grab big stakes in two local sports teams—the Washington Wizards basketball team and the Washington Capitals hockey team. Everyone seemed riveted by what AOL's executives were up to. At a speech I gave in 1999 to a local business group in Washington, D.C.—the locus of AOL power—one major grocery chain executive I had known for years asked me if I thought he had been really stupid for not getting in on the action and whether he should jump now. I was obviously the wrong person to ask.

"Don't you wish you'd taken my job offer?" Leonsis kidded me in 1999, when I met him at the National Press Club in D.C. I saw him right after a meeting he'd had with his new hockey team, where he gave each player a new and very expensive laptop computer to introduce them to the new world order. By now, I was not sure what to tell him.

A Moment of Reflection

While AOL was finally soaring in the late 1990s, life for Jerry Levin in these heady days wasn't good at all, either professionally or personally. While he'd managed to come out on top after the power struggle that the contentious $14 billion merger of Time and Warner created, he seemed perpetually in trouble.

He had been attacked in a much talked-about 1996 *Forbes* article as presiding over a "beached whale" of a company, and soon there were betting pools on Wall Street about when Levin would be ousted. A combination of bad Internet investments and overpriced cable acquisitions, along with crippling debt, had depressed Time Warner stock. From December 1993 to 1996, while the S&P was up 59 percent, Time Warner was down 15 percent. Worse still, the bitterness of the Time and Warner merger continued to linger.

Levin was undaunted. "You have to have a strong inner core. The press is very often too high or too low on a CEO or on his or her strategy," wrote Levin to me in an email, recalling the difficult time. "On the other hand, you have to have responsible leadership that is respected within and outside the company. So your public image is important."

But Levin's life took an even more tragic turn in June of 1997, when his eldest son, Jonathan, was found dead in his New York City apartment. Tragically, the 31-year-old teacher at a low-income Bronx high school had been killed by a former student.

Levin was shattered by the news, and his grief had many layers. His son was not only dead, but he'd been cruelly murdered. Compounding Levin's agony was the fact that in recent years, he had not spent a lot of time with his son. He also seemed haunted by the fact that Jonathan, unlike Levin himself, had chosen to devote his professional life to helping others. In my conversations with him in 2002 and 2003, Levin often talked about this. It is no exaggeration to say that his son's death created a personal crisis that would forever change Levin.

I was astonished that many people, after the merger fell apart, charged that Levin made too much of his grief and used it to shield himself from other criticism. But this is sniping that Levin does not deserve. News clips taken of Levin at Jonathan's funeral show a man in a daze. With fellow mourners supporting him, he appears barely able to stand; his face is creased with pain. Levin's anguish ran so deep that some colleagues wondered if he'd have the strength to ever fully reengage in his work again.

The tragedy most definitely provoked Levin's restless mind to wonder if anything he was doing really mattered. He'd spent his entire life fighting his way to the top of the corporate hill. His was a world where people lived and died according to box office figures, record album sales, and magazine circulation numbers. How was it possible to care about any of that now? "I think I started to see everything differently from that moment, although I did not realize it at the time," Levin told me. Others at the company also began to treat Levin better, too, startled by his son's death into realizing that perhaps their CEO was more of a human being than they had thought. "It gave Jerry a lot of humanity, because he became more approachable," said former Warner Bros. head Terry Semel.

Oddly, the beginnings of the forces that would soon improve Time Warner's prospects came only a week after Levin's son's death. Microsoft's Bill Gates invested $1 billion in Comcast in an effort to jumpstart the digital rollout of information services. Gates followed this with a $425 million investment to buy WebTV and made other cable investments. His overall aim was obvious: To speed the development of high-speed Internet services to open new markets for Microsoft software. Microsoft's other founder, Paul Allen, was also on a cable-buying spree, which further heated up once moribund cable market valuations.

That was good news for Levin, since Time Warner's cable assets were strong and its media assets top-notch. But in the rush toward the Internet space, Time Warner still lagged badly, with few initiatives and little indication of any true strategy. The disastrous experience of both the Full Service Network and Pathfinder had proved debilitating. Though individual divisions, such as the film studios, pursued their own experiments, Levin seemed to have all but abandoned the grand interactive plans that had long occupied him.

It seemed unusual to me that Time Warner executives were almost nowhere to be found in the Internet space during this frothy period of the late 1990s. One would hear stories of their occasional visits to Silicon Valley, and they seemed to take particular interest in possibly acquiring one of the many Web-centric publications that had sprung up in the boom and seemed to be minting money. Sometimes they would talk to a small dot-com about a partnership or even an acquisition. But with all the money scattered around for anyone who bent down to pick it up, it was hard to compete. The stories I heard from both inside and outside the company usually ended with some Time Warner functionary lecturing the dot-commers about their insane valuations and jetting back empty-handed to New York. They were right about the mania, which they also wanted to be part of, but still got dinged as dinosaurs for not benefiting from the Internet boom.

Other media companies were less circumspect about entering the fast-moving digital stream. In the summer of 1998, Disney made a major move by purchasing a large stake in a second-tier portal called InfoSeek, and then moving quickly to remake it into a major Web site called the Go Network to compete in the big Web leagues ruled by AOL and Yahoo. General Electric's NBC bought CNET's Snap portal, while both Viacom and News Corp. made a series of moves to beef up their Internet assets.

Perhaps the most audacious attempt was made in early 1999 by USA Networks' Barry Diller, in a stillborn deal that would turn out to be a kind of precursor to the AOL Time Warner merger. Diller, who had been one of the earliest and savviest among the media moguls to enter the Internet space, sought to purchase the Lycos portal. When the agreement was first announced in February, it was valued at $18 billion. It was also touted as a critical merging of old and new media to create the first e-commerce and entertainment powerhouse. The deal was scotched by May, though, by its largest shareholder—Internet-holding company CMGI—which thought the price USA wanted to pay for Lycos was too low. Diller, a wily businessman hardened by innumerable Hollywood scams, didn't concur and walked away. Interestingly enough, Time Warner was soon suggested as a possible new suitor for Lycos and held many talks with the company about a possible acquisition or investment deal. But Lycos's high valuation prevented a deal that properly valued Time Warner's digital contents.

Thus, nothing came of it, despite a new unit Levin created in June 1999 called Time Warner Digital Media, which was intended to give new energy to Time Warner's Internet strategy. It was headed by Richard Bressler, who had been the company's CFO and who would later play a critical role in the AOL Time Warner merger even though he had little Web experience or expertise. He began his Web efforts in earnest by sniffing around the portal space, after the company nearly completed a deal to buy the AltaVista portal, in a deal so close to signing that the St. Regis ballroom in New York was rented to announce the acquisition. (Before the formal announcement, though, Time Warner canceled the deal, due to company infighting over who would be in charge.) The company also considered spinning off and taking public some of its vertical Web assets, especially popular ones like those created at CNN more for the stock pop than for business reasons—but those plans also came to naught. The company then began to focus on creating topic-specific "hubs" that linked in with e-commerce, even as it was in the process of shuttering Pathfinder.

But all this was clearly not enough for Time Warner or for Jerry Levin. As Internet stocks shot up even further in mid-1999, some media companies became increasingly worried that rather than being an acquirer, they might find themselves in the crosshairs of these increasingly muscular Web companies. With no special controlling stock that might prevent such a move, many felt vulnerable.

Many close to him at this time said Levin even became concerned about AOL after hearing rumors that it was considering plans to go hostile on Time Warner. Every top-ranking AOL executive has told me this wasn't true, mostly due to issues around losing talent and angering big shareholders. In addition, they feared it might prompt a wholesale reevaluation of what Internet companies were actually worth. But it remained a possibility. "It was a red hot time for Internet companies and I think it laid one on Jerry that in the real world that AOL could do that," said John Malone, who noted it seemed unbelievable that even Time Warner wasn't large enough to face down the soaring Internet valuations.

Levin was also facing some serious cash-flow problems at his heavily indebted company. While the cable business had rebounded, there was considerable weakness in the once cash-spewing music division. And things were only going to get worse in that arena, considering the damage that the explosive growth of Internet music-swapping services like Napster was having on sales. No matter how hard the media companies fought back, Levin was certain that the Web posed a threat to a lot more than just the music business over the next decade. All of Time Warner, he surmised, would sooner or later be under siege by the Internet.

Levin told me in 2003 that to counter that fear, he'd become even more convinced that Time Warner needed another major transforming transaction, because the spark to make huge changes was not present inside the company. "I thought that you have to change the culture, or you were going to be in real trouble because of what was coming," he said.

One Levin adviser agreed that the Time Warner CEO was tired of doing nothing and wanted in on the Internet game. "In a way, it was capitulation, since Time Warner had been vilified as a dinosaur because it sat on the sidelines of the Web's ascendancy," this person said. "It did not believe in the Web, did not believe it, did not believe it. Then it finally believed it."

After three years of the Internet boom, the adviser added, "Time Warner just lost its ability to say no to the Net and that was exactly the moment when Jerry Levin met Steve Case."

Climb High, Climb Far—Oh, Just Climb!

Steve Case seemed to have been ready for him well before late 1999. In a December 23, 1998, email to his major executives—including Novack, Gilburne, Pittman, and public policy head George Vradenburg—Case advised them to think big, even as he appeared nervous about AOL's growing valuation. AOL now needed, he insisted, something much more stable.

"I like the idea of buying fallen stars that have real assets versus chasing the highfliers that are fluffy and inevitably will come crashing back to earth," Case wrote, noting he was amazed that the online auctioneer eBay was worth $12 billion at that point. "Given the Internet zaniness, I also like the idea of looking beyond the so-called Internet and identifying companies that have a profound impact on how people get information, communicate with others, buy products, are entertained. . . . They tend to be suffering from the Internet momentum." Case ended the email with a hokey poem often featured on inspirational business posters: "Climb high/Climb far/Our aim, the sky/Our goal, the stars."

Case's point, said one AOL executive, was that "everything was going to be profoundly changed. We could do either more Internet or media buys to transform." Or do both.

And although Case was already higher than anyone had thought he could be, sitting atop a company that looked like it could do no wrong, he was also worried. While the company's momentum was soaring in terms of both business and valuation, he and others at AOL were nervous about coming changes in the interactive market that could badly damage the online service. These included a possible shift to non-PC devices such as more powerful cell phones and handheld organizers, the coming saturation of the dial-up audience, and the inevitable shift of users to high-speed broadband connections. Where these changes would leave AOL was anybody's guess—especially if the company couldn't make the transitions smoothly.

The Netscape deal had provided some short-term revenues and added luster to AOL, but it hadn't done much of anything else. Badly managed and relatively ignored by AOL, Netscape suffered from a mass exodus of talent (including Marc Andreessen in 1999), no real progress in its enterprise efforts to reach the business market, and negligible development of its famed browser. AOL's short attention span—coupled with its long history of mangling rather than managing acquisitions—made it ill-suited to really get in the trenches and make something of Netscape.

Instead, it did more deals, a favorite tactic for pasting over past failures in acquisitions. To AOL and a lot of other tech companies, making deals was another addiction, mostly because it was a lot more exciting than using its energy to manage what they already had. In a manic series of placing its bets all over the table, AOL seemed to touch on every new trend of the moment. Since AOL's stock was so high, it was capable of buying just about anything, and in a very frantic 1999, AOL launched its AOL Anywhere push. This included a plan for AOL TV and investments in several digital video recorder companies; deals with Palm Computing on small handhelds; a $1.5 billion investment in General Motors's Hughes Electronics satellite in hopes of spurring a high-speed satellite Internet service; and an $800 million stake in Gateway Computers, to push the development of new computing devices and get more subscribers. And that wasn't all. There were also multiple phone-company deals related to high-speed DSL services and cell phones, and a plan to deliver AOL over Black-Berry paging devices. The company even considered buying one of the big broadcast networks and making a $250 million investment in the radio broadcaster Chancellor Media.

One of the most intriguing and important developments occurred in the spring. It had to do with potential AOL involvement in a bid by cable operator Comcast to beat out AT&T in acquiring the MediaOne Group. While AOL ultimately was not needed by Comcast and shoved aside, it had made sense for AOL to consider such a move, since executives were increasingly worried about their inability to get any of the cable companies to open up their lines to AOL. More worrisome were the exclusive agreements that several major cable companies had with their jointly owned high-speed Web service called Excite@Home. In fact, when the Excite portal merged with @Home in early 1999, a panicked Steve Case instructed lobbyist George Vradenburg and others to hit hard at the cable industry to force them to provide open access.

"Although we thought broadband was coming on much more slowly than others did, we knew we needed to get access to high-speed access systems, especially cable," said Vradenburg. "But the cable companies were not willing to do deals, because they thought they could leapfrog us. Why do any deal with AOL when you thought you had the upper hand?"

AOL quickly backed an open-access lobbying organization, agitated in various cities to prompt cable companies to do a deal with AOL, and even took its arguments to federal regulators. Cable companies (including Time Warner cable executives), long used to little government intervention, despised AOL for the move. They had all seen how AOL rode the phone lines to glory while phone companies got little of the benefit, and they weren't going to let it happen to their prized cable lines. They were not, as Excite@Home head Tom Jermoluk often told me at the time, going to become "dumb pipes."

One of Case's biggest opponents in the open-access battle turned out to be John Doerr of Kleiner Perkins, the venture capital firm that was one of AOL's early investors in the 1980s. At a party to raise money for Silicon Valley's Tech Museum, the wiry and jumpy Doerr wouldn't let me leave as he ranted about AOL's behavior. "They don't have a product anyone wants to buy anymore if they have to pay for it *and* access too," complained Doerr, in an agitated rant that I got to hear many times. "Steve Case is in big trouble and he knows it, which is why he's attacking us." Doerr was right, but Excite@Home later turned out to be a flameout of a company and went bankrupt, done in by sheer incompetence on the part of its owners and management. But the challenges that broadband access presented to AOL—specifically that high-speed users churned off of the dial-up service forever—scared it a lot.

And Case wasn't attacking only the "cable cabal," as AOL lobbyists called it: As always, there was a continuing omnipresent fear of Microsoft. With Microsoft's big cable investments and rumors that it might even drop the price of MSN dramatically, AOL was on tenterhooks over just what the software giant would do next. Both Colburn and Case testified against Microsoft in its antitrust trial in Washington—a battle that got even juicier after AOL bought Microsoft's alleged victim, Netscape. "I'm trying to get everyone to understand that Microsoft is the real enemy," joked Vradenburg to me when I saw AOL's lobbyist at a congressional event in D.C. in 1999. "And not us."

Hovering above it all was Case's deepening worry about unstable Internet valuations, those close to him said—most especially his own. Wall Street had boosted AOL's value compared to its performance, forcing it to garner impossible-to-reach results. Thus, AOL clearly needed to put a very big and stable business underneath itself in order to keep from slipping off the valuation treadmill.

Subscriber growth was sure to slow before AOL could make up the difference with much-less-lucrative high-speed customers once it created a viable broadband service. And too many of the ad deals that were coming in relied much too heavily on financially questionable dot-coms. AOL had made an art form of reinvention, and many at the company thought the jig was just about up once again. "We all knew we were living on borrowed time and had to buy something of substance by using that huge currency," AOL's investor relations head Richard Hanlon told me. "We definitely needed to trade up, and fast."

Others agreed. "I think he looked at the prices the shares were selling for and thought it was time to do something to keep AOL as the frontrunner in the Internet space," observed John Sidgmore, the former WorldCom executive who knew Case well.

Another executive spoke even more urgently. "The bottom line is that there was always going to be a deal, since we felt the market was overvalued and that there was a kind of craziness," he said. "And, believe me, we knew an Internet nuclear winter was coming."

AOL needed to heat up its efforts immediately, especially because of concerns about the possibility of a diminishing currency. "If we fail to capitalize on this market," Steve Case's closest adviser, Ken Novack, told him, according to others who were present, "it will be the biggest missed opportunity in history."

It Takes Two to Tango

AOL needed a grand strategy, one unlike any they had ever considered or anything they had ever done. Enter, once again, Miles Gilburne, the brainy deal maker who had taken to coming and going at AOL on his own schedule. He had collected around him a small group of mostly young Harvard MBAs, who started formulating—with the help of bankers from Salomon Smith Barney—an analysis of what AOL should do. The strategy was to address the basic problem of finding future growth and diversifying AOL's business from a single dynamic industry.

According to internal documents generated by Salomon bankers and AOL analysts, the possible directions settled into four major areas. The options were:

1. To double their bet on the Internet sector, with "tuck-in" purchase—adding it to existing AOL units—of smaller Web or tech companies. The companies AOL was considering for this included Yahoo, Amazon, eBay, Intuit, Lycos, Electronic Arts, RealNetworks, and even Apple Computer.

2. To diversify in the business-to-business arena, by doing a major deal with a company like IBM to sell online software and services specifically targeting small businesses nationwide.

3. To diversify "downstream" to the telecommunications sector, looking especially at wireless assets. Here AOL hoped for some kind of deal with AT&T, WorldCom, or Bell Atlantic/GTE.

4. To diversify "upstream" in media. It was a strong belief that content and destination sites would yield valuable cross-promotion opportunities, as well as the longed-for Holy Grail of the single ad buy. Here the main targets were Time Warner, Bertelsmann, NBC, and Walt Disney.

The business-to-business option was quickly discarded, since AOL had a long history of mucking up all its attempts to break into the enterprise space. Its Netscape fiasco only underscored the fact that AOL was more of a consumer brand, much in the same way that Microsoft operated better in the corporate realm than in attracting consumers to MSN.

Telecom also elicited groans from AOLers, because of the then-high prices and also the unhappy prospects of owning massive amounts of costly infrastructure in a market of diminishing margins. AOL had sold off its network once in the CompuServe deal and had little competence in the sector. The company had engaged in off-and-on-again discussions with AT&T in both 1998 and then again in 1999. The talks included the idea of AOL taking over AT&T's troubled long-distance business and getting carriage on its cable systems. But each time, the discussions got caught up in a series of complex issues about control and price, made worse by an ego clash between Case and AT&T CEO Michael Armstrong.

The Internet and tech sectors were more appealing to AOL executives, since it was clear that consolidation here was inevitable. But the company thinkers were still nervous about the elevated Web stock prices and worried that acquisitions in the arena wouldn't be enough to materially impact AOL's business. Individually, each Web company had issues: Yahoo was an unlikely partner because the combination of the two biggest Web companies would likely create a regulatory thicket; Amazon was coming under increasing scrutiny for its high debt and risky sales prospects; Lycos was a less attractive, second-string property of dubious popularity; Apple meant a very heavy bet on hardware; and AOL worried that RealNetworks faced too much competition from Microsoft's Media Player in the streaming media market and might become another Netscape. Only financial software maker Intuit, eBay, and games maker Electronic Arts really intrigued AOL, although all seemed small. "You do not get to the end game with another Internet company," Gilburne told his staff many times, given AOL needed to solve its broadband infrastructure challenge.

Merging with a media company had always been the *real* end game anyway—the path to convergence that Case had long dreamed of. He had discussed the concept a lot with his close friend and AOL board member Thomas Middelhoff of Germany's Bertelsmann, but the cultural issues seemed too big and the family foundation-controlled company was not for sale. NBC was low on the list, because of the troubles the broadcast market was undergoing. No serious discussions were pursued with News Corp. or Viacom, although later Viacom head Sumner Redstone would try to burnish his reputation as a savvy mogul by recounting that he had turned AOL down flat.

Actually, it was not Redstone, but Disney's Michael Eisner who'd done that. Gilburne had traveled to see his counterpart, Peter Murphy, at Disney's California headquarters, to explore various possibilities of collaboration at very early stages. Eisner, according to sources, found out about the discussions and was furious, thinking the pair was discussing a merger behind his back. Apoplectic, he called senior Disney executive Sandy Litvak to get Case's home number. Litvak called AOL's Vradenburg, who finally gave it to him. Eisner then called Case at home and told him angrily to stay away, irked at the prospect that he could be acquired and nervous that AOL might attempt a hostile takeover. Sources familiar with the conversation said that Case tried to assure him that that wasn't what he was attempting, and that AOL would do only a friendly deal with Disney. Or do none at all, given Eisner's angry mood—which was how it turned out.

AOL executives didn't care that much, really, because their first choice had always been Time Warner. Steve Case, who was trying to make contact with executives at all possible companies, was on the hunt and Jerry Levin was the prey. The pursuit of Time Warner would soon be dubbed "Project Tango," one of several monikers Ken Novack drew from the military-style names for the letters of the alphabet. Walt Disney was "Whiskey," News Corp. was "Foxtrot," Viacom was "Victor/Charlie," and Bertelsmann was "Bravo." AOL was, not surprisingly, "Alpha."

Time Warner had all the things AOL needed, according to internal documents—strategically, financially, and in many other ways. Among the key positives: Time Warner's cable could solve AOL's broadband problem; it had strong consumer brands; its management was top-notch; it had low-risk businesses; and it would also put AOL on a more level playing field in relation to Microsoft, giving it money and manpower, as well as a range of solid assets that would be hard for the software giant to match.

Last on AOL's list was one perceived plus that would prove quite the opposite: "Good cultural fit."

Let's Blame the Commies

It certainly seemed the cultural fit might work from the beginning of the deal dance, which focused almost exclusively on the rapport between Case and Levin. Like many intense relationships, it would begin as a mutual seduction and end up turning into a mutual deception. Both men, profoundly awkward as communicators, would engineer the creation of what could be the most powerful media company ever.

While a lot of attention has been paid to the more glamorous late September 1999 meeting in China, Levin and Case had met many times on the executive circuit—at the whirlwind of investment conferences, industry alliance meetings, and political events that is part of being a CEO in American business.

They bumped into each other in a more substantive way in mid-September of 1999, at the first meeting of the Global Business Dialogue on Electronic Commerce at the Louvre museum in Paris. The initiative, chaired by Thomas Middelhoff, had been launched at the beginning of the year to focus on developing policy for the global online economy. At the meeting, Case and Levin were announced as cochairs for the following year, and they spent a lot of time there talking about the digital future. "I thought Steve was bright, young, determined," recalled Levin. Case was equally impressed—since Levin spouted the same kind of digital hoo-ha that Case so adored. Had they each found a soul mate?

The pair next met up just a few weeks later in Shanghai, China, at the *Fortune* Global Forum being held on the 50th anniversary of the founding of the People's Republic, sponsored by Time Warner's magazine. Titled "China: The Next 50 Years," the event boasted an impressive roster of business celebrities and global players, including former Treasury Secretary Robert Rubin, former Secretary of State Henry Kissinger, General Electric's Jack Welch, Ford's Jacques Nasser, Coke's Doug Ivester, Pepsico's Roger Enrico, Dell Computer's Michael Dell, and Yahoo's Jerry Yang. Naturally, Jerry Levin and Ted Turner (and his wife, Jane Fonda) were also there, as was Time Warner's board, which had come along for a longer "news" tour of the country. The Time Warner group were treated like visiting pashas by the Chinese government, whose leader, Jiang Zemin, kicked off the event with a keynote speech.

Steve Case was not initially on the invitation list. But with the aim of getting to spend more time with Levin, AOL had called seeking to be invited. *Fortune* was thrilled to have him—especially as the positive buzz around AOL had been rising through the summer, and

Case was becoming a popular executive to have around especially for a planned side tech program. He got many chances to talk to Levin at the conference and later when a smaller group traveled north to Beijing for several anniversary-celebration events, including lunch with the city's mayor. And a big opportunity came at one of the first major gatherings, a sumptuous dinner in the Great Hall of the People.

At the end of the dinner, as guests were leaving, a torrential downpour turned out to be a good omen for Case. Everyone was forced to wait in the entryway for their cars, and Case, Levin, and Turner, as well as Jane Fonda, ended up deeply engrossed in conversation. Many others took note of the unusual group, their heads bowed together in what was clearly an intense encounter. "What were you all talking about?" one reporter who was there asked Case later. He just smiled cryptically.

The three weren't actually talking about any kind of deal, but rather of big, airy ideas about the global market and the role of business in society. And their conversation continued on October 1, when they were again thrown together at a massive and endless parade of soldiers and citizens and tanks and flag-waving held in Tiananmen Square. This was surely the kind of theatrical backdrop one might imagine for the moment that the spark of a big deal was struck—but Levin and Case were still only talking about big issues. Luckily for Case, who stuck around to be with Levin, Communist parades are notorious for being deadly dull and interminably long, so he had lots of time to woo Levin. And this parade was the granddaddy of all Communist parades—it lasted eight hours, providing the pair plenty of time to talk while huddled in the open viewing stands on Tiananmen's gate. The parade's end was punctuated by a magnificent fireworks display that lit up the clear sky, which the previous night's drenching rain had cleaned of the normal polluted smog of Beijing.

Levin later said he wasn't immediately thinking of any kind of merger, although he was aware that AOL was looking for a big deal. He told me he considered Case more of a "star-fucker—you know, he liked being around all this power and such that was not so common in the Internet space." Levin added that he did enjoy talking about corporate values—both expressing the idea that a company had societal and cultural responsibilities beyond the bottom line—but that he wasn't thinking of anything more substantive related to AOL. "I put it out of my mind," he said, "because I didn't think anything would come of it."

Maybe nothing would have, but within weeks Case was on the phone to Levin proposing a merger of equals, already intimating that Levin would naturally be the CEO of the resulting megacompany. Levin demurred at first, telling Case, "I don't see it. But I will call you back." He then went immediately to both Richard Bressler and Dick Parsons. Levin told his close executives that he felt cautious, since he'd heard all the stories about how AOL was a very arrogant group. They thought it best to keep all options open, looking at the range of possibilities that crossed their path.

Still, he agreed to meet Case for a private dinner on November 1 at New York's Rihga Royal Hotel on West 54th Street in Manhattan. "I said, 'You and I can get together to talk about aspirations,' and I found him unusually idealistic," recalled Levin, who noted that Case seemed to share his vision that a company was about more than profits. "He was certainly mouthing the words, and it made me think the culture of AOL was more humanistic than I thought." Case made sure that impression prevailed by avoiding talk about the nuts and bolts, playing on Levin's weakness for vision and spinning a world of convergence that their combined company could rule.

When I'm in one of my more cynical moods, I think Case was just selling Levin. And yet, in many years of covering him, I could never get Case to shut up about this kind of stuff, even though he often delivered this idealistic message of the future in the flat tones of an animatronic dummy at Disneyland. I do believe, at least initially, there was a mind meld going on between Case and Levin. And I believe Levin had great hopes of moving to a higher plane of business with Case, even if such reveries were naïve and a bit delusional given how rapacious both AOL and Time Warner—not to mention Case and Levin—could be.

The mundane details of how a deal might work out were left to Rich Bressler for Time Warner and Miles Gilburne and Ken Novack for AOL. By the middle of the month, Gilburne and Novack traveled to New York for a series of "think sessions" with Bressler, to outline what a combination of AOL and Time Warner might look like. Not initially focused on the cost synergies, the group first looked at more forward-facing ideas, such as digital media and music and interactive television. "It was a lot of circles on the white board," said one person privy to the meetings. "Very high concept, very pie-in-the-sky."

These sessions went so well that Levin and Case planned another meeting to talk turkey; they also decided that Case should have a meeting with Ted Turner, Time Warner's biggest shareholder. Levin wanted Turner, whose shares represented almost one-tenth of the company, to be on board early and with enthusiasm. Both Levin and Case had seen what had happened at Lycos and other companies when large shareholders were not cooperative. Besides, if Turner was on board, it would likely have a major influence on other key share-holders such as John Malone and Gordon Crawford, the powerful media investor from California-based investment fund mammoth Capital Research and Management.

Turner was actually more interested in making another run at NBC, but he went along with Levin's request since things had been going well between them and at Time Warner. Levin and Case knew they had to convince him it was for the good of the shareholders and the good of the company. "They painted it as the deal of the century for Turner, telling him things like we will not close until you sign off," said someone who knows both sides well. "I think they coerced him into making him feel he would be the power."

The question of power was actually a sticking point even before Case's scheduled November 17, 1999, meeting with Turner took place. Things went awry the day before when Case and Levin met alone in Manhattan at the St. Regis Hotel. There Case stopped talking in airy visions and got down to brass tacks. He suddenly began focusing on making sure that AOL would get carriage on Time Warner cable systems. And as AOL stock headed further upward, he worried openly about the hit his company's shares could take if it didn't end up with a much larger stake in the combined company. Case proposed a 60/40 percent split, in AOL's favor, unless it got more governance power in exchange for a lesser stake. Levin thought Case had overreached. "If this was just about cable, it was not what is was all about to me," said Levin. "And suddenly it felt like it was an AOL takeover plan."

The pair parted, and Case went back to the Pierre Hotel, where he had a glum meeting with his team. "Is it 'off off' or just 'off' for now?" asked CFO Mike Kelly. Case had no good answer, but still kept his date the next day with Ted Turner, who had been briefed by Levin on the conversations. Though Levin seemed to have soured, Turner now was enthusiastic about the idea, and he urged Case to persevere. He even suggested that Case insist on being CEO instead of Levin, people familiar with the meeting told me, an indication that Turner might not have gotten over his pique at Levin quite yet. Case told Turner that wasn't a "viable possibility," sources said, and that the idea was surely a deal breaker.

Unless, that is, the deal was irreparably broken already. As one deal participant said, "It had fallen off the rails."

If You Can't Be With the One You Love

AOL and Time Warner wasted no time in trying to find alternatives to each other, scouring for as big a blockbuster as they could find across the interactive landscape. Both were serious, but each also needed a stalking horse that might shake the other up enough to get back to the bargaining table.

Time Warner quickly turned to Yahoo. Levin had met and been deeply impressed with a very young Jerry Yang, one of the cofounders of the spectacularly successful Internet directory and portal. With the biggest Web audience, Yahoo had become a powerhouse, known for its simple, fast, and uncluttered delivery of all kinds of information, and it had done so with little of the rough behavior AOL had gained a reputation for. Its valuation had headed skyward, too, making Yang a multibillionaire in his first job after leaving college. Yahoo was also, unlike most Internet companies, profitable.

I had called Yang as soon as I got to California in 1997. Aside from Amazon's Jeff Bezos, eBay's Meg Whitman, and RealNetworks's Rob Glaser, Yang was the Web icon most central to the whole boom.

Levin, who had long been interested in Yahoo, liked Yang. So he sent Bressler to meet with Yahoo's leadership many times, which included CEO Tim Koogle and his number two, Jeff Mallett, as well as Yang. The two sides had several meetings in late November and early December about what the companies could do together and how both sides saw the world evolving. But Bressler was coy, and if he had a bigger idea, the Yahoo team was hard-pressed to figure it out. "He was not specific at all," Yahoo's CEO Koogle told me. "We huddled and asked ourselves, 'Are they serious, or are they just fishing?'"

The Yahoo team was torn, since they, too, were worried about the insecurity of Web valuations and wondered if they could survive without a big media partner. They also wanted to stay independent if possible, and didn't want to venture so quickly outside the company's core competency or outside the Net. Doing a deal, even if that meant that Yahoo would grab a major stake, meant selling the company. Unlike AOL executives, whose egos were much larger, the Yahoo team thought they would surely get lost in the shuffle and that they were ill-suited to try to run a complex media company. They were also dubious that old and new media were really natural partners. "We were more practical in our approach," said Koogle. "We were in a quickly moving industry where speed of decision and execution was key. And we thought being tied to a very large company might slow us down."

Time Warner was also reticent, because of Yahoo's valuation and also because it didn't have a huge base of paying subscribers like AOL. Being totally ad supported, Yahoo was a much riskier proposition for Time Warner, making it hard to justify the unequal valuations. And soon enough, Levin would be put off by the same whiff of arrogance from the Yahoos that he'd picked up from Case.

At a dinner with Yang and Mallett at the elegant Upper East Side French bistro Le Refuge in Manhattan, Levin started lecturing the pair on Yahoo's inflated currency, asking how its business was sustainable. Mallett, unfamiliar with the subtleties of the media world dance and frustrated by Levin's cryptic nature, shot back quickly and arrogantly.

"Why are you peppering us about our business when you're the ones without any growth?" he snapped, then uttered the most annoying Web mantra of the era: "You just don't get it." The remark, more confrontational than it needed to be, made Levin cringe. A few more meetings did take place, but the Yahoo option was pretty much off the table.

AOL had moved onto its doubling-down-on-the-Internet option by stepping up talks with a number of Web companies, most especially eBay. AOL was impressed with the online auctioneer's huge growth, and eBay had been one of the few ad partners who had seen gigantic gains from its AOL deal. It had signed increasingly large agreements with AOL and had seen major payoffs to its business, since AOL subscribers and eBay users were demographically similar. Executives at the companies also had a good rapport. The two companies began talks, and soon AOL's Miles Gilburne was coming out to Silicon Valley to work on what it would call Project Dock, as in "dock of the Bay."

Today, in late 2003, with eBay in ascendancy, it's clear this deal would have been a huge boon to AOL. But, at the time, things were rockier for eBay, which was facing competition from several companies, worrisome technology issues, and an inability to leverage its brand worldwide. A big company like AOL, eBay executives thought, might just be the ticket to solve their woes. AOL promised the possibility of keeping eBay a standalone business, run by Meg Whitman, eBay's steady and well-respected CEO. Whitman had racked up considerable experience in a range of traditional companies including Disney and Hasbro before joining eBay, and she was a proven and experienced executive much admired by Case and especially Pittman. It was even possible that Whitman might make a good candidate to run the whole company someday, as she was just the kind of mature executive AOL sorely needed.

The only big worry the AOL deal makers had was that such a small deal would not give AOL enough assets and also that it would make them only a bigger Internet power. But AOL's ambitions were much larger. And there were concerns at eBay, too. "We did not know what a large company was going to do to us and were still trying to figure it out," said one eBay insider involved in the talks. "The question was, did we want to be attached to someone else's ocean liner?"

Talks continued into December with a planned visit after the New Year to AOL by eBay's executive staff. But Case and others were unmoved. "What's the point?" Case told his staff. "It doesn't help us in broadband and it hardly moves the needle." Plus, as WorldCom's John Sidgmore pointed out, "Case really believed in the huge value in Time Warner's content."

So the needle mover was still Time Warner. Still unhappy that things had gone astray in the far-and-away sexier deal, Case urged Novack to reestablish contact with Bressler and see if they could break the impasse and keep the deal alive. AOL's stock by now was swelling to almost ridiculous proportions, hitting an all-time high in mid-December. AOL had to buy something big and buy it now. Levin agreed to the overture by Bressler and wanted to bring in Dick Parsons more actively and get his assessment. A steady and dependable executive, the tall and imposing Parsons was known for his gentle manner and diplomatic skills.

The two sides scheduled a meeting in Novack's Boston office for December 23—two days before Christmas and a week before the millennium New Year's celebration, the biggest ever. In attendance were Novack, Mike Kelly, and Salomon banking heavyweight Eduardo Mestre for AOL, and Bressler, Parsons, and Morgan Stanley banker Paul Taubman for Time Warner. Parsons, several people at the meeting remember, immediately affected a professorial air with no judgments, making it easy to lay everything on the table. "Tell me all about it," he opened. The two groups started hashing out the various roadblocks, which mostly centered on figuring out the right exchange ratios, considering the disparate valuations. After taking in everything, Parsons was quiet for a moment, and then told the AOL side that Time Warner would get back to them after the holidays. His biggest issue was over getting equal board power and also making sure Levin remained CEO, according to sources familiar with Parson's thinking.

And so AOL waited, as Levin, Parsons, and Bressler kibitzed about what to do, with a determination to accept a 55-45 split. During the interim, an interesting omen appeared in Time Warner's own flagship magazine. *Time* editor Walter Isaacson chose Amazon's Jeff Bezos as the magazine's Man of the Year, although Steve Case had also been considered. On the cover, Bezos posed with a box on his head: The joyous face of a company that was changing the world.

Soon Levin would do him one better.

The Price of Eggs

While AOL waited impatiently, Levin recused himself to ponder the deal over the holidays at his compound in Vermont. Though he would later insist that others were involved, this kind of solitary contemplation was typical for Levin, who had never been an opinion seeker. It is clear that Levin had been the prime mover and visionary of the deal. After it was done, some would complain about the hubris of Levin in doing a deal almost alone, without a healthy debate among stronger-minded executives who might present a serious challenge to it. Bressler, though competent, was junior, and Parsons had never been one to forcefully oppose anything Levin wanted to do. "He built this little children's crusade around him," said one Time Warner executive later. "He made it so there would be no dissent."

It is astonishing that Levin operated so independently, able to change the fortunes of such a major company in such secrecy, which one former Time Warner executive called "Nixonian." This would be critical to striking the deal and also to its failure. Given that Levin had dubious control over the operations of the company, where true power had long resided in the divisions, leaving out more powerful voices like HBO's up-and-comer Jeff Bewkes or Time Inc.'s legendary Don Logan was a major error. "Jerry was convinced that he had the right strategy, it would work," said one executive close to him. "But he wanted to be able to say once again, 'I am right against all protests of the company.'" In truth, as many executives close to him told me, Levin's style was not collaborative. "Jerry is a guy who collects facts and data . . . and then goes off alone and contemplates," said one Time Warner executive.

Levin told me that he worried about leaks from his very leaky company that might start a groundswell against what he considered a revolutionary idea. He was not alone. One Time Warner executive said widespread consultation would have resulted in the deal being "a dead fish in the water." And Levin wanted no obstacles and created a situation where he got none. He would, though, display an almost snotty disdain for those who did not agree with him, noting they were not big enough thinkers to comprehend yet what he had done. So while many later would accuse Case of snookering Levin, some going as far as calling Levin a moron, it was clear it was a con that the victim was very much in on.

When he got back to the office after the New Year, Levin decided AOL was the right choice, and told Bressler to set up one more dinner meeting with Case to see if they could iron out everything. They decided to keep it small and intimate: Just Levin, Bressler, Case, and Novack. It was to take place at Case's faux French chateau mansionette in suburban northern Virginia. There, the foursome would hammer out the deal over dinner, well into the evening on January 6, 2000. Gilburne and Kelly, who were at an investment conference in Arizona, coached Case by phone before the meeting, telling him to be as amenable and flexible as possible to Levin.

He was. And so the terms, which the two sides had been working on, fell into place rather quickly. It would be a tax-free merger using purchase accounting. The ratio was fixed at 1.5 AOL shares to each Time Warner share, which added up to a price of $110.63 for each Time Warner share—an amazing 71 percent premium from Time Warner's close of $64.75 on the Friday before the deal was announced. Under the agreement, AOL got 56 percent of the company, with Time Warner's stake pegged at 44 percent. Even still, the group agreed, it would be considered a merger of equals, since the board of 16 members would consist of eight members from each side.

The issue that caused the least tension was the one that would later become most controversial: The lack of a "collar" on the deal. A collar is a deal point that allows for a readjustment of the terms, should the stock of the seller or buyer fall below a preset range. As I would write later, "for better or worse, AOL and TW were tethered together for the storm," because of the lack of a collar. Most acquisitions do have a collar, mostly to protect the acquired company from a price drop. And although Bressler had pushed for one, Levin demurred. Not only did Levin think it was unnecessary, but he also believed the lack of one would be a strong signal to Wall Street that the deal was going forward without any doubt. The huge 71 percent premium was supposed to protect Time Warner from any precipitous decline in AOL stock, and was too high a price for Time Warner to demand a collar too.

Time Warner's investment banker Joseph Perella of Morgan Stanley thought the no-collar provision made sense at the time, when it was not altogether clear that Internet stocks were about to fall. "When you replay the tape and remember the frenzy of opposition to this deal and the feeling that the company would be a giant, a collar would have been insane," he noted to me in 2003. "The bust was a slow leak and if the boom had continued into 2001, we would have gotten squashed for not seeing the upside of such a hot stock. No one knew what was going to happen then, but today everyone has perfect vision."

Levin agreed. "We were getting married or not," he told me in 2003, despite the raft of criticism he would get over the no-collar deal point. "If we had one, it would have said that we did not believe in our vision." And Levin was most definitely a believer. It would be impossible, in short, to break up this deal without a lot of pain. But pain was not on Levin's agenda, and he even happily agreed to several other seeming concessions. The new company would have joint headquarters, in Dulles and New York. The ticker symbol would be AOL. And the name would be AOL Time Warner. "I picked the name," Levin noted.

Gilburne and Kelly were anxious as they jetted across the country from their conference in Arizona to get back to northern Virginia before the dinner's end. As the private plane headed east, Gilburne and AOL investor relations head Richard Hanlon reminisced about how far AOL had come. Kelly said he was rendered almost mute at the very thought of it.

After they landed, Gilburne caught a ride home with Kelly, since they lived near each other in Potomac, Maryland, not far from Case's Virginia home. During the drive, they called Case and asked how it was going. "Okay," he replied. They asked if they should come by or not. "No," said the terse but excited Case, "I don't want to change the dynamic." So they went home separately and got online. Case IM'ed them soon enough. He simply typed: "It's done."

The next morning, a Friday, things were jumping at AOL headquarters. They would need to close the deal immediately over the weekend due to the extreme possibility of leaks now that a wider group at both companies was due to find out. A group of about 40 AOL staffers gathered in the Malibu conference room on the fifth floor of AOL headquarters to be split up and sent to do various due diligence investigations in Virginia and New York. AOL and Time Warner afforded themselves only a few days of due diligence, since both were public companies, despite the fact that the deal would be one of the biggest in history.

David Colburn started screaming to those gathered in mock horror about what lay ahead: "Do you know how much work this is going to take?!?" he barked. Colburn, like Pittman and his staff, hadn't been much involved in the merger attempt, and had assumed the "eggheads" couldn't get such a monumental deal done.

But they had done it—and now they had to quickly put another deal on ice. By coincidence, eBay's Meg Whitman, her top executives, and eBay's investment bankers from Goldman Sachs had come to AOL headquarters that day for what had been billed as a final negotiating session for the acquisition deal. But top AOL executives wandered in and out of the long meeting, shuttling between the company's main boardroom (where the eBay executives sat) and the Malibu room on the opposite end of the floor (where the Time Warner deal team was working). It was a comical scene: Executives shuffled in and out, alternately apologizing to and ignoring Whitman and her team.

The eBay group had no idea what was going on down the hall, and some wondered whether AOL's culture had bred attention deficit disorder. They worried that perhaps AOL thought of eBay as a very small company and thought they might be seeing a high-level version of the classic AOL ad deal brush-off tactic. At the end of the day, quite unsatisfied, Whitman and others from the group went to Bob Pittman's office to say good-bye. "You have a lot going on here, it seems," she said, according to those there. She had no idea.

The due diligence in New York was tense, as Time Warner and

AOL tangled with each other under heavy pressure to get the deal to their respective boards, and iron out remaining issues. Both boards had been largely in the dark about the specifics of the deal until it was being shoved across the table at them on Sunday, January 9. Among the documents given to AOL board members were impressive charts showing how big the merger was going to be. "A Media Powerhouse for the New Millennium," one was grandly titled, and the page noted that AOL Time Warner would become the world's first truly "new media" company.

The documents for both boards promised both grand new revenue and cost synergies: More cable services, more digital distribution, new interactive properties, common customer database, lower infrastructure, lower overhead, lower sales and marketing, lower ad sales, and a consolidation of interactive efforts. And other intracompany synergies were also touted: CNN distributed on AOL; Moviefone promoting Warner Bros.; Time Inc. magazine subscriptions sold online. In one line of the AOL board documents lay the first recognition of problems that might slow down these important synergies. There was a risk, the papers noted, that there might not be an "ability to achieve synergies in a decentralized corporate environment."

At a marathon nine-hour Time Warner board meeting at the law offices of its counsel Cravath, Swaine & Moore, there were achingly long banker presentations by the Morgan Stanley team, led by its investment banking head Joe Perella, and from other advisers. Morgan Stanley Internet analyst Mary Meeker, a longtime AOL fan, noted that there was no sign of weakness in AOL's business, as long as it moved quickly to embrace the broadband business and the ad market stayed strong. By coincidence, Meeker had compared Steve Case to Time founder Henry Luce in an earlier Internet report she had written.

Levin talked about the profound implications of the deal. Parsons talked about the people and warned the board, quite correctly, to expect some fallout from Time Warner employees. He warned the group that nothing was going to be the same again, and that this deal was unlike any before it. "This will be dramatic," Parsons said.

Turner was feeling a little grumpy about the price, given that AOL represented only 18 percent of the revenues and yet was getting more than half the combined company. But he noted happily that it would be nice to let AOL fix all the Internet woes Time Warner had suffered. Those present at the meeting said the docile board was largely complimentary to Levin for the deal and offered no objections.

"At the time of the meeting, I don't think that any CEO in America had more credibility than Jerry," recalled Morgan Stanley's Perella, noting that Levin had gone against conventional wisdom and bet on cable with a successful outcome. "He had been consistently right for too long in his vision, so he had a lot of support when he went in with this deal."

One board member, opera diva Beverly Sills, did admit to being a little confused by what was happening. Sills would soon be retiring from the Time Warner board, and she found all this talk of Web valuations and digital convergence incomprehensible. And the idea that a company not even out of its adolescence could purchase a major chunk of a company that had been around since before most people in the room had been born was mind-boggling to her. Sills was shaken upon learning that the old TWX ticker symbol would disappear to be replaced by AOL. "I have to get off this board, because I don't understand a lot of this stuff about the future," she said. "It's just over my head. . . . I have outlived my usefulness."

Over at the AOL meeting, held at the Manhattan law offices of Simpson Thacher & Bartlett (coincidentally, the firm Levin had worked for early in his career), there was similar bonhomie and no objections. Briefed by Salomon bankers and its analyst Lanny Baker, it was a slam-dunk from the start. Most questions were trivial, such as board member Al Haig's query about what would happen to everyone's stock options. Only Fannie Mae head Franklin Raines raised a legitimate concern about the 71 percent premium, noting that at some point it might look as if AOL was selling the company at a discount. Netscape's Jim Barksdale, famous for his down-home aphorisms, assuaged Raines's worry. "That's the price of eggs," he said simply. "And that's what we have to pay if we want Time Warner." What he meant was that it did not matter what anything was worth anymore, but what the market would bear. The group waited until

Levin called to tell them that the Time Warner board had approved the deal, and then voted for it, also unanimously.

AOL and Time Warner had leapt into uncharted territory. When I finally got the AOL executive's Instant Message confirmation in the dead of that Monday morning, the first email I sent was to Jerry Yang of Yahoo, to ask him what he thought. I knew he'd be up and online, like so many techies, and he'd learn of the deal pretty quickly from the *Wall Street Journal's* Web posting, if he had not suspected it long before. And after everyone digested the news, I knew that they'd surely want to know what Yang's highflying and stock-rich company would be doing; it would be the obvious follow-up story. After all, on the Friday before the merger, Yahoo itself was worth $150 billion.

Yang soon called me on my cell phone, and as I stood talking to him out in the cold San Francisco night on my porch deck, the fog drifting around me, it felt as if I was standing at the end of the earth. Adrenaline had taken over me by now; I quickly asked Yang a raft of questions and furiously took notes. I also couldn't help myself: "People are taking Weimar Republic money, so what are you going to do?" I said, comparing Internet stocks to the highly elevated but ulti-mately worthless currency in pre–World War II Germany. It wasn't a perfect metaphor, and Yang seemed confused. "It means you better buy things fast," I explained, because over AOL's rocky life Steve Case had seemed to have an almost psychic ability to know when to bail out. Clearly, if Case was discounting his stock, it might be time for Yahoo and others like it to act.

Yang was unusually calm, talking about how Yahoo would remain neutral like "Switzerland" and the AOL Time Warner deal would make Yahoo an obvious choice for all the other now surely terrified media companies, like Disney and Viacom. Yahoo would stand pat, he said. While Yang might wonder if his company was wrong not to pursue a big media merger, he also was not certain what it had missed. But, he agreed, the merger was a game changer that would have an enormous impact on the media and Internet markets. But neither he nor I, to tell the truth, knew much more, since the pro-posed merger of AOL and Time Warner had upended everything we understood.

PEOPLE CONNECTION

Q-Link's "People Connection"—a 300-baud precursor to the online "community" (read: sex chat) that would propel AOL to the top of the digital heap.

A gaggle of adoring quilters who met online at AOL presented Steve Case with this quilt in 1995, along with cookies and kisses. It was clear he was on to something.

PHOTO BY LISA DICKEY

In the mid-1990s, boy wonder Steve Case was in the back of the pack at this Al Gore tech event. Time Warner head Jerry Levin had the prime center spot—amid a crowd of such diverse luminaries as Michael Eisner, Larry Ellison, and Quincy Jones.

What's going on behind Steve Case's patented placid gaze? His inscrutability earned him the nickname "The Wall" among his staff.

Steve's older brother Dan (nicknamed "Upper Case" to Steve's "Lower Case") got him his start in the online world. Dan's death from brain cancer in 2002 robbed Steve of one of the few people who truly knew him.

PHOTO BY JOHN CASADO

Worse than alligators
in the sewer:
The Urban Legend
of the deal,
AOL's Myer Berlow.
COURTESY OF
MYER BERLOW

David Colburn's "Putz, we
are!" became an AOL legend
(not to mention a T-shirt).
His "jokes" rubbed Time
Warner employees raw
before his abrupt fall from
grace in August 2002.

No one could quite believe it when the "cockroach of cyberspace" turned into the new Godzilla.

Give a man a white board, and he will change the world. Miles Gilburne, the man behind the curtain, drew up some of AOL's biggest deals.

The Consigliere. Ken Novack, Steve Case's closest adviser, wielded tremendous power for a guy you've never heard of.

{Above} The monk and the clown: Steve Case (in his trademark Hawaiian shirt) and Ted Leonsis live the high life as AOL stock begins to soar, taking in a Mike Tyson fight in Vegas in 1995. {Right} With the millions his AOL stock brought him, Ted Leonsis bought his way into hobnobbing with sports gods, including Michael Jordan. BOTH COURTESY OF TED LEONSIS

"There's got to be a pony somewhere in this shit," Jim Kimsey declared in the earliest days of the company. By the mid-1990s, he'd found it. COURTESY OF JIM KIMSEY

Amazon founder Jeff Bezos was judged to be the human who had the biggest impact on the news in 1999. Things were getting out of hand.

The $10 million napkin: A business venture offered to me at the height of the Internet boom. If I'd agreed to take part in this deal, you might not be reading this book right now.

PHOTO BY MEGAN J. SMITH

Kara,   10-18-99
We would back
your dream team
with a $10 mil
Investment which buys
= 40%. => 40%
        60% Mgmt
          20% unallocated
          40% Dream Team

Patrician, staid Henry Luce cofounded *Time* magazine in 1923 with fellow Hotchkiss graduate Briton Hadden. His blue-blood manner continued to permeate the company nearly eight decades later.

Warner head Steve Ross helped Jerry Levin vault to the top of Time Warner—as his co-CEO—after their companies merged. His death in 1992 left Levin fully in charge.

The Time Warner deal team—no matter what they say now. Rich Bressler, Ted Turner, Jerry Levin, and Dick Parsons. COURTESY OF JERRY LEVIN

"I was robbed!" CNN founder Ted Turner.
COURTESY OF TED TURNER

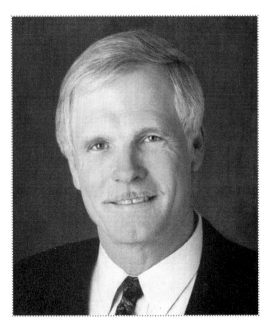

A screen shot from the "most expensive pizza delivery system ever invented": Time Warner's Full Service Network.

Time Warner's "black hole": The ill-fated Pathfinder Web site.

High fives and hugs at the merger announcement on January 10, 2000. It was all downhill from here. © LES STONE/CORBIS

As of January 11, 2001, AOL Time Warner officially owned the air you breathe.

© JIMMY MARGULIES, *THE RECORD*, NEW JERSEY

Hype, hype everywhere, but few cautious words. The press mostly devoured the talk of "synergy" whole.

If ever a marriage needed a pre-nup . . . Time Warner employees thought they'd hit the Internet jackpot, but stock options would prove a disheartening bust.

PATRICK CORRIGAN /
COURTESY *TORONTO STAR*

Show time! AOL's Bob "Pitchman" Pittman was the heir apparent—and the first AOL Icarus to flame out.

Dick Parsons was described by some as the "nonalcoholic beverage." How else could he have been the last one standing as of February 2003?

The new headquarters:
AOL Time Warner's enduring
monument to hubris.
PHOTO BY LISA DICKEY

Now a struggling
division in a vast
Time Warner
landscape, AOL goes
back to its roots:
fighting MSN. Here,
MSN butterflies crash
the October 2002
AOL 8.0 launch at
Lincoln Center.
PHOTO BY LISA DICKEY

As AOL and Time Warner scratched each other bloody in internal fighting, Microsoft was poised to be the beneficiary. Here, Bill Gates and MSN head Yusuf Mehdi demonstrate MSN 8.0. PHOTO BY JEFF CHRISTENSEN

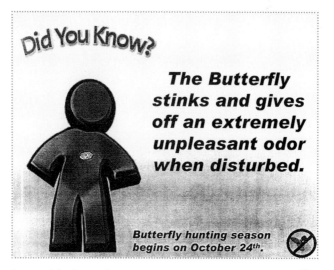

Even with three times as many users as MSN, AOL still saw itself as the underdog. Anti-MSN posters began sprouting up at AOL headquarters in the fall of 2002.

The face of the past may be the face of the future: Don Logan.

The next great hope (and a very handsome man): Jeff Bewkes.

Was this the moment when the Web would finally take over the world, a powerful movement that had been building for years now without a pause? It certainly felt like it. Or, I wondered for a brief second, as I stood shivering in the chilly air, was it actually the onset of snow flurries of that dreaded Internet nuclear winter?

So we knew it was going to happen, and it did. The Black
Horsemen came and cut down the revelers, even those
with names of virtue engendered like Prudent and Faithful
and American and Growth.... Not only did the market go
down, it kept going down.... Another day it would come
back, but not until an unscarred generation, so bold with
memories, had become scarred like its predecessor.

ADAM SMITH, *The Money Game*

Chapter Five

PURSUING THE PUTZ

Was it: "We are, you putz"?

Or was it: "Putz, we are"?

This subtle distinction has taken up more minutes of my
life than it ever should have. Starting out, the only things I
knew for certain were three basic facts.

The first: That this was a colorful riposte supposedly
uttered by AOL's top deal maker, David Colburn, to a Time
Warner counterpart during the weekend of due diligence that
was conducted in advance of the consummation of the
biggest merger of all time. "You're making it sound as if
you're buying us," the Time Warner exec had joked to Colburn, who had actually held his tongue. But with AOL colleagues later, the eternal bad boy had quickly dropped all
pretenses, and made the remark. Definitely not hewing to the

laughable "merger of equals" party line put out by the deal's architects, Colburn's quip offered his own brass-knuckles take on the situation.

Second: That T-shirts were made, white with a blue logo, with this very phrase on them—"Putz, we are," as it turned out—and given later to Colburn's notorious Business Affairs team. There was a generous amount of chortling over the shirts, which expressed, to the group's admiration, Colburn's screw-you toughness against the Time Warner empire that AOL had just conquered.

And third: That *putz* is vulgar Yiddish slang for a *penis.*

I also know for certain that this is not a good story to begin the relationship of AOL and Time Warner. But the "putz" incident took on a life of its own soon after the deal was consummated and became a corporate urban legend, with multiple, and often incorrect, versions bandied about. But like any good urban legend, it owed its existence to some very real problems—ones that were apparent right from the beginning of the AOL Time Warner merger.

The heart of the problem was this: That even if the most basic idea underlying the combination of AOL and Time Warner—the premise that there will and should be an eventual and inevitable convergence of all media and digital products—is a valid one, this particular marriage seemed doomed from the start. Today, that's easy enough to see and to say, as people pick apart the merger much as you would the breakup of a couple you predicted were headed for divorce court even before the wedding banquet's appetizer course.

As with any ultimately doomed union, if you slowly wind the merger backward from its messy end to its promising beginnings, you can more easily see how the meltdown happened. From its faulty conception to its deeply flawed execution to its bungled handling of a recovery attempt, there is no point in this melodrama that in hindsight was not a painfully obvious misstep. But it was an evolution of small steps in the wrong direction, so it was hard to see the merger running aground from the very start.

But even hindsight doesn't allow one to discover the full truth of what happened to the AOL Time Warner merger—a tale that soon reminded me of a souped-up version of the classic 1950 Japanese drama *Rashomon.* The big question in that film, in which characters describe the same heinous crime from differing viewpoints, is the same one you might ask about this deal: What's the real truth? Or, perhaps, is there any truth at all?

That's because in this tale, there aren't just two versions of the same event, as is often the case in reporting a business story. Instead, there are multiple versions. And each and every version depends on a complex and arcane number of factors, including but not limited to who lost money and who didn't; who sold what and when; who lost power and who gained it; how they acted when they gained it, and, more important, how they should have acted; who came from Time and who came from Warner and who came from Turner (unless, of course, you were dealing with AOLers, and then everyone at always fractious Time Warner was suddenly one united company against the vile barbarians of Virginia); who thought the Internet economy was a bubble and who did not; and who had no clue, but took advantage of the situation anyway.

But a few things are eminently clear and easy to outline in a few broad strokes. As it turned out, the problem began on the very first day, with the announcement itself: An orgy of high-fiving and self-congratulation so over the top that it was as if completing the deal itself was the winning move. By declaring victory immediately, the group in charge set in motion a pattern of overpromising and under-delivering that would make meaningless any forward movement at the combined company under the questionable mantle of "synergy." The result was that whenever anything was actually accomplished, it looked very small, throwing off a sad little *is-that-all-there-is* vibe both externally and internally.

This was most destructive when it came to the financial bragging that seemed recklessly ambitious from the moment the big num-bers—$40 billion in revenue, $11 billion in cash flow, $1 billion in savings—went up on the board. When some top executives, including Steve Case, began selling a lot of stock even as they continued to tout those handsome projections, they later looked suspect. Worst of all, these numbers, which would ultimately hang the merger, were entirely of the executives' own making. Essentially, their need to prove the deal's worth got tethered to impossible-to-reach numbers, result-ing in a kind of financial suicide.

Most problematic, since the AOL unit was cast as the principal driver for growth and synergy in the merger, was the bust of the dot-com sector—which began almost immediately after the deal was struck and intensified over 2001. Since AOL was a bit higher up on the Web food chain, the reverberations of this decline were less noticeable at first. But the implications of the Web bust would eventually reach AOL, too. It was in this time, perhaps not surprisingly, that AOL—never shy in striking aggressive ad deals—started to commit some even more edgy accounting tricks to preserve momentum. These moves would later come to haunt the merger.

Meanwhile, even as the declining economy rang a distant bell of trouble, AOL took over the reins of AOL Time Warner in a take-no-prisoners style that would chafe those on the Time Warner side. There was, no doubt, terribly bad behavior on the part of AOL, ranging from the silly to the very serious. With little media experience, but a lot of hubris that their way was the way of the future, the AOL crew rampaged through Time Warner with little care and no sense of respect. They mandated change without a solid knowledge of the businesses they sought to control; they were often rude and arrogant while doing so; they bragged of their copious accomplishments and talents even as their own business began to suffer badly.

And while much has been written in the daily press about the AOLers' power mongering—the prevailing notion became, as AOL investor relations head Richard Hanlon described it to me, "the attack on the fair maiden Time Warner by the molester AOL"—it is not altogether accurate to say Time Warner was simply a victim of this boorishness. Continuing in the long tradition of protecting its fiefdoms while feigning cooperation, Time Warner played a delayed game with its new AOL conquerors. In what became one of my favorite expressions of the merger, one top executive at AOL noted that Time Warner's passive-aggressive style—honed from years of ignoring dictates from the corporate center—amounted to simple "grin-fucking" of AOL executives who were pressing them.

Perhaps most damaging of all was the lack of both a common goal and the emergence of a central leader. Despite all the hoopla, no one in this group of individually powerful people ever really had the ultimate power to give the deal a true vision or to force lasting change.

Without strong leadership, which is not the same as strong-minded leaders, the merger's failure degenerated into a blame game at the highest levels of the company, where everyone thought he was right and no one would admit being wrong. Was it a takeover or a marriage? Sadly, no one ever knew.

In other words, there are no heroes here. And the putz T-shirts were the first clue of that. Even I know the cardinal rule of successful merger integration: Do not compare one of your new colleagues to genitalia.

In fact, it got much worse than that, and very soon.

The Dating Game

On January 10, 2000, there were only smiles, backslaps, and those unfortunate high fives all around. At the Equitable Center in midtown Manhattan, an array of euphoric executives lined up to announce Jerry Levin's latest, greatest "transforming transaction"—the $183 billion marriage of AOL and Time Warner. Together, according to the *Wall Street Journal,* the companies were worth almost $319 billion.

Seated in a row on the stage were the new stars of this media colossus, including Steve Case, Jerry Levin, Ted Turner, Bob Pittman, and Dick Parsons. Also on stage was AOL's CFO Mike Kelly, whom Levin had selected to be chief financial officer of the combined company. My first thought on seeing that line-up on television was that there were an awful lot of people up there on stage. It reminded me of a Wall Street version of *The Dating Game,* with all the contestants perched on stools, waiting for their chance to impress the audience. With klieg lights and swarming photographers, this was more than just a merger—it was a high-concept production number. "There were a lot of people who had to talk," observed Time Inc. editorial director John Huey to me later. "It was like a commune."

In some sort of strange fashion homage, Levin had even dressed down for the announcement, lending another odd touch by showing up in the dot-com uniform of khaki pants and an open-necked shirt, having shaved off his mustache for the first time in more than three decades. Steve Case, on the other hand, tried to appear statesmanlike in a dark suit, blue shirt, and yellow polka-dotted tie. But this conservative attire didn't prevent him from doing a happy little hip-shaking dance onstage and joyously hugging the heretofore unhuggable Levin.

Just about any big merger announcement incorporates a certain amount of hyperbole. But the rhetoric surrounding this deal, the largest merger in history, was truly epic. Steve Case, the new media kingpin, opined grandly, "We're kicking off the new century with a unique new company that has unparalleled assets and the ability to have a profoundly positive impact on society." And also: "This is a historic moment in which new media has truly come of age. . . . We are going to be the global company for the Internet age. . . . This will be the Internet Century."

He later declared to reporters that he hoped AOL Time Warner would be bigger than Microsoft or General Electric. And Case had even larger goals, noting later to Wall Street and the press that he hoped that AOL would someday have a market capitalization of $1 trillion, with $100 billion in annual revenue.

Ted Turner, of course, did him one better by offering his own now legendary take on things, comparing how it felt to approve the deal with his first major sexual experience. And he was equally pumped up in the bathroom before the announcement, where he slapped Bob Pittman repeatedly on the back, crowing, "We have to make this work! We have to pull together! This is just amazing!" He even joked giddily that he had never "made $1 billion before breakfast."

The stock price would turn out to be a good barometer of Turner's mood about the deal over time. Gone, for the moment at least, was his grumbling about the fact that AOL—with only one-fifth of the revenue and less than one-third of the operating cash flow—grabbed 56 percent of the combined company. Turner was even heartened a bit, because if the deal had been based solely on stock valuations, AOL would have owned at least 12 percent more.

At first, in a reflection of the frothy times and moment, the press and Wall Street focused mostly on the premium AOL paid over Time Warner's share price. To many, the merger was the final sign that the old economy was tossing in the towel, and that Time Warner had finally managed to make a bold and necessary move into the future. Despite the fact that synergy—particularly at Time Warner—hadn't worked before, most reporting on the deal centered on the notion that this was destined to be an invincible combination.

I certainly thought as much, although I was more in awe that AOL had been able to pull it off than anything else. But the combination did seem to suggest immense promise, given the possibilities that one could imagine between the various parts of AOL and Time Warner. In one major move, the two companies had seemingly addressed their weaknesses and intensified their strengths. I won't deny I really believed that, as did many others—many of whom now pretend they never did.

But behind the scenes, other media company moguls began to shake their heads in wonder that Levin had made such a shocking trade. Many noted that he might have done a deal of this magnitude to distract from his inability to manage what he already had. They also marveled at what he had given up, since there had long been a pervasive feeling among them that dot-com valuations were insane. Still, Time Warner's acquiescence was a powerful reminder that the Internet boom seemed to be gaining power rather than losing it, as had been long predicted. Soon enough, the AOL Time Warner deal would set off a stream of strategic reevaluations that led to more talks between the remaining media and Net companies, although mercifully no deals like this one were struck.

"In the lens of the moment, I was amazed by it, and so were others," said Barry Diller, the one media mogul who had deep experience in the Web arena, and who had tried a similar combination with his 1999 attempt to acquire Lycos. "A lot of people sat around the table and said, 'This is great.'"

Big institutional shareholders surely did. AOL and Time Warner had called their largest ones, including Capital Research and Management's Gordon Crawford, immediately before the announcement. The investment company held massive amounts of shares in both companies, and Crawford's view—which was enthusiastic at the beginning—was crucial to the merger's ability to gain credibility on Wall Street.

Executives quickly called other potentially influential shareholders, such as John Malone (whose large parcel of shares actually had no voting power), asking them to be as supportive as possible. In fact, Ted Turner called Malone to ask him what he thought. "I asked [Turner] if he supported it, and he said, 'Yes, I guess, but they did not give me a lot of time,'" said Malone, recalling that the response worried him a bit. "But, like a lot of people, I decided to hang on for a bit of the ride anyway."

So did the employees of both companies, most of whom had no idea the deal was brewing until word began to leak out over the weekend. Inside both AOL and Time Warner, the reaction was most definitely mixed.

On a positive note, Time Warner employees were thrilled with their stock's upward trajectory immediately following the deal. It rose 39 percent by the end of the first day of the announcement. Their joyous mood at this development was further elevated by the fact that all their stock options immediately vested—in other words, they could buy and then immediately sell them at a major profit. Many outside compensation analysts considered this early vesting dangerous. The result of old rules enacted in case of an ownership change, early vesting could, some speculated, prompt the departure of Time Warner executives who would have no financial incentive to remain. But others considered it a deft way for Levin to buy silence from any dissent, especially as Time Warner shares surged further upward.

At AOL, the reaction over the share price was almost the exact opposite, since many in the company would not be able to vest a bulk of their options until a year after the deal closed. In addition, as major AOL shareholders, they were used to owning a high-growth stock—and now they had apparently been hitched to a slow-growing one. That disparity was made clear when AOL shares started to tumble almost immediately as news of the deal spread, even though bankers had advised the company that the market reaction would remain neutral.

AOLers were also worried that the disparate and slothlike nature of Time Warner might hinder what they considered their own more nimble culture. "Welcome to middle management," said AOL service head Jon Sacks to a colleague as they walked out of the room where they'd just heard about the deal. More troublesome to AOLers was Time Warner's well-known reputation for corporate intrigue; many considered the media giant a minefield of competing agendas. In fact, the top ranks of AOL considered Time Warner a culture that didn't care to change, where the executive credo seemed to be "Deny, delay, and retire." One strong voice against the merger on this particular issue had been Bob Pittman's close adviser Kenny Lerer, who had dealt with Time Warner in the past. Lerer was deeply worried about both the political nature of the media giant and the mismatch of cultures.

"It is unrunnable," Lerer told AOL vice chairman Ken Novack on the day the deal was announced, in what had become his refrain. "We have destroyed AOL."

Concerns over the cultural issues also ran high at Time Warner, given AOL's reputation there as an aggressive team with boundless arrogance and looser ethics even then. "The Nazis have invaded Paris," warned one Time Warner executive who had worked with AOL and had seen some of their tactics. "They are going to strip us clean." Jealousy obviously also played a role here, given the vast wealth Time Warner's new partners had—a painful déjà vu to Time's merger with Warner. In addition, many employees were also annoyed that AOL had seemingly bought them, despite the efforts to paint it otherwise. One Time Warner executive called me the day of the merger, looking for my opinion of the AOL team. "Well, you broadcast *The Sopranos*," I joked, referring to the popular HBO gangster drama. "But they are actually the Sopranos, since they just stole your company fair and square." I thought it was funny, but he was mortified.

Inside AOL, in fact, calling the deal a merger was considered a joke, despite dictates from Case and Novack to do so. "We only said it around Time Warner executives to make them feel okay about the situation," said one executive to me in the spring of 2000. "But to us, it's an acquisition pure and simple." AOL thought its power would give it the leverage to finally unify the disparate Time Warner culture, which the online company's executives often likened to the bickering European countries.

Although the indignity of being bought by AOL would later have a profound impact on the failure of the merger, more damaging at the start was Levin's lack of communication to his major division heads about the deal. Time Inc.'s Don Logan, HBO's Jeff Bewkes, and most others didn't hear about it until the weekend before the announcement, leaving them little time to object, ask questions, or provide any input. Logan contemplated trying to get out of his contract, as did others, over the sudden shift in the company's fortunes without any consultation. According to those close to him, he also thought the Internet valuations were "bullshit," and ripe for a fall. Most of all, Logan could not believe Levin had done this without a word to him and others.

This was classic Levin, of course, a way to avoid the possibility of any opposition before the deal was done. "He brooked no real objections, since he looked at anyone without vision as pygmies," said one top executive, who was appalled, like most, to find out about the deal in a phone call from Levin after it was already struck. "And, anyway, how can you step up and say no in the maelstrom of all that excitement?"

You couldn't, and they didn't.

Synergy or Bust?

One of the top corporate goals was to keep up the deal's momentum in its first weeks, which meant selling it as hard as possible from the outset. But convincing others of the soundness of what clearly seemed an unproven idea and a gamble was not going to be easy, since there was no model for what Case and Levin had created and its success was based mostly on unknown trends far in the future. And ultimate success was predicated on visions of a high-speed digital culture, where AOL Time Warner could and would dominate with its potent mix of assets.

Almost immediately, the companies started selling the sizzle, flacking a bunch of airy synergistic initiatives cooked up by Colburn's team. But this was nothing compared to the most extravagant promise, which was trotted out to universal gasps: A vow to deliver spectacular financial results that would be hard to pull off even under the best of conditions.

"We can't show any weakness," Pittman told his fellow executives, and Case, Levin, and Kelly shared that sentiment. They were hell-bent on providing instant proof of the deal's worth through spectacular returns, and the figures they predicted were accordingly stunning.

Initially, according to internal documents, Miles Gilburne's team pegged $800 million as the amount of cash flow improvement the two companies could achieve in their first year as a merged company. Developed from an unproven wish list of ambitious cost-cutting and revenue-enhancing strategies, that was the figure the executives used to help convince the board to approve the merger. But even $800 million wasn't considered an excessively ambitious estimate. Kelly, supported by Pittman and Case, soon bumped the figure up to $1 billion, giving it to Levin to present what one AOL deal maker called an "optically attractive" number.

Levin told me he was surprised by the figure, which was arrived at with minimal analysis and no Time Warner input, but he accepted and later embraced it as a reasonable goal. "Everyone thought that by running the business tight, the money was attainable," said Levin, noting that top executives at both companies felt it would be easy to find this many cuts in $30 billion of expenses. In addition, they considered the looming prospect of finding $1 billion in savings as a good tool to force collaboration among divisions in order to save money.

But others within Time Warner didn't think these numbers were realistic, or even real, and they believed that Levin wasn't close enough to the operating units to understand what kinds of potentially damaging sacrifices he was asking of them. On the morning the deal was announced, Time Warner's longtime investor relations head Joan Sumner (who later went by the last name Nicolais), whose tough reputation was well known on Wall Street, questioned Kelly directly about the $1 billion number.

During the due diligence phase, she'd already had one run-in with the burly AOL CFO, a clash over who should be running a finance meeting. Undeterred, Nicolais now pressed Kelly hard on where AOL had come up with its financials. "Where did you get the one-billion-dollar figure?" she asked, wondering how Kelly could give out the data without Time Warner approval. "I've looked at the numbers, and I don't see where you find one billion."

"You don't know where," he said dismissively. "But I do." And Kelly would make certain he did know, by applying the kind of pressure to Time Warner divisions that they'd never experienced before. Kelly was convinced that Time Warner's history of not making its numbers resulted from weak central control, so he put on his tough-guy persona—a tactic that had worked well at AOL. "No one can grind like me," he'd brag to anyone within hearing distance, a rough style encouraged by Levin.

Later, in an interview with me in 2003, Kelly would curiously deny ever making that particular remark—despite the fact that I told him at least a dozen people at both AOL and Time Warner had heard him utter the phrase in a variety of meetings. He did allow, though, that he believed it was critical to be firm right from the moment of the deal's announcement. "Part of it was pushing the organization to take the costs out, because if we pulled back, we stalled," he told me. "We had had a strong year and there was a strong wind at our backs, so we felt there was nothing we could not overcome."

Along with the $1 billion in savings, AOL and Time Warner trumpeted a range of other big numbers. Claiming their combined first year's cash flow would hit $11 billion, Levin said the merged company was capable of smoothly riding out any economic storm and would post $40 billion in revenues. That amazing 30 percent growth rate, Steve Case later noted in a conference call with investors and analysts, was actually only a middle ground between his company's 50 percent growth rate and Time Warner's 15 percent one. But it would mean the company would have to reach unheard-of revenue and profit goals as time went on. To get there, all of top management would trumpet one more lofty number for AOL Time Warner: Its 130 million paying subscribers across offline and online distribution platforms. Pittman would later tout AOL Time Warner's future ability to garner hundreds of dollars from each and every one of those consumers by leveraging its array of soon-to-be interlocking cable, magazine, online, and music subscription businesses. This was all—and I am being kind—a big guess.

But to explain how all this might occur, since none of these services actually existed, the companies started spewing out press releases about new deals and partnerships that were designed to underscore the merged company's potential power. Many people at Time Warner considered these mostly hype, blaming AOL's Kenny Lerer, who thought it important to keep up the momentum through good news about the merger even before it was a done deal. A struggle over how to position the company in the public eye soon became acrimonious, with the Time Warner side urging less grand publicity, while the AOL side insisted on touting every single item it could get to prove the merger's worth.

This communications fight—in which Time Warner's Ed Adler, a 20-year public relations veteran, was placed under Lerer's command—centered on how to handle the press and position the combined company, and was another signal of the very different philosophies at work. In my experience, AOL under Lerer was all about control and fending off the press, while keeping on message constantly and loudly. It always reminded me a lot of campaign-style political spin, with highflying but sometimes empty promises. Adler represented a much less heavy-handed approach, which AOLers found lacked strategic thought. But being less meddlesome and cozier with the press worked much better within a media company located in New York, where Adler would have gotten quickly flamed by Time Warner's legions of journalists for more aggressive methods.

There were other differences in AOL and Time Warner public relations philosophies. While AOL had tamped down leaks almost viciously, this was never Time Warner's practice. And while the Time Warner corporate often badly underplayed its announcements—the entertainment divisions providing the most hype—AOL never met a press release it did not trumpet extravagantly. It is often said that whoever controls communications, controls all. And the battle for that function was perhaps one of the more obvious signs of trouble right away, since it set the tone for credibility of the whole merger. Once again, it angered many at Time Warner, especially as Levin began to become close to Lerer.

"Our credibility took a big hit," said one Time Warner executive. "Journalists, investors, and employees all felt betrayed; over time no one trusted us." But AOLers thought Time Warner's complaining was overdone.

Guess which side won? Thus, the "good" news came fast and furious. February 15: "AOL and Time Warner Team Up for Winter Goodwill Games Promotion." February 16: "America Online and Time Warner Announce Online Unveiling of the 2000 *Sports Illustrated* Swimsuit Issue Cover on AOL." March 20: "Warner Bros. Records and AOL's Spinner.com Present Faith Hill Live Online!"

Still, some were not convinced of the benefits quite yet. Long-time AOL observer Allan Sloan, in a typically excellent *Newsweek* column, wrote, "The more high-flown the rhetoric surrounding a deal, the more suspicious we should be." And *Fortune*'s talented Carol Loomis opined ominously in February 2000 in the Time Warner–owned magazine, "Regardless of what numbers may dazzle you about the deal, that is the one to focus on: The market cap that the company must push up a steep hill to continue rewarding investors."

Mickey Mousing Around

While most were initially convinced of the merger's promise, Case, Levin, Pittman, and others had to make sure the doom-and-gloom attitude of the unconvinced didn't become pervasive. They hoped to solve that by getting the merger going as soon as possible, even before the deal was done. The companies aimed for a quick close of the deal by October, after approval from the Federal Trade Commission (FTC), the Federal Communications Commission (FCC), and the European Union. Many agreed the time it took to close the deal hurt the momentum of the merger, since it allowed too much uncertainty to linger for too long.

Not surprisingly, considering the deal's size, government regulators started asking questions, prodded by competitors who were eager to slow down the merger's pace for both tactical and strategic advantage. Would a combined AOL Time Warner simply be too powerful? Was there danger that this new behemoth could squeeze out other companies in the online services, cable, and entertainment sectors? Could any other combination of companies achieve the same scale as AOL Time Warner? And, if not, who could control this giant?

AOL and Time Warner tried to assuage growing fears by asserting that the two companies were in different businesses and didn't confer on each other a stronger advantage in controlling any one arena. Generally, it was "apples and apples" mergers, such as two huge telecom companies combining, that aroused the interest of federal regulators, as these were the kinds of deals that could lead to total domination of a single industry. But the AOL Time Warner deal—involving magazines, television, movies, music, sports teams, and online services—was positioned by Case and Levin as a clearly apples-and-oranges union.

But on May 1, that argument was destroyed by what normally would have been a simple business dispute. As happens often in the fractious cable industry, Time Warner and Disney got into a fight over the price of carrying some Disney-produced cable stations. In the heat of the moment, claiming that its license to carry Disney's ABC station had expired before a new contract on all its cable properties could be settled on, Time Warner suddenly pulled the plug on the broadcast network in seven markets—leaving 3.5 million viewers in places like New York, Los Angeles, and Houston without ABC.

Instead of seeing host Regis Philbin quiz talk show queen Rosie O'Donnell on a celebrity episode of the then popular *Who Wants to Be a Millionaire?*, viewers that night instead saw a screen with the words "Disney has taken ABC away from you." Furious at the blackout, Disney appealed immediately to the FCC for help. Within 39 hours, ABC was back on the air, and shortly thereafter the FCC's Cable Bureau rebuked Time Warner for its action. FCC Chairman William Kennard chastised the company, saying it "committed a clear violation of FCC rules" and that "no company should use consumers as pawns in a private contract dispute." He stopped just short of accusing Time Warner of monopolistic practices.

Not so New York Mayor Rudy Giuliani, who went even further, charging in the *New York Times:* "This is an example of what happens when you let a monopoly get too big." Indeed, Disney lobbyists quickly began throwing around the term *arrogant monopolist* as they used the opportunity to push regulators to take a harder look at the merger. Among Disney's more draconian recommendations was that the government split AOL Time Warner into two pieces, separating conduit from content.

The Disney blackout was a cloddish move on the part of Levin and his often obstreperous cable unit head, Joe Collins, who were either oblivious to or, worse, ignored the damaging perceptions that the move might evoke in the middle of the merger approval process. AOL executives, particularly Steve Case, were livid, especially since they hadn't been fully informed of the blackout plans.

This distracting external fight would soon be eclipsed by the first round of internal strife, which resulted from a series of announcements on May 4 outlining the structure of the company after the deal closed. Designed to give Wall Street and the companies' employees clarity about the setup, it painted a new media order that was an audacious shift for Time Warner. Early encounters between the companies were rocky, with AOL already exhibiting aggressiveness and Time Warner stubbornness. So when the new management was announced, it gave credence to the worry that AOL had taken over.

As expected, Steve Case was named chairman, Jerry Levin chief executive officer, and Mike Kelly chief financial officer. Levin, in a move that angered many, had earlier picked Kelly, who would report directly to the CEO, dumping Time Warner CFO Joe Ripp. Levin also presided over the decision to create an unusual power-sharing arrangement between Bob Pittman and Richard Parsons, who were named the cochief operating officers. Although he later said he hadn't intended for it to seem that way, Levin had created a division of labor between them that seemed to indicate that Pittman was the heir apparent.

Pittman would oversee the supposed future growth engines of the business going forward—the key subscription, distribution, advertising, and commerce businesses: AOL, Time Warner Cable, Time Inc., HBO, TBS, and the WB television network. Left to Parsons was the softer side, including the entertainment contingent: Warner Bros., New Line Cinema and Warner Music, Time Warner Trade Publishing, and the legal and human resources departments. The balance was skewed enough that one AOL executive actually resorted to an appalling racist quip, which later got wide circulation internally, describing the African American Parsons's position as "separate but equal."

Although Pittman hadn't played a key role in creating the merger and actually had mixed feelings about it, he was still the only executive with significant experience in both companies. Glib and charismatic, he was also seen by Wall Street as the consummate schmoozer and salesman. Parsons, considered more of a diplomat and a gentleman, not only lacked Internet DNA, he was just a bit dull compared to his ambitious cohort.

Besides, it wasn't even clear whether Parsons was in Time Warner for the long haul. He'd been at the company for only five years, and before that, he'd worked in banking, law, and government service, including a stint as a senior aide to President Gerald Ford. For Parsons, Time Warner could well be just another notch on an impressively eclectic résumé—rumors abounded that he was likely to get a job in the Republican administration if George W. Bush won the presidential election in the fall. For Pittman, on the other hand, a march to the pinnacle of AOL Time Warner would be the ultimate achievement—the culmination of a career spent climbing the ladders of both old and new media. While Pittman would tell people close to him as the merger progressed that he had no interest in the top spot, it seemed as if it was his job to lose.

As was his manner, Parsons remained quiet about the implications of his new role. But many inside Time Warner were furious, since most of their team had suddenly been blasted out of the corporate center. The new job designations made it clear that AOL was firmly in charge—especially since its executives also took over lobbying (George Vradenburg over Tim Boggs), communications (Kenny Lerer over Ed Adler), and investor relations (Richard Hanlon over Joan Sumner Nicolais). Levin appeared to have given up everything to get the deal done, in what many inside the company regarded as an almost traitorous act. "It was the first real sign that Jerry was protecting his own job and sold everyone out," said one executive who lost a position to an AOL counterpart. "He likes transforming transactions in which he is the only survivor."

Joe Ripp, who had lost his financial job to Mike Kelly, appealed to Levin to not let AOL get all the key corporate jobs. "Jerry thought he would be running it, and I told him, 'No, you won't, they're street fighters and you're not,'" he recalled. "I said, 'You don't have a prayer.

You have given it all up, you're sandwiched in, you will lose control.'" Many others both inside and outside of Time Warner made similar appeals to Levin. They all fell on deaf ears. AOLers, meanwhile, hardly noticed their growing anger.

Neither, it seems, did Levin. In 2003, after his ouster, Levin said he didn't think he'd made bad decisions in the senior job appointments, adding that in most cases the AOL person he picked was more qualified than the equivalent Time Warner employee. In addition, most of the operating divisions still had Time Warner executives at the helm. "By combining it all, I thought over time something new would emerge," he said. "We needed change." But, clearly, Levin hadn't thought through the implications of his choices and was amazingly insensitive to the kind of rage they would cause at Time Warner. Indeed, it was probably this one move that set in motion the intransigence from the Time Warner troops toward their AOL leaders.

One change Levin made sure to complete as the restructuring commenced was replacing Ted Turner as head of his beloved CNN and other properties. Levin had long felt Turner was an erratic manager, and the merger finally gave him the opportunity to do something about it. Publicly, the decision to shift Turner didn't attract a lot of notice, which was surprising given how major, and unexpected, a change it was. But in the May restructuring announcement, Turner received the vague title of "senior advisor" and the shared role, with AOL's Ken Novack, of vice chairman of the combined company. Gone was Turner's direct responsibility for running the Turner cable programming units, which was later given to Jamie Kellner, creator of the WB television network.

Levin dumped Turner unceremoniously in a phone call, dispatching Parsons to Atlanta to explain the news, then later faxing the press release to Turner's ranch in New Mexico as a fait accompli. Levin was annoyed with Turner, to be sure, but this was still shabby treatment for a man who'd long been a media visionary and an important icon at the company. John Malone, who was with Turner at the time in New Mexico, said the feisty entrepreneur was devastated by Levin's actions and considered bringing a lawsuit, since the diminution of his role and responsibilities appeared, to Turner, to be a breach of his contract. Turner didn't end up suing, but his wholesale removal would later prove to have been a dangerous act, one that enabled his uncontrollable anger to spark the rage of many others in the new company. He soon started to grumble privately about the deal to anyone who would listen, including other large investors.

"Levin definitely wanted to empower management at the corporate level to drive growth and cross-division innovation," said AOL lobbyist George Vradenburg. "Turner's control over the Atlanta properties and his unpredictability ran counter to that strategy. Levin knew for sure he did not have control of him, but the problem was that corporate did not have operational control of any division." To begin that shift to the center, Turner was out.

"It was clear to Ted from that moment on that he had been tricked," said Malone. "It was worse because he was probably the most hopeful of all at the start, thinking that AOL would finally be the thing that set Time Warner on fire."

But it was Turner who ended up burned.

A Matter of Timing

Igniting the combined company was precisely what AOL was supposed to do. By adding the magical digital element that had allowed it to grow so quickly over the years, AOL was supposed to be the key driver for the entire company to finally take off. Both Case and Levin envisioned AOL extending and morphing all the Time Warner businesses with its high-growth power. Levin had even dubbed the online unit "the crown jewel."

And yet the merger announcement was exactly when the Web-fueled rocket that had propelled AOL so high began to sputter—although few outside of AOL perceived it at the time. It was an irony that later would not be lost to those both inside and outside the company. Many believe that if Levin had simply delayed the deal talks even for a few months, as the dot-com valuations started to wane, he might have been in a position to completely control AOL rather than the other way around.

In fact, the Web descent began on April 4, 2000, less than three months after the AOL Time Warner announcement. On that day, the NASDAQ dropped 575 points, losing more than 13 percent of its value, before recovering to finish the day down 75 points. Though the NASDAQ did recover that week, the plunge would turn out to be a harbinger of things to come; that day marked the beginnings of the Internet bust that would leave AOL—which had garnered 42 percent of its big ad deals from dot-coms in 1999 and 37 percent in 2000— deeply vulnerable.

But the significance of the NASDAQ's plunge was lost on most people, partly because the first quarter of 2000 marked the high water point of Internet venture funding, rollout of Web IPOs, and—mostly because of the AOL Time Warner deal—the headiest time for the celebration of all digital businesses. For these reasons, AOL's business continued to look strong on the surface throughout the year and into the next—even though this time would later be regarded as the last great gasp of a bubble market.

Just two days before the NASDAQ plunge, for example, AOL became the first Internet company to make the Fortune 500 list, debuting at number 337. And by April 18, AOL reported record earnings for its third quarter. Revenues were up 47 percent to $1.8 billion, advertising and commerce revenues had more than doubled, and the service had added another 1.7 million members. In fact, Pittman was so sure the positive trends would continue that in July he reportedly bragged at a joint meeting of the AOL and Time Warner boards that AOL's annual ad revenue could reach $7 billion by 2005. This was a risky, rash prediction, and it had huge implications for AOL Time Warner, since the high margins from ad sales at AOL dropped straight to the bottom line as pure profit.

Later, a two-part series in the *Washington Post* would raise doubts about the quality of these 2000 results—posing the question of whether AOL artificially inflated its revenues by striking dubious deals and accounting for them improperly in an effort to keep the merger from blowing apart. But already by May, an old accounting problem made the news again when AOL paid a $3.5 million SEC fine relating to its mid-1990s practice of counting marketing expenses as assets. Considered a relative slap on the wrist, the fine was generally ignored by Levin and Wall Street, seen by many as evidence of past problems rather than a troublesome pattern of behavior.

The fact that this accounting incident and fine went largely unnoticed at Time Warner prompted some later to wonder why Levin didn't press for more due diligence in the year it took to close the deal. "That was our real opportunity to look under the hood," said one top Time Warner executive, "and we blew it."

It was not for lack of trying. In the early fall of 2000, as it became abundantly clear that Internet stocks were in a free fall, Parsons, Bressler, and others on the corporate staff went to Levin and advised that he consider not doing the deal. The reason was mostly due to the declining Web valuations and not about AOL in particular, although there was already a growing discomfort at the media company over the change in power and the brash style of the AOLers. Linking with an online company was a good idea, they argued, but did they need such a big deal to do so? There would have been several ways to accomplish reneging on the deal, the group suggested, including not going along with the many government requests for approval of the deal, paying a breakup fee that might apply or even risking an AOL lawsuit by dumping the deal and not forking over a dissolution fee.

But Levin declined because he felt a deal was a deal and that AOL had not changed substantially even if the Internet market had. Other sources said, more important, Levin could not bear not doing a deal he considered revolutionary and critical to Time Warner's future. And there was, it went unsaid, more than a little bit of ego involved. Later, Levin told me that he never thought there were serious questions about the deal at Time Warner before it was consummated, even though others say there was. "I think Levin saw such a cause of action as some kind of impugning of his integrity," said one top executive who tried to warn his boss off the deal.

And while the lack of collar and the possibility of a lawsuit and breakup fees—along with Levin's stubborn insistence that the deal be completed—partly explain the reasons for this lack of action, in truth, no one at Time Warner pressed the issue strongly, because no one knew that things would get so bad so quickly. All through 2000, in fact, there was still a feeling that the strategic unification of AOL and Time Warner was still filled with possibilities and that the deal made sense, especially since AOL's stock—on which the AOL Time Warner share value would be based—had held much stronger than other Web companies.

While Time Warner executives later seemed to suffer collective amnesia on the subject, I recall their company's employees speculating happily about what they'd do after retiring with their stock windfall. Many were worried about the Internet's downturn, to be sure, but they also felt more anticipation of the benefits than they care to admit now. "There was not an us-versus-them mentality at first, even if it did end up that way," said Walter Isaacson, Time Warner's former head of Pathfinder. "A lot of people appreciated the idea of some centralization and finding ways to work together."

In any case, the boom still looked pretty healthy in 2000—so much so that the AOLers were still whooping it up. David Colburn made waves, for example, when he hired the boy band 'N Sync to play at his daughter Rachel's bat mitzvah in June of 2000. Three hundred guests were treated to a set by the teenyboppers in Potomac, Maryland's Beth Shalom Synagogue social hall, which had been decorated with a Venice Beach motif. It was another in a long line of dotcom excess stories that did not abate in 2000. I can tell you that no one in Silicon Valley thought the boom was going to end, even though everyone expected a correction and some had secretly hoped for one to calm things down.

And the contraction began soon enough, as more and more Web companies that had been AOL's cash cows began to openly warn about potential cash squeezes. As early as the end of March of 2000, for example, the most jarring warning came from the medical Web site Drkoop.com, which had promised AOL $89 million as part of a much-touted four-year deal in 1999. In a report to the SEC, the company noted that its "sustained losses and negative cash flow"—once considered a dot-com plus—put its future prospect in jeopardy. By the end of April, it had restructured its AOL deal by handing over 10 percent more of the company as compensation—an act of desperation that was a sign of later troubles.

AOL deal makers punched back with another blockbuster

announcement in May, trumpeting a deal with real estate Web site Homestore.com. AOL valued the arrangement at $200 million, even though it received only $20 million in cash and almost 4 million shares of Homestore stock. It was the terms of this deal, among others struck in this period that would later be investigated, though no one questioned it at the time and it was considered evidence of AOL's strength.

But by late summer of 2000, some within AOL were becoming acutely aware of the potential downside of any drop-off from the 80 percent annual advertising and commerce sales growth the company had enjoyed between 1997 and 1999. "AOL TW Strategy: Future Trends and Recommendations in the Advertising Sector," an internal document prepared in July of 2000, noted ominously that any contraction in the ad market would drain billions of dollars from critical cash flow. "Although AOL has been able to maintain [ad rates] due to its market-leading share of eyeballs," the report said, "some combination of these factors (even under moderate downside scenarios) could result in [cash flow] growth slowing from 25 percent to 23 percent and a cumulative AOL Time Warner [cash flow] shortfall (vs. Street estimates) of nearly $5 [billion] from [2001 to 2005]."

The document offered several suggestions for finding incremental revenue for the online service, including increasing targeted ads, which had long been problematic considering AOL's strict privacy rules; and forging better relationships with traditional ad agencies, which AOL had long attempted to bypass. It even floated the possibility of acquiring online ad serving and selling companies, such as DoubleClick, Avenue A, and 24/7.

This kind of strategic reassessment became even more critical given that more than 100 dot-coms had failed by the fall of 2000. Hundreds of others were tottering, many of which had struck pricey AOL deals in the boom's heyday. AOL deal makers, in fact, keep a running list of all their worrisome dot-com agreements, with scores tracking their viability and risk of nonpayment. Most were deemed troubled, and needed to be renegotiated from long-term contracts to short-term ones. By the end of the summer, renegotiations of these contracts became commonplace, as evidenced by the fact that AOL's

$3 billion ad revenue backlog—that is, the value of the future ad rev-
enue expected from its many multiyear deals—remained flat. That
was a clear sign that the growth years were over, and AOL's executives
were aware of the dangers looming. "We warned of trouble, but no
one wanted to hear it," said one high-ranking AOL executive. "It was
like a distant bell to them, since the noise of the merger was so loud."

Still, AOL's top brass maintained its euphoric outlook into the
fall, even though Time Warner was also beginning to warn about the
weakening ad market for its magazines and TV networks. In an October 2000 conference call in which AOL reported better-than-expected
results, Steve Case inexplicably insisted that AOL was completely
unaffected by the overall ad slump.

"AOL's advertising growth is right on target," Case said, stressing
AOL and Time Warner's potential strengths as a unified company.
"The current advertising environment benefits us, because it will
drive a flight to quality."

Case was bolstered by Pittman, who pooh-poohed any ad woes in
a quote that would later come to haunt him. "For this company, I
don't see it and I don't buy it," he declared definitively, in a memo-
rable but dangerous line suggested by Ken Lerer. And AOL CFO
Mike Kelly also continued to insist that the merged AOL Time Warner would be able to make the ambitious numbers laid out after the
deal's announcement. Still, some analysts were shaken when AOL also
told them it would no longer report its ad backlog number. It had
been the prime indicator of strength, but times were changing fast.

At the time, I got only one real clue that AOL was troubled by
any decline: A comment that I reported in my "Boom Town" column
in October 2000. I had no idea how serious the falloff would become,
but one high-ranking AOL executive was worried enough that he vol-
unteered an enticing reason for wanting the deal to close quickly. "For
all the deal does," he told me in a near whisper, "the thing that makes
me happiest is that it puts a floor under our stock." It was clear AOL
once again hoped to replace one declining business with a new, more
promising one, something it had done so many times before. "They
seemed to expect for the answer to fall out of the sky," said one AOL
observer. "It was management by wishing and hoping."

But from a peak of more than $90 a share in late 1999, AOL's stock had fallen to below $50 by December 2000. That dropped the value of the combined companies from $319 billion in January to under $250 billion by the end of the year. The absence of a collar meant that no matter what happened with the two companies' stocks, the deal would go forward on the terms originally negotiated. But the huge premium AOL had offered Time Warner was withering fast, and AOL executives pressed hard for the deal to settle, willing to be more amenable to government demands than Time Warner.

Luckily for AOL, government opposition waned too. FTC attorneys informed the companies they'd have to make their cable lines available to competing online and entertainment companies, and appointed a "monitor trustee" to oversee the situation for five years. European authorities wanted Time Warner to cancel its planned $20 billion merger with the British music giant EMI. And the FCC would push AOL to open its Instant Messaging service to rivals, eventually requiring the company to do so when it deployed the service on Time Warner's cable network, as a condition of approval.

But ultimately the feds didn't require anything the companies weren't willing to concede. When the FCC voted to approve the merger on January 11, 2001, almost exactly a year after the merger announcement, the last hurdle had been cleared.

It's Show-Me Time!

In the early-morning hours on the day of the close, workers took down the giant "Time Warner" sign above the company's Rockefeller Plaza headquarters in Manhattan, replacing it with the name that would soon become ubiquitous in American media culture: "AOL Time Warner."

Angst ran high throughout the Time Warner side in January, as one AOL executive after another traveled up—often, annoyingly enough, via their own private planes—to the New York headquarters of the most powerful media company in the United States. The Time Warner side's irritation was countered almost equally by the feeling of pleasure that coursed through the AOL staff at the very same prospect. Who wanted to stick around sleepy Dulles, Virginia—where even the Wal-Mart store across the road had closed down—when there was a chance to jet triumphantly into glamorous Manhattan?

Steve Case's unlikely, longtime dream had finally been realized. He and his ragtag team had done the unimaginable, turning an anemic online video games company into a new media empire in just over 15 years. They had led the revolution of getting millions of ordinary Americans online. They held the upper hand in the largest merger in business history. And they had gotten where they were by continually ignoring the swipes of those who were sure they would fail. Who could blame them if they believed they were invincible?

And the AOL executives seemed to believe that above everything else. Almost immediately they set out to show their Time Warner counterparts—who hadn't thought much of them over the years—the right way of doing business, with little respect for the complexity of other industries. Soon, by intoning the Web industry's arrogant mantra of "You just don't get it," AOLers would lose friends and influence no one. They would make huge changes across the Time Warner landscape or die trying. And the latter is precisely what happened.

"AOL thought it was bringing a stodgy company into the Internet age, but everything we had was running solidly in place. Warner Bros. was doing a great job, so was HBO. Why tamper with that? I don't think they understood how delicate it all was," said one top Time Warner executive. "The concern we had was that this was a 15-year-old company or so, which is the life of a fruit fly. It was a single-product company. And it had been sitting on the top of a tidal wave. The range of its experience was limited."

Today, the AOL team's belief that it could easily take over a company about whose businesses it knew so little seems massively naïve and deeply egomaniacal. One ace-in-the-hole they thought they had was Jerry Levin and his evangelical vision for the company. But that soon proved unreliable. "Since Jerry was so committed to it, we thought the various teams would line up and make it happen," said Mike Kelly. "We underestimated how people at Time Warner felt about the merger."

The AOLers also underestimated how the Time Warner people felt about them—and most especially about their battlefield leader, Bob Pittman, who many at Time Warner felt did not have the capacity for running a creative, multi-industry business. The issue of Pittman's role would soon take center stage, especially since the responsibilities he got in May of 2000 made him the point man for the merger's execution.

Or, as *Business Week* put it, it was "Show Time!" In a cover story that immediately spread ripples of discontent throughout the Time Warner side, *Business Week* lionized Pittman as the man to watch at AOL Time Warner. "By turns charming and steely, he convinces proud and powerful business-unit executives that they'll win more battles by playing ball than by balking," the magazine gushed. "It doesn't hurt that he gives them much of the credit." Even though Pittman was sharing COO duties with Dick Parsons, the story didn't even mention Parsons until the 12th paragraph.

What *Business Week* failed to notice was that the return of Bob Pittman to Time Warner was a less welcome homecoming than it appeared to be, especially since he had remained a controversial figure there long after he left. There were many reasons for this, including still-simmering corporate jealousies over Pittman's close relationship with the late Warner icon Steve Ross; envy over his huge financial payoff in the Six Flags sales; and his reputation for self-aggrandizement, relentless ambition, and a whiff of hucksterism. Now that he was returning to the merged company even more fabulously wealthy and as the big boss, Pittman became a natural lightning rod.

It's hard to say if Pittman relished his bit of payback, because he wasn't a prime mover of the merger, and he hadn't actually believed Case could make it happen. "Wake me when it's over" was Pittman's frequent response to updates on the progress of the on-again-off-again talks in 1999. And of all the AOL executives I talked with after the merger was announced, Pittman seemed the least excited. In one interview, he rolled his eyes at the thought of his "retaking Manhattan," as news accounts had surmised. While Pittman had never liked being stuck in the sticks of northern Virginia, he was also quite wary of reentering the snake pit that he clearly regarded Time Warner as being. My impression was that he was always worried that Manhattan might actually retake Bob Pittman.

Perhaps that's why he hit the company at such a full bore, so much so that almost everyone I interviewed at Time Warner had the same description of his style: An efficiency machine without an ability to make small talk or engage in the kind of "foreplay" that his job clearly required. Many described him as slow to compliment, fast to criticize, and eager to be seen as a tough operator. Of course, it was a lot easier to be a head banger when you were preaching to the converted, as he had been doing at AOL. At Time Warner, there were a lot of disbelievers in the merger, although some welcomed the prospect of change shaking up the company.

But there were not enough believers at Time Warner and that was problematic, since any chance of success for the combined company's big goals depended on having someone like Pittman in control. His hard-charging style was anathema to those accustomed to Levin's neglect. While Levin would periodically act out and fire a division head, his reign was marked by minimal interference and little of the kind of active management that would be Pittman's hallmark. Pittman would edit ad storyboards at the cable unit, comment on HBO programming, and even give advice on talent to the music unit.

Pittman also had a nagging reputation within Time Warner for short-term thinking. "I think the biggest problem was his time horizon," said a high-ranking Time Warner executive who had worked with Pittman. "Long-term planning to him was thinking about the first month of the quarter, not the next year. This year, next year did not interest him." Pittman supporters deny that characterization, but it was a trait he was known for at Time Warner when he returned as the prodigal son.

But encouraged by both Case and Levin, Pittman recast himself as an agent of change, charged with making the ambitious numbers work by reducing costs and launching synergistic initiatives. His involvement was soon considered mindless meddling by most at Time Warner, a feeling that was exacerbated when Pittman sent his tight-knit team around the company in an effort to "cross-pollinate" the cultures.

While you might think employees at a media company in New

York would have a tolerance for colorful characters, at Time Warner they did not. Among those belonging to the AOL executive shock troops were the pugnacious deal maker David Colburn and slick ad salesman Myer Berlow, both of whom practiced a take-no-prisoners style and left disgruntlement in their wake. The irritation they caused would be rubbed even more raw by CFO Mike Kelly, whose bullying and haranguing of division heads over making the numbers eventually caused them to revolt.

By contrast, most AOLers thought Pittman was never tough enough, as he seemed to prefer trying to encourage changes without forcing them. Many urged him at the start to be more ruthless at Time Warner. "If you choose the battlefield of 'Do they like you?' you will not win," Berlow told me he advised Pittman. "You have to be willing to say: 'Do it my way.'"

To those at Time Warner, this seemed to be AOL's style from the beginning, as the group from Dulles quickly began to make its presence known throughout the company via a series of small moves that would produce large reverberations. With a goal of bringing power to the center, as had been the rule at AOL under Pittman's strong hand, the AOL executives thought they would be the ones to finally deliver excitement and growth to what they often scoffingly called an iron-age company.

Can't We All Just Get Along?

But first, they had to make one company from many—or so the AOL team thought.

After the hoopla of any merger announcement, it often takes a decade for a new company culture to emerge, and at least that long to get real traction with new business practices. That had certainly been the case with the Time and Warner merger in the early 1990s, and it held true after the Turner acquisition as well. And even after all that time, most still considered Time Warner more of a holding company of different businesses than anything unified, right up until the AOL merger.

It was ironic that they expected unity from a company that had always been disjointed, and that they expected it after the biggest merger in history—one with a pronounced culture clash of old and new worlds. Nonetheless, Pittman, Levin, and Case, as well as members of the board, all seemed to be in an inexplicable rush to prove the worth of the new and unknown combination. It was this need for speed—a signature characteristic of the Internet era—and the desire to make this merger appear as successful as possible as soon as possible that led to many of the thoughtless errors that later took place. This need was obviously born out of a deep insecurity that had been part of AOL culture since its beginnings. Always counted out as losers, the executives of AOL now had their ultimate comeuppance to administer to those who had doubted them.

Full of hubris over their success, the AOL team—with Levin's enthusiastic encouragement—began trying to create one culture from many. Intensely worried about the potential of Time Warner's decentralized nature to wreck the merger, the corporate team tried to quickly push through a series of initiatives designed to bring everyone together. If they couldn't, they feared their chance of making the kind of money they'd promised Wall Street was doomed. In fact, a January memo from the investor relations department to all the top executives warned that the new company was under intense scrutiny. "AOL Time Warner can expect to be something more than the most watched company in 2001," it read. "But quite possibly the one from which most is expected."

The first true effort to unite the cultures was aimed at the pocketbooks of the company employees, in hope that financial benefits would inspire them to join together. Steve Case and others believed that the best way to share the wealth and inject a little bit of Levin's longed-for Internet DNA into the Time Warner culture was via stock.

So Case and other top executives at AOL Time Warner advocated a new stock option plan to replace Time Warner's traditional cash bonus plan, which had been based on both divisional and company performance. This was a major move, because over the years the profit-sharing program could yield huge returns to top executives who beat their financial plans. Even at the lower levels, the cash bonus could account for a huge part of an employee's salary, and when it came to top executives, it meant millions of dollars. Best of all, it was cash money in someone's pocket, with none of the potential risk of stock options.

But at AOL, stock, which had made millionaires of even lowly assistants, was considered the only true way to reward talent. So the compensation at AOL Time Warner would now be aligned with the company in a much more direct way, linking financial benefits directly to stock performance. This would also presumably save the company cash, as options were not counted as an employee cost in financial reporting. The move was a hallmark of AOL's entrepreneurial culture, which believed these "founder's options" were a necessary part of bringing the company together as one in an immediate and obvious way.

"If you align with shareholders, that's the right thing if the idea is to try to get the company to think like a company as a whole," said former CFO Mike Kelly. "If you are pushing the organization, cash can work, but it is hard to know if people are submitting divisional plans to be realistic or to get more cash at the end of the year."

At the start, at least, many at Time Warner were nervous about the level of risk—but they were also eager to benefit from a stronger stock. Helped by encouraging results for the combined company in its first quarter, AOL Time Warner shares still remained higher than the value of their previously owned Time Warner shares in the first months of 2001. "I thought I was headed for an early retirement, since it looked like the shares were going to be okay at first," said one top employee. "I won't deny the greed." Indeed, since many of the higher-ranking executives at Time Warner got gigantic grants of stock, greed was an important motivator.

But the mood quickly changed as the stock started to sink in the late spring, eventually playing such a factor that I taped a note to the wall above my desk saying "THE STOCK WENT DOWN" as a reminder of the most critical factor in why the rest of AOL's efforts later began failing so miserably. AOL's leaders had badly misjudged Time Warner's appetite for risk.

If the combined company's stock had gone up, there would never have been a peep of protest about the options plan or anything else, since the employees would have reaped huge gains. But in taking away the Time Warner side's highly lucrative profit-sharing plans, then saddling employees with paper options whose value became worthless, top executives sowed the seeds of serious discontent. This was exacerbated by the fact that company pension plans also held giant blocks of company stock, which employees seldom sold as it piled up over the years. Now, all of corporate morale was tied much too closely with AOL Time Warner's stock price.

And there were other unsuccessful attempts to promote together-ness and save money. One of the executive board's directives decreed that everyone in the newly combined company should use AOL's email system. In a perfect world, this made sense, since each Time Warner division and even its subdivisions had its own costly information tech-nology structure. But AOL's simplistic email was designed for unde-manding chatters and consumers. While it was fine for AOL's internal needs, a larger communications entity like Time Warner had more complex uses for email. Irritated Time Warnerites soon found their attachments mangled, photos lost, and Excel spreadsheets jumbled.

It's difficult to fault anyone for being upset at this change; not only was AOL's email offering clearly inferior, but urging employees to migrate all their information, addresses, and saved email files to a new system was a huge irritation. Despite the more serious issues between AOL and Time Warner, I think I heard more about the email debacle than about any other issue—suggesting that small details can truly matter a great deal. I first saw evidence of this at an HBO event in Aspen in March of 2001, where employees were in near revolt over the glitchy AOL mail they were forced to use. "Fuck AOL, fuck AOL, fuck AOL," one employee muttered under her breath as she tried and failed to send a single email there.

That soon became the mantra for many at Time Warner, as AOL sprung its final tool intended to promote harmony. With a need to get synergistic initiatives going as quickly as possible and enhance cooperation among many divisions, the newly invigorated corporate center began to dictate a series of required face-to-face meetings for managers to strengthen ties.

Soon enough, divisional heads and their subordinates were summoned to weekly and monthly intracompany gatherings. Some were led by Levin, some by Pittman and Parsons, and others by Pittman lieutenants Mayo Stuntz and Marshall Cohen. These "councils" of division CEOs, marketing honchos, and ad poobahs were intended to foster the sharing of ideas and better ways of doing business together. They were also intended to nudge the company into functioning as a unified whole, with executives from the various divisions working together rather than remaining isolated in their own fiefdoms.

On its face, this idea isn't a bad one—except that most of the meetings soon degenerated into useless free-for-alls where little was accomplished and acrimony only increased. Problems that started as questions of style evolved into battles over basic issues of how to do business. Against the backdrop of a rapidly weakening economy, these tussles became increasingly ugly. As one AOL manager who watched from the sidelines while bigger bosses bickered told me, "It degenerated into a series of street fights."

One Nation Under Siege

Street fighting was a particularly apt metaphor for AOL Time Warner internal relationships in the first months of 2001. Like warring gangs, each side had its share of righteous, arrogant, and aggressive attitudes. Of course, the bigger problem was that no one from either company valued the history of the other's institution. They felt they had nothing to learn from each other.

Even a cursory discussion with either side revealed irreconcilable sets of values and goals. To Time Warner, AOL was rude and rambunctious, facile and ignorant about the complexities of the various businesses, and primarily interested in milking the divisions for the greater glory of its online service. To AOL, Time Warner was political for the sake of politics, slow moving and obdurate, and unwilling to make the changes needed to face down the challenges of the future. Both were right, of course, but neither was able to help the other overcome its joint set of problems.

The fighting began over simple issues of civility. As I started reporting this book, I soon found myself cringing at the multitude of stories about the antics of AOLers, especially those of David Colburn and Myer Berlow, who appeared to relish their enfant terrible reputations at Time Warner. And they were in fact like terrible infants, as they inflicted almost immediate damage on the merger by behaving more like tantrum-prone toddlers than new leaders of one of the world's most respected companies. The stories about the pair, who actually did not work as closely together as some perceived, soon became legend. Arriving late to meeting after meeting, trading high fives, spitting food, and interrupting others, the legend of their behavior, and the behavior itself, horrified many in the more formal corridors of Time Warner.

Berlow, for example, quickly became famous for his expensive but rumpled suits, his chain-smoking lunch table at the Four Seasons, and his tendency to mouth off to Time Warner executives about how their business was doomed. Colburn, meanwhile, was constantly cracking wise, asking for free tickets to movie premieres, concerts, and awards shows, and strong-arming colleagues into deals they didn't agree with. While this kind of silliness was common in the looser dot-com era when AOL's power had given them a limitless ability to misbehave, in New York their actions were soon magnified in the echo chamber that is a major media company.

One encounter would create widespread reverberations in the media culture, making it seem as if hundreds had experienced each slight and rudeness. Like that of the putz T-shirt, stories about Berlow and Colburn soon became exaggerated and the pair became the equivalent of corporate urban legends. At AOL, this was often annoying to many, but seldom was it threatening. To the vast majority of employees at Time Warner, where AOLers now commanded immense influence, they were considered out of control and possibly dangerous. "Time Warner was a hierarchical company and not used to senior executives mouthing off without meaning it or to provoke debate," said one former Time Warner executive who had previously worked with AOL. "At AOL, that was normal and expected."

When I later asked Berlow about his behavior, he discounted the many stories about him that cropped up, saying that he, Colburn, and others at AOL were easy marks for Time Warner backstabbers who resisted change in all its forms and were motivated by jealousy. "It was a culture so humiliated that we bought them that they couldn't think of anything else," he told me. "Arrogance makes a good story, but they didn't want synergies, because synergies meant you don't have principalities." To him, it was Time Warner's "ack-acking" that ultimately took this merger down.

But Berlow, whom I'd known for many years and whose company I had always enjoyed, was well aware of his colorful reputation. Frankly, he relished it at times and I doubt he wanted to behave any differently at the new company, especially since he was proud of his accomplishments as one of the pioneers of the online ad business. His efforts to build this new business took a certain amount of chutzpah that he never lost. Over many years, I'd seen him and other AOL executives make public speeches that sometimes made me want to hide under the table, almost always due to the fuck-you tone and message. "People who have no charisma hate those who do," he often joked. "We believe in what we do and that bothers those that don't." I didn't know about that, but it was clear his peculiar brand of charm was lost on those at Time Warner.

When AOL was just another Internet company, it was easy to write off this kind of superciliousness as the kind of bluster needed in a medium that was struggling into creation. But after the AOL Time Warner merger was announced, the perception and audience changed dramatically—while many AOLers did not. I teased Berlow to behave when I saw him right after the merger was announced. "That word is not in my vocabulary," quipped Berlow, who bragged to me that he'd sold billions of dollars of ads without having to behave. He then compared his job to a wartime scenario, using a battle metaphor. "I was told to take the hill, so I took the hill," he said. "And I will keep taking the hill."

Another top AOL executive was more regretful of the behavior. "Time Warner people looked at us like Internet snot-noses, and we did not disappoint them," said the executive. "We should have chilled out, because the behavior did not work anymore, if it ever did."

Time Warner was not blameless in this, of course, packed full as it was of people who resisted the ideas AOL brought simply because of the manner in which they were delivered. While one might sympathize with them over the rudeness, Time Warner also had its share of well-known divas and other assorted characters. This was, after all, a company that included fussy recording-industry mandarins, egomaniacal Hollywood movie moguls, grumpy journalists, and, well, Ted Turner.

While AOL executives could certainly be obnoxious, the complaints about Colburn and Berlow also provided a handy excuse for noncooperation from Time Warner. This resistance, of course, had deep historical roots, given a longtime culture that had not rewarded unification over independence. Its culture, in a way, prohibited companywide collaboration, which was Time Warner's own version of arrogance.

"It was all so political and it's kind of hard to operate when the enemy is within," said a top AOL executive. "If people think the enemy is within, there is no AOL Time Warner."

With little corporate meddling for much of its history, Time Warner's divisional executives had developed a high regard for their talents and a fierce interest in protecting their power. It seems obvious enough that experienced executives like Time Inc.'s Don Logan were never going to take true direction from someone like Berlow or Colburn, or even Pittman. They had worked long and hard enough that they would be less than welcoming to what they perceived as a foreign intruder. "This was not a company that wanted suggestions from neophytes," said one Time Warner executive, "especially neophytes with planes."

Time Warner executives, almost to a person, denied being uncooperative to me, noting that AOL simply did not understand how cooperation worked at the company. "One could have the impression that we have some reticence or resistance, but that is not true. We cooperate where we must," said one top executive at Time Warner. "We all wanted to figure out how links would work, but what they proposed was immediately destructive. They called it parochial, but I call it doing our jobs."

And, among Time Warner executives, there was also a reluctance to take more risks on the digital technologies that AOL's team was advocating so intently. Time Warner had already lost big in this arena and was not the most open to the virtues of the Internet's ability to transform their businesses. In fact, because of past experiences, it had seen only downside to any such forays. Given that those who had succeeded in the Web space had become phenomenally wealthy, Time Warner's extreme lack of success must have made their executives chafe at any further lecturing by the mouthy AOLers. And as their own stock drifted slowly down from the latest brush with interactive businesses, the situation became untenable. That said, if the stock had remained high, I have no doubt that the arrogance of AOLers might have even come off as downright charming.

But the stock didn't stay high. And the culture wars only got nastier and nastier.

Have It Our Way

Both the Time Warner ack-acking and the AOL smacking got even worse when AOLers started to seriously delve into each individual Time Warner business and demand changes. Conforming to the dysfunctional pattern, some of their points were, in the long-term scheme of things, correct. But the manner of the message rendered them useless. While company executives were told they still could run their businesses as they saw fit, a pervasive feeling of being forced to do so took over quickly.

"These are all different cultures, businesses, and structures, and you really have to have an ability to operate differently. You try to make rational connections, but when it is immediately brought to a coercion level and not based on market conditions, it will not work," said a Time Warner executive who was initially open to more synergies. "How you do it—because it is to the advantage of the company to cooperate—is that you respect the systems and debate the issues, you respect the rule of information and decision-making." AOLers, many asserted, did none of this.

AOL was particularly interested in Warner Music, for example, since it wanted to dominate the business of digital delivery of music. Now, with Warner assets, this was an arena where the combined company could show the ability to create important synergies. If AOL and Warner Music could cut through some of the thorny issues that had long separated the technology and entertainment sectors, and make some real progress on legal ways to distribute music online, it would be seen as an important win. The problem was, like most music companies, Warner Music felt under siege because its core business was under relentless attack from the growing phenomenon of free music swapping online.

Warner Music's apprehension at working with AOL worsened even before the merger closed, with the mid-2000 release of file-swapping software by an AOL subsidary called Nullsoft. Nullsoft founder Justin Frankel had developed Gnutella, which helped users search and manage downloadable music files without distinguishing whether they were legal or illegal, much like Napster did. AOL pulled the plug on Gnutella by August, but it certainly sympathized with its function. When I visited AOL and asked a top executive about the yanking of Gnutella and the public declarations against services like Napster, he opened a drawer and tossed me a Napster T-shirt with its winking logo as a gift. "Napster is good," he whispered. "No matter what we say."

Indeed, AOL's Internet roots were much stronger than its copyright concerns—and its hurry-up attitude clashed immediately with the more wary style of Warner Music. Almost immediately, AOL wanted to use Warner artists on its service, waving aside complex copyright agreements and artist relationships as easy barriers to overcome. Lower-level AOL employees even began relentlessly emailing counterparts at Warner Music about how they were fighting a losing battle with online music, which bothered its executives. At AOL, though, it was perfectly normal for junior employees to challenge the higher-ups.

"It felt like a piranha attack," said one Warner music executive. "And it was all designed to help AOL and not us." Like many at Warner Music, this executive thought it wiser to treat AOL's service like any other Internet company, and to partner with the best one, rather than giving them special access, despite top company directives to do so. And once again, Warner Music didn't complain when AOL helped launch new bands, including one called Eden's Crush, by flacking them hard on the online service's welcome screen.

AOL executives were perplexed by Warner Music's obstinacy and inability to blow apart the business model for the music industry, which had long enjoyed the ability to charge ever-higher prices. But now, as attitudes changed among key customers—young people—as they began to download music for free over services like Napster, AOL executives thought Time Warner should be bold and push for different methods of selling music.

"Our reach often exceeded our grasp, but at least we had vision," said one AOL executive charged with making a music deal work. "There are a million excuses to hide behind if you don't want to do anything, but neither Warner Music or anyone else there ever accepted that if we could crack the code, there might be whole new ways to market."

Those at Warner Music scoffed at this idea, noting it was working hard with companies like Apple Computer and others to solve its critical digital challenge. While AOL talked a good game, the music group employees found the decision-making process in its online music group slow, its management constantly in flux, and its focus more on promotion than commerce. Worst of all, they felt AOL's technology was clunky and not able to take advantage of fast-moving Web trends. What AOL kept offering, they felt, was no good.

"They could have been leading the way, like Apple did later," said one Warner music executive, referring to the computer company's much praised music-buying service launch in the spring of 2003. "Instead, they offered us nothing that would really help our business."

New ways to create, distribute, and market movies was another major focus of Pittman and his crew, one Levin also strongly supported. And, once again, while there was some truth to the AOL executives' contentions, their know-it-all delivery was deeply flawed. Things immediately got off on the wrong foot after both Steve Case and AOL online service head Barry Schuler lectured Warner Bros.

studio executives, including its chairman and CEO Barry Meyer and its president Alan Horn, on how the coming tide of digital filmmaking would sink them if they didn't change the way they made and sold movies.

Fights erupted over a range of issues, including AOL's desire to take over the lucrative *Harry Potter* Web site for the Warner Studios movie. Warner's executives argued, much as the music division had done, that it had complex and binding agreements with its artists—in this case, restrictions imposed by *Potter* author J. K. Rowling—that limited its ability to turn over material to another division. With echoes of the Road Runner debate, the studio won that skirmish after Pittman sided with Warner and garnered lucrative endorsements for the site. This infuriated AOL executives, who felt its online division marketing, which had flacked the movie relentlessly on the AOL site, had been a big help in making the *Potter* movie a hit when it debuted in the fall. For this, they felt they got nothing.

And the two divisions would also clash over Warner Bros. marketing in newspapers, a longtime practice that AOL considered expensive and ineffective. Berlow attended a controversial presentation to the Warner executives on the issue, which included an analysis showing how other competing studios did more business and experimentation online with AOL than Warner did. And he and others were aiming at the studio's reliance on newspapers, which many felt were often vanity buys undertaken mostly to satisfy spoiled stars and directors rather than as effective marketing to get more people to actually go to see movies. Why not, they asked, try to change marketing practices on one movie in one market to see what would happen?

To the executives at Warner Studios, the presentation felt like a corporate dictate to move those ad dollars to AOL instead. "It was draconian—you do things our way or else," said one studio executive. "The threat was always hovering that 'Dulles' would be unhappy if we did not cooperate." And yet, despite all the Sturm and Drang, Pittman never pushed hard enough to make anyone do anything and no such changes were actually made. "I bit my hand keeping quiet," said Berlow. "They claimed we were forcing them and then nothing was ever forced."

Other AOLers pointed to this as another example of a company-wide lack of vision. "Sure, we were asking for stuff from Time Warner, and maybe we were unreasonable," said another AOL executive, who agreed with Berlow. "But we were trying to look to the future, which they didn't seem to do too much of."

Time Warner saw it differently. "If a bunch of people with no attention span wants to paint it as resistance, that's not what it was," said one Time Warner executive.

The battles worsened, especially at the division that put up the biggest fight against AOL's attempted incursions—Time Inc. As the stalwart of the entire Time Warner empire and the most powerful magazine publisher in the United States, the division and its executives were not open to advice about advertising from a northern Virginia start-up. Under the steady leadership of Don Logan, who had reinvigorated the division after years of drift, Time Inc.'s executives and editors did not welcome AOL's many directives and requests.

While they were initially pleased when Time Inc. magazines got big circulation boosts from experiments in selling magazine subscriptions online, the executives basically closed down their division to AOL on other issues. So when AOL, for example, pushed immediately to use exclusive photos from *Time* and other magazines, executives there refused, pointing out that *Time* didn't own the images most of the time, so would not turn them over. When AOL made similar requests for special content, Time Inc. executives became exasperated that AOL didn't understand that it wasn't there just to help make the online site better.

But the real clashes centered on attempts by AOL to broker big ad deals through the Ad Council. Charged by Pittman with coordinating large cross-company deals, and headed by his close adviser Mayo Stuntz, the effort was designed to press a range of marketing initiatives across many of AOL Time Warner's mediums to pull in big advertisers. In addition, Myer Berlow was made president of a closely linked unit called Global Marketing Solutions, which was supposed to streamline the process for advertisers to get these kinds of deals done.

The idea that AOL Time Warner could provide one-stop shopping with ease garnered resistance from the start, in part because a prior Time Inc. effort at ad cooperation among its magazines ad sales staff, called MaxPlan, had been a disaster. In the experience of Time Inc. ad sales executives, joint ads deals only led to discounting that lost money and forced clients to advertise where they might not want to. Most executives believed that they could get better deals selling ads separately. And figuring out how to share the wealth in a group deal was always an issue no one wanted to contend with.

"I didn't find the Time Inc. folks resistant to big-ticket advertising packages, but they were wary because all their experience told them that big-ticket packages almost always resulted in demands for huge discounts," said Time Inc. Editor-in-Chief Norm Pearlstine. "In addition, they worried that some of the selling strategies associated with these packages made them counterproductive."

Still, cross-company ad sales were one of the main promises of the merger, and major deals were needed to prove its worth. Initially, the group did a number of them, such as a $6 million deal with Wrangler jeans to be on AOL, TNT, and also in *Sports Illustrated.* Others with Toyota, for example, were considered promising. But some deals that were held up as major coups were actually with vendors of AOL Time Warner—such as those with Nortel Networks and WorldCom, neither of which could be described as bold new initiatives.

Given the sagging economy, the reluctance of the units, and the fuzzy premise, synergy was struggling soon enough. In one small deal Business Affairs cooked up to dump longtime Time Warner corporate air carrier American Airlines in favor of United Airlines, AOL's carrier of choice, things came to a head. The AOL side favored United since it included a one-year commitment to spend $5 million on company properties, including AOL, although it provided less of a corporate discount for air tickets. Time Warner, whose executives had plenty of frequent flyer miles on American, thought the deal would actually lose money since United's flights were costlier, and that American Airlines—which had spent $10 million at Time Warner—would do so again, although without a definite commitment.

"It was hardly worth changing ad partners," said Jack Haire, Time Inc.'s ad sales head. "It was done to generate buzz for AOL." Haire, whose calm, suburban preppy demeanor was worlds away from that of the peripatetic Berlow, became apoplectic over the deal, since the only benefit to him seemed to be the press release that could be written touting another combined ad deal. "You just want to make an announcement to pump up the stock," Haire said he told Berlow with barely concealed contempt about a number of such deals. "You just want to make these deals for Wall Street and not the business."

But Berlow didn't consider that a problem, referring to the need to find synergies in the merger. "What else is there?" Berlow said he told Haire, since he felt every manifestation of unity trumped all. "Yes, we want to make good on the promise to shareholders, since my constituency is shareholders." Could the philosophies and style of AOL and Time Warner be any more different?

Later, the group would clash in a similar manner over a deal Berlow brought from Burger King that was valued at $80 million, which needed to deliver certain bells and whistles from all the divisions. Most were doable, but Berlow fought with other executives on the Ad Council to get it passed. Some units wanted to do their own deals, which mucked up the unified approach.

Eventually, Berlow cobbled together a deal, but he wanted to announce it before a Wendy's fast-food-chain deal that the group had also been working on that was already completed. This enraged the Time Warner executives, who felt it betrayed an ad relationship, because Wendy's had been the first at the table and deserved the lift an announcement might provide. "To AOL, it was 'Who cares, because that was yesterday's deal,'" said one Time Warner executive close to the negotiations. "They were not interested in long-term relationships and we would have passed on Burger King if it meant screwing another advertiser."

And that was precisely the problem: AOL had enjoyed a long and lucky period when it could and would demand anything from advertisers who were desperate to get on its online network. At Time Warner, as at most traditional media companies, there were always competitors vying to take away advertisers. When Berlow and others at AOL continued to act as if they were the only game in town when representing divisions other than AOL, it caused alarm. There was no telling what they might do or say, or how they might damage longtime business relationships. To those at Time Inc., years of success had made the AOLers sloppy and arrogant, striking deals that were more like promotions than advertising.

"I give them an 'A' for ambition and a failing grade for sophistication," said Haire to me in 2003. "They were successful in the new economy, but in ours they had a clumsy and damaging way of doing business." Haire thought AOL had a dangerous tendency to "disregard a long-term ad relationship by throwing a client under the bus for a short-term gain."

Berlow considered the Time Warner attitude pathetic. "They didn't want to understand the value of a transformational deal, and they didn't want to hear it, because they stood for status quo and all they hope for is the status quo," he said to me in 2002, as we sat in his home on the Upper East Side of Manhattan. At that point, he'd resigned from the Global Marketing Solutions job, but was still employed under contract at AOL Time Warner, although he spent a lot of his time making wooden bowls and furniture at his own workshop. "They saw the whole acquisition as a bank robbery, so we couldn't blind them with vision."

Breaking (Into) the Bank

One thing Berlow had right was the bank robbery metaphor. As the stock started to peter out over the course of 2001, the Time Warner corps soon became paralyzed with anger and angst, which made working with AOL pretty much impossible. "Managers knew they had been undersold, so every time someone from AOL wanted anything, you'd rather hate them instead of help them," said one top executive. "We could only put up with the arrogance if the share price were there."

I heard this sentiment time and again from Time Warner employees, who felt that their company had been taken along with their money—all in the service of AOL, rather than of the combined company. As the year progressed, and AOL's business—along with the entire Internet's—began to look less strong, Time Warner executives began to suspect that AOL might have been a one-trick pony and that their divisions would be sacrificed to help bolster it.

Don Logan of Time Inc., ever the math nerd, had actually done a Venn Diagram—overlapping circles used to show relationships between things—after Pittman had touted the fact that the companies had only had 10 advertising clients in common. While everyone thought that was wonderful, sources close to Logan said he was appalled, since Time Warner knew all the stable advertisers and it meant that AOL did not have an ad business that was sustainable. To him, AOL only seemed to have had worrisome dot-com clients and only those traditional advertisers experimenting in the online space. With such an unstable base, Logan thought whole market was still in its infancy and that the money would dry up quickly.

Some AOLers were acutely aware of this, too. "Past performance is no indication of future performance," one executive at AOL warned me when I asked if the company was about to sail off the cliff as Yahoo had done in 2001. The trouble at Yahoo got so bad that its longtime CEO Tim Koogle had stepped aside under pressure at the start of the year and had been replaced by, of all unlikely people, the former head of Warner Bros., Terry Semel. Yahoo had already been drastically cutting its yearly revenue projections for 2001 when Semel arrived, after dot-com ad deals had dried up. And Semel, who had dabbled in some dot-com investments after he left Warner, spent much of the year drastically overhauling Yahoo's entire strategy.

Though Yahoo was AOL's biggest rival and presumably the new canary in the Internet coalmine, Pittman and others continued to promise that all at AOL was fine. They insisted that profits were sustainable and AOL would make the transition smoothly because of its regular subscriber fees (which Yahoo lacked) and the new revenue streams coming in from Time Warner. It was a typical AOL mentality, because AOL was a company with a history of finding new businesses to save it just before the old ones crumbled. But this deliberate ignorance of key trends was reckless.

With the cross-company deals coming through more slowly than expected—due in equal parts to the weakening economy and intra-company noncooperation—new incremental revenues weren't being funneled into the online company fast enough. With dot-com ads in free fall, this was a dangerous situation.

Similarly, in June 2001, when AOL launched an internal investigation into one of its own ad deals, no one could have guessed that it was a harbinger of far bigger problems to come. The investigation, which examined some unorthodox transactions related to its March 2000 deal with Las Vegas–based electronic marketplace site Purchase-Pro.com, seemed serious. AOL had even put senior vice president Eric Keller on leave while it investigated the situation.

The real fallout from this and other deals wouldn't become clear for another year, but only six months into the merger Time Warner executives became increasingly worried that AOL was in it only for the quick cash. "Their view was you don't say no to cash versus what was right for business," said one executive at Time Warner. "And our businesses were doing fine until cash became the issue."

Indeed, it became the only issue, as Mike Kelly—reporting directly to Levin—applied even more painful pressure on the cost side than Berlow and others had been putting on the revenue side. Kelly's massive cost-cutting directives began hitting the divisions, which now had to initiate layoffs of several thousand employees almost immediately, offer buyout packages, and even cut budgets for pizza and other foods served during late-night magazine deadline pushes. Accompanied as they were by the arrogance and "you just don't get it" attitude of the AOL conquering army, such cuts and layoffs, which are a normal and expected part of any merger, completely wore down the patience left among Time Warner employees. The hostility of top executives soon trickled down to the rank-and-file, who got a bitter taste of Kelly's we-make-the-numbers-or-else haranguing.

The cuts were particularly painful at CNN, which bore the first wounds of the deal in early 2001. The Atlanta-based division was a tightly knit group and the cuts, which came suddenly and without warning or real explanation from the top, devastated morale. People with decades of service were dumped unceremoniously and given severance payments that required them to sign nondisparagement agreements.

Like the attempts to goose revenue, these draconian cost-cutting measures were all part of Levin and Pittman's quest—with Parsons silently acquiescing simply by not raising his voice loudly in disagreement—to make their aggressive numbers for revenue and cash-flow growth. To deliver these lofty figures, Levin let Kelly loose on the division heads in a manner they'd never seen before. Nobody could grind them like Kelly, and no one did—making him even more reviled across the company than Berlow, since Kelly was now asking divisions to start sacrificing things that they had spent years building.

With the rallying cry of $11 billion EBITDA—earnings before interest, taxation, depreciation, and amortization—Kelly was soon clashing with division heads over making their numbers. The difficult-to-reach numbers were hard enough to swallow, but Kelly's pushy style made it worse. I think there is no one—apart from Kelly—who didn't complain about his rough persona, which was variously characterized as bullying, rude, obnoxious, and highly personal. He would often call people morons in meetings—which he told me he considered a joke—and deliver withering assessments of their performances in front of others.

Some from AOL understood Kelly's method, and didn't mind it. "Kelly was hard on us at AOL, but we needed that," said Richard Hanlon, investor relations head. "But it was less welcome at Time Warner and they took umbrage, which he didn't think they would."

Kelly agreed with that, noting that he was more worried about missing the numbers than about alienating people at Time Warner. "If we held back, I wasn't sure what it would mean, because if we weren't pushing, we were going to fail," he told me in 2003. "I thought I was just hearing pain from people who hadn't had to perform before."

Still, as the economy continued to weaken, some division heads were upset at being asked to push numbers they didn't believe were possible to make. "There was a huge amount of rebelling," said Walter Isaacson, who was moved to become head of CNN. Some complained that Kelly had bulldozed them into agreeing to plans they couldn't achieve, and that no one in the corporate suite was listening to them. There, the top executives waited and hoped for the ad market to rebound.

Ted Turner, worried about the impact of cuts at CNN and hearing of the worsening ad market from his close associates at Turner Broadcasting, started complaining in management meetings that the financial goals were not achievable without damaging the businesses badly. He thought the numbers were killing the company, and many agreed. Even executives at AOL started to warn corporate to move off the numbers.

"If you want a dead stock, we can move off the numbers," Pittman replied. "The market is waiting for us to stall." Having recovered by May to what would later be the combined company's peak of almost $57 a share, executives hoped the worst was over.

But by July of 2001, when the company's quarterly results showed some weakness in meeting its revenue predictions by $500 million, shares began to plummet. The decline was further intensified by a small warning made by Kelly in the analyst's call after the results were released. Pushed by Kelly to go on the record about some doubts without abandoning the beloved numbers, the company noted that the $40 billion revenue figure was "at the top of our range" and they would make it only if the company's last quarter was strong. Still, the company executives once again stressed that the media behemoth was certain to excel with its diverse businesses. Levin, who had not favored backing down, wanted Wall Street to understand the merger's main goals were still strong.

Analysts were wary, but they kept their price targets high for AOL Time Warner anyway, blaming the weak quarter on the economy and not on any apparent management or business problems. But an internal memo at AOL Time Warner from its investor relations unit knew better, warning top executives that more disappointing news meant "all bets on this year and next are canceled, with obvious consequence for ownership, ratings and support."

Later, Levin and other company executives would use their minor warning as proof of their backing off the too-positive projections they'd made in January. It was a fig leaf for the real problem. Rather than focusing smaller, on short-term victories, the AOL Time Warner executive team had badly overpromised. And they had ruined their chances of ever making those numbers, because they had been beating too hard on a recalcitrant company to achieve them.

It would take until late September—two weeks after the devastating September 11 attacks on the World Trade Center and the Pentagon, which sent economic shock waves throughout the world—before the company made the announcement that some had long expected. After 20 months of insisting it could meet its aggressive financial targets, facing a decimated ad market, AOL Time Warner finally admitted it could not.

"AOL Time Warner Inc. today commented on the impact on its business of the September 11 terrorist attacks and the advertising market slowdown, which was compounded by these events," read the press release. "As a result of these developments, the company said it now expects to achieve full-year 2001 EBITDA growth in the 20 percent range and revenue growth of five to seven percent."

Many found it cynical for AOL Time Warner to have waited until after September 11 to blame the results on terrorism, rather than on deeply problematic business issues. Other companies had done the same, but it is clear that AOL Time Warner should have considered pulling back on its impossible financial goals much sooner.

While Pittman and Kelly would get the bulk of the blame for the restatement, the real responsibility for not changing the number sooner rested with Gerald Levin as the company's CEO. To make matters worse, none of the executives under him were strong advocates of refiguring the projections, despite their worries, creating a situation where no one took a leadership position on the issue. And Case and the board abrogated their role in not pressing Levin harder and allowing the company to wait until a tragedy gave them reason to move.

"That's really when we finally threw in the towel," Kelly told me in 2003 about the restatement. In reality, the towel had been thrown in long before that, almost from the first days of the merger when it was clear David Colburn's putz joke was not very funny to anyone.

I managed to track down the AOL executive who had those putz T-shirts made up. It was not, in fact, Colburn who did it, as many had thought. Another urban legend bites the dust. "It was my idea, because people were a little depressed about the merger and I was trying to bring a little levity," admitted Paul Baker, an AOL lawyer and deal maker. "But we really underestimated the touchiness at Time Warner over it, even though it was not done in a mean-spirited way."

Baker, who left AOL Time Warner in 2001, sighed at the sudden change of mood that took over right after the merger that was supposed to bring the next great era for AOL. "Everyone thought we were so smart, and then within two years, we were assholes," he said. "I mean, it's not illegal to be an asshole."

No, it is not. While disturbing questions of legality would soon be raised regarding AOL's business, being an asshole was merely devastating to any chance the merger had of success in the first place.

The world breaks everyone and afterward many are strong at the broken places.

ERNEST HEMINGWAY, *A Farewell to Arms*

Chapter Six

WAY, WAY AFTER
THE GOLD RUSH

The Life of the Party

"You have to remember," said Ken Auletta, the *New Yorker* media writer and a longtime observer of Time Warner, as we considered the unusual career of Gerald Levin in the fall of 2002. "He was like Gromyko, always on the podium."

Auletta was referring to the late Andrei Gromyko, the dour Soviet foreign minister who had a talent for survival, outlasting leaders from Stalin to Gorbachev and also nine U.S. presidents. Like the indestructible Communist diplomat, Levin had always seemed likely to be the last man standing, no matter the crises that had begun to engulf AOL Time Warner in 2001.

After all, despite widespread discontent internally and on Wall Street, a lack of traction for the synergies and financial returns he'd touted, and a rapidly weakening economy, most expected that after 30 years of climbing to the top of the corporate ladder, Levin would overcome these as well. Even with the rumblings of trouble that commenced almost as soon as AOL and Time Warner merged, it was still too early to count out the wily corporate politician.

It turned out a lot different at Time Warner, where animus toward Levin runs deep. He was the guy who decimated the employees' 401Ks. The guy who handed the keys of an iconic, 80-year-old American business to a 15-year-old upstart. Who sold the company's soul after asking almost no one at Time Warner if they thought it was a good idea. Who didn't bother with adequate due diligence or other strategies to protect Time Warner stock. Who allowed AOL's troops to rampage through the corridors of Time Warner. Who wagered Time Warner's future on a dream that had already failed too many times before.

"It was an incredible case of intellectual arrogance," Michael Fuchs, a pugnacious former Time Warner executive whose relationship with Levin was both highly emotional and deeply troubled, told me in a common assessment of his former boss. "He bet the company when he didn't have to."

That was the nice way of putting it. In 2002, *Time* magazine critic Robert Hughes expressed more raw feelings in a scathing email to Levin. Levin insisted to me he didn't receive it, but he could still have read it—like the rest of New York's chattering class—in Tina Brown's *Sunday Times* of London column after Hughes had forwarded it to her.

"How can I convey to you the disgust which your name awakens in me?" wrote Hughes, whose reputation within the company was legendary for both his prodigious writing talent and his obstreperous personality. "The merger with Warner was a catastrophe. But the hitherto unimagined stupidity, the blind arrogance of your deal with Case, simply beggars description. How can you face yourself knowing how much history, value and savings you have thrown away on your mad, ignorant attempt to merge with a wretched dial-up ISP?"

This was ugly enough, but Hughes saved his real wrath for the end. "I don't know what advice you have to offer, but I have some for you," he wrote. "Buy some rope, go out the back, find a tree and hang yourself. If you had any honor you would." Even in the cutthroat environment of big business, that's an astonishing thing to suggest to someone, no matter how angry you are. Yet these are exactly the kind of emotions the AOL Time Warner deal and its aftermath aroused.

In fact, if you took a stroll through the *Time* magazine bureau in Washington, D.C., in the fall of 2002, you'd have seen Hughes's "hang yourself" email posted proudly above the copy machine. In the halls of the Time-Life building on Sixth Avenue in Manhattan, the bulletin boards were papered with news clips critical of Steve Case and Bob Pittman, too, with a smattering of editorial cartoons about corporate greed and crashing stock holdings. By this time, it was hard to get very far in reporting this story without getting an earful of angst from everyone at AOL Time Warner, especially concerning the financial pummeling employees had suffered—whether it was a magazine reporter who became unable to send his kids to college or a studio mogul who'd lost millions.

The plunge of AOL Time Warner stock decimated Levin's own wealth as well, since he sold little of his holdings as the stock tanked. Worse, he borrowed in order to buy stock. And his lavish spending in greener times (as well as the expected cost of his impending divorce) had led Levin in late 2002 to start selling his various properties, including an expensive Upper East Side triplex (once featured in *Architectural Digest*), a group of upscale condos in Santa Fe, and his interest in a California vineyard. In winter 2003 he told me that his personal net worth had fallen from the neighborhood of $400 million to around $10 million. "And I will probably not hold on to much of that," he added in a resigned voice.

Yet it's hard to feel too sorry for Levin, since he still controls large holdings of stock options that could be worth a fortune someday if the share price ever rebounds. And, after years of excessive multimillion-dollar salaries, he still pulls down an annual $1 million consulting fee from AOL Time Warner as part of a five-year contract, as well as $400,000 a year as part of his pension, when he left the company—a fact that enraged his critics. When Levin abandoned New York for the West Coast in 2003, some would joke that Marina del Rey, where Levin had moved to be with the new woman in his life, could now be considered "the newest city in the witness protection program."

Many other things about Levin would infuriate his detractors, but none more so than his steadfast refusal to say he was wrong. In all the interviews I had with him, Levin never once expressed any doubt that the merger had been the right move. He may be the last one who believes in the merger, but he still believes in it all the same. "When the economy comes back and everyone figures out how to work together, they will reconsider me," he said, ever the oracle. "I believed in the Internet and I believe in it now." He also refused to say he might have been tricked by AOL, as many at Time Warner think. "Of course, I did trust the integrity of Case, Pittman, and Kelly," Levin wrote me in an email in 2003. "I don't believe they engaged in deception."

This stubborn insistence that he sees what no one else can see is typical of the contrarian, go-it-alone style that has been the trademark of Levin's career. Many years ago, the *Orlando Sentinel* quoted him as saying in weird fortune-cookie style, "He who makes a living from a crystal ball must learn to eat ground glass." His critics believe that this time, his last prophetic vision—the merger of AOL and Time Warner—will leave him chewing into eternity.

But he won't be alone in partaking this unpalatable meal. Before it was all over, almost everyone associated closely with the merger would be taken down in some fashion. Soon enough, the acronym AOL would come to stand for "Another Ousted Leader." And when it was over, the last man standing on the podium would turn out to be Levin's loyal lieutenant, Dick Parsons. He, like Gromyko, would be the only true survivor.

It's the End of the World As We Know It

When AOL Time Warner finally told the financial world that it wouldn't make the aggressive numbers it had long been predicting, it came as no surprise. With the deteriorating economy, slow movement on promised synergies, and, finally, the September 11 terrorist attacks, it was more of a shock that the pullback had taken as long as it did. Many felt the constant backing of the projection was more than a little egotistical on Levin's part especially, an impossibly elaborate justification for the merger. Some felt the numbers were Levin's battle cry in a war he was losing.

Levin had already been getting heat over the issue in management meetings, especially from Ted Turner, who had become increasingly agitated as the stock started plummeting in the spring. The dyspeptic billionaire would later trace his discontent to his ouster at Levin's hands in the May 2000 management restructuring, but the truth is Turner had long been harboring rage at Levin that needed little cause for eruption. Later, Levin noted that Turner always needed a demon to battle against, which was entirely correct. To Turner, Levin was satanic. In many 2001 meetings, he began calling him names, like "thief" and "liar," and also began leveling a series of accusations about his short-comings as the CEO. As usual, Levin ignored the rants, sitting quietly without acknowledging them until Turner eventually petered out.

Initially, because it was Turner doing the ranting, no one paid much attention. "That's Ted" was the usual refrain, since Turner's out-bursts toward Levin had been so frequent over the years. While Turner would be credited with helping get rid of Levin, he was used mostly as a tool of others more deft and focused in their machinations. But Turner was attuned at a very emotional level to the extreme discomfort that the corporation was feeling, especially in its increasing ire at Levin. His pain was soon to be everyone else's.

Yet Levin couldn't have cared less, because after the terrorist attacks, he claimed something inside his soul snapped. As he described it, the concerns of normal business practices seemed ridiculous and crass. The attack on his beloved New York also allowed old wounds about the death of his son, Jonathan, to reemerge. "After 9/11, I was a basket case, and could not see anything anymore," said Levin to me in an interview in 2002. "I just lost all the drive I had had." He repeated this sentiment frequently to both the press and personal friends.

Within Time Warner, many scoffed at this newly soulful Levin, claiming he was seeking an excuse for his incompetence at running the company. Many were appalled at his frequent chest beating over the tragedy, finding it untoward and insincere. "It was just another thing Levin used for his own benefit," said one top Time Warner executive. "He should have been ashamed of himself."

Like those that followed the death of his son, I think these attacks on Levin are unfair. While he deserves all kinds of criticism for his executive performance, his emotions seem genuine enough, especially since they were exceedingly awkward and not particularly convenient for him. In fact, his overblown reaction to September 11 made many people who worked closely with him exceedingly uncomfortable. He dragged Parsons, Pittman, and others down to Ground Zero, for example, to survey the disaster, and he spent much of his time in the weeks after the attack working on charitable endeavors to help in the recovery. And at a very difficult financial time, with the ad market coming to a complete stop, he instructed AOL Time Warner's news organizations to spend whatever was necessary to cover the event with no revenues coming in.

Levin had changed substantially after the attacks in another key way, becoming even less willing to compromise and more isolated than ever. This was a problem, since AOLers were now deeply engaged in the business in a way Levin hadn't previously had to contend with. Instead of being able to do whatever he liked in seclusion, with minimal input between himself and his division heads, Levin had surrounded himself with people eager to use power. "Levin never had a collaborator and did not preside over a collegial operation until the deal," said one executive who had been close to him before the AOL merger. "And that didn't matter until it mattered."

Indeed, increasingly over the course of the fall, some board members began worrying about the possibility of missed financial results and started offering advice. "It was fair to say we were concerned, but we accepted what we were told, that we would be able to meet the numbers," said one board member, who noted that Levin seemed increasingly irritated. "But it became more and more obvious that we needed to press on the management." As he had with Turner, Levin didn't respond. "He was not interested in anyone's perspective," said another board member, who also noticed Levin's growing isolation. "I would have been offended, but he did not even talk to me."

That included most especially the man who'd dreamed up the idea of AOL Time Warner, Steve Case. Case had removed himself from the fray rather quickly after the merger for a number of professional and personal reasons. First, as at AOL, Case was not much of a line manager, having little interest in operations and the day-to-day worries of running a large corporation. He was typically much more interested in involving himself in the policy arena and other big-idea visions for digital convergence and the future, preferring a more Reaganesque role.

In addition, sources close to him told me that Case felt he should stay away from corporate headquarters in New York. He wanted to make it clear that Levin, Pittman, and Parsons were in charge, even though he had mandated an "active" chairman's role in the merger, which meant having an impact on major strategic decisions. Thus, he kept his main office in Dulles and traveled to New York infrequently. He'd kept a similar distance at AOL with Pittman, and their split duties had worked just fine. In that arrangement, Case had been able to fly high above the clouds, while others carried out the dirtier work on the ground. But such 20,000-foot haughtiness would become problematic once Case suddenly reengaged with the company, and especially with Levin.

Case also had a much more personal reason to be absent in the first months of the merger: In March 2001 he learned that his older brother, Dan, was seriously ill with brain cancer. Case was close to only a few people, and he trusted fewer still—and Dan was one of them. While he would publicly downplay his brother's illness when news articles questioned his absence from the growing turmoil at the company, Case was surely devastated by it.

I know I was, since the sunny Dan was one of the kinder and more thoughtful souls I'd met in Silicon Valley. I had spent a lot of time with him over the years, first when I met him while covering AOL for the *Washington Post* and later when I started working for the *Wall Street Journal* in California. As the leader of the San Francisco–based boutique investment firm Hambrecht & Quist, which was involved in taking public many early Web companies like Netscape, Dan was a keen observer of what was going on in the Internet sector. I met with him now and again and emailed often, mostly asking for his take on the crazy swirl of the late 1990s. He almost always provided a sharp insight and was ultimately amused by the circus atmosphere that had taken over, despite the fact that his own company had taken financial and public relations hits along the way.

When I asked him to talk about his illness for the first time for my column, he replied, "Who wants to hear about a head case?"—making a play on both his illness and his name. He finally jokingly relented, as long as I promised "no little dot-drawing with my skull wrapped in bandages," referring to the surgeries he'd have to undergo and the dotted art portraits the *Wall Street Journal* uses in place of photos. I promised.

In the interview, the ever-gracious Dan spoke eloquently about what he faced and his low odds for survival. "I do not think people change their character that much, but they can change their priorities," he told me. "While I have always liked the integration of work and my personal life, health is obviously going to go way up and work go way down." Later, he kidded that, "We had already created an organizational plan of succession at H&Q for a future year, and I beat expectations by putting it in effect in March."

He also talked about the recent spate of troubles in the industry he'd helped build, noting that they had been constructed on too-flimsy foundations. "It was a classic match between creating quality and getting market share, and it got out of whack," he said, referring to the very venture-backed companies that AOL and others had feasted on to get huge. "Both the old and new economy have been taking potshots at each other, but the companies that succeed will be the ones that embrace both sides. It's important to remember that the whole notion of the entrepreneurial cycle is messiness and creative destruction." Dan was not talking specifically about AOL Time Warner's problems to me, but his comments were also how his brother looked at the situation.

Steve Case was there in May 2001 when Dan made his final appearance at the H&Q annual investment conference, and he gave a moving tribute to his brother's influence on his success. He also spent a lot of time with Dan in San Francisco, working on a brain cancer project to search for new and more aggressive ways to battle the disease. But by the fall, when Dan seemed to be on a bit of a rebound and it began to become clear that things might be seriously askew at AOL Time Warner, Case began returning his attention to AOL Time Warner, where he wanted to reassert himself as chairman.

And that was precisely the moment when Levin wanted as little of

Case's input as possible. He was already furious that Case hadn't agreed to cancel the September board meeting in deference to the trauma caused by the World Trade Center attacks, and he became openly disdainful of Case's motives. "Just emotionally, I could not accept the inhumanity of business as usual," Levin told me. "They were all only worried about if ads sold." Of course, this was Case's job—and also Levin's—but Levin seemed unable to accept such bottom line worries any longer. Or about uniting AOL and Time Warner either. "Until the attack, Jerry was committed to making a new culture," said one top AOL executive. "And then he changed his mind."

To further drive home this new sentiment, Levin wrote a November 19 holiday letter to AOL Time Warner employees that floated the idea of AOL Time Warner as a force for good in the world—of "investing in the public trust" rather than simply being a money-making machine. Levin continued to push that idea, often insisting the company was about more than just profits. Case was furious that Levin would make such declarations—basically telling Wall Street at the worst possible moment that profits didn't matter—without any input from him. The truth is, the fracas had little to do with the letter and a lot more to do with control. They began to clash regularly as Case pummeled Levin with numerous emails about the need to drive integration more strongly. That typical Case habit angered Levin, who didn't want a person he considered inexperienced in media and management telling him how to run the show.

Wire Mire

But Case was determined, since a link between AOL and cable had been the linchpin of the whole merger strategy. "Cable was the driver of everything," said one person knowledgeable about Case's thinking. "Without it, the merger made a lot less sense." And given the online unit's increasing weakness as the dial-up business stagnated, it desperately needed to shift over to high-speed alternatives as soon as possible. The whole cable issue had started out on the wrong foot for Case, who had been livid when Levin and cable head Joe Collins had blacked out Disney's ABC broadcast network from its systems in the midst of the merger approval process. The move had brought increased scrutiny to the deal and added to the time and trouble it took to get an okay for the merger from regulators.

Case had pressed the issue of a combination of AOL online assets with Time Warner Cable at a joint meeting of the boards in July of 2000, promising that high-speed AOL-based services were going to happen and happen fast. He again noted in an October 2000 earnings call, "It's highly likely we'll complete a [cable] deal before the merger and highly likely we will complete the deal this quarter." And then in January of 2001, an investor relations' memo to top executives more stridently linked AOL Time Warner's stock success with a cable and online linkage. "The sooner we get AOL not only on Time Warner Cable but on other systems, the swifter we'll remove the big question mark over the stock," it read.

The fact of the matter was this: The company's failure to make any progress in linking AOL to Time Warner's cable assets was the single clearest indicator that the merger was never going to work. AOL executives were acutely aware that the online service's dial-up business—as large as it was—was now about to become static as more consumers switched to broadband connections. More troublesome was the fact that large numbers of those who signed up for high-speed connections were dropping AOL, never to return. This was a problem on many levels, since its number of subscribers was AOL's only currency in its efforts to sell advertising. Subscribers also provided a monthly certainty of cash flow, sending gushers of free-flowing money into the company. And moving into high-speed would be risky, since it offered dramatically lower margins and less control over the customer, who was not as limited to AOL's longtime walled garden as he was in a dial-up environment.

But broadband was the only way into the future for AOL, as more and more consumers demanded speedier Web hookups. The AOL team, which tried to muscle its way into a deal with Time Warner Cable, was soon thwarted by Joe Collins, a tough executive who had little regard for AOL from his premerger experience tangling with the company over open access. He had already been bothered by

AOL's aggressive political attempts before the merger to force cable operators to open their lines to online companies like AOL.

Sources close to him said that Collins, like many key players in the cable industry, had no intention of letting AOL waltz in the door to hijack an increasingly important new business for cable. He and others had seen how AOL had hijacked consumers from the phone companies, and they were determined that wouldn't happen with high-speed cable. Anyway, Time Warner Cable had its own offering with the highly successful Road Runner service. Why give AOL the opportunity to steal thunder from that promising business? Plus, it made AOL appear more of a threat than ever to other cable companies rather than a partner. As with the direction of online music, AOL's and Time Warner's interests diverged dramatically in this all-important arena.

To AOL, that gap was another example of Time Warner's short-sightedness and its division heads' inability to see their goals as one. After much back-and-forth, Levin in August approved Collins's transfer to a new interactive video unit to move him out of the way. Levin told me he did not consider it a demotion, noting that Collins understood interactive best. But others thought differently about Collins's ouster. "While everyone else smiled and knifed us in the back, Joe would not cooperate explicitly, which only made things worse," said one AOL executive. "He just said, 'Fuck you,' which was basically the attitude of all of the cable industry." A Time Warner executive concurred: "Joe had long operated independently and just did not want to do an AOL deal."

Even with Collins's replacement, though, there was still no movement on any kind of cable deal with AOL—which made Case even more annoyed at Levin, whom he now began to disdain for his inability to control those under him. Case wanted Levin, for example, to completely "blow up" Road Runner and replace it with AOL. Case became even more incensed when Levin lashed out rudely in a meeting at Miles Gilburne, the AOL-deal guru and company board member, after a question he tried to get out about cable issues at AOL. Gilburne was worried about acquiring a new cable company if synergies between AOL and Time Warner Cable had not been found. Levin considered Gilburne a dilettante for lecturing him on issues he knew nothing about, and cut him off.

No one was going to be lecturing Levin, the cable expert, on that issue. And no one was going to stop him now if he wanted to buy a cable company, a desire that jumped to the forefront when AT&T's massive cable systems came into play in mid-2001. After all, he'd been right before about the cable business, when his much-criticized move to build up Time Warner's cable assets throughout the 1990s paid off, and he knew he was right now. Levin was even more annoyed since he'd thought the merger was more than simply about cable, and he considered Case's obsessive focus on it not properly visionary. While he agreed that AOL needed to be available on Time Warner's high-speed lines, he also thought that it did not mean that other services like Time Warner's Road Runner—a big success—should be sacrificed to do so.

And, in any case, the opportunity to grab AT&T's cable assets was too huge. The long-distance giant's cable systems had been subject to an unsolicited bid by the Comcast cable firm earlier in the summer and AT&T had initially rejected its offer as too low. Obviously, AT&T wanted a competition for its assets, and the names of other suitors soon popped up—including Disney and Microsoft. The idea of AOL Time Warner as a possible buyer came to notice after John Malone promoted the idea publicly in early September, which some felt was an effort to stir up excitement and prices.

Levin had long been wheeling and dealing behind the scenes by then, submitting bids and attempting to make the deal happen. Merging the AOL Time Warner and AT&T Broadband assets wasn't a bad idea, since it would create a behemoth by combining the largest and second-largest cable systems. This would immediately supercharge the company's high-speed power, since Time Warner Cable only passed through only 20 percent of homes in the United States. As an added benefit, such a deal could also settle the complex ownership of Time Warner Entertainment, a stake that AT&T had inherited as part of its cable-buying spree.

But—in arguments pressed by Case—the combination would also surely bring even more intense attention from regulators, including the FCC, FTC, and even the Department of Justice, as well as the

ire of competitors. On top of that, AOL Time Warner was still carrying huge debt from its previous cable acquisitions. The integration
alone would take much-needed focus off the still-festering problems
at AOL Time Warner, Case thought.

Still, Levin pressed on. "He did it to poke a finger in Steve's eye,"
said one corporate executive who watched the brewing fight. "And
Levin was always in love with cable."

But while Case and Levin's growing battle was publicly characterized as a tiff over the AT&T acquisition, it was about much more
than that. Comcast ended up winning those cable assets—but the
more important issue at AOL Time Warner was about who was in
charge. The cable battle marked the end of the short-lived era in
which Levin and Case's relationship seemed so promising. Their
mutual seduction had long worn off, and now the more mundane and
disappointing reality of their relationship was about to be revealed.

Poetic Justice

As Case and Levin's arguments intensified in the fall of 2001, Case
began calling and visiting members of the board in an effort to persuade them that Levin had to go. Case had multiple arguments. Levin
had held on to the aggressive financial projections too long, for reasons of ego. He'd become increasingly unwilling to work with anyone.
He had refused to take direction on the cable deal and had kept the
board in the dark about his deal making. He wasn't the leader AOL
Time Warner needed to halt the precipitous decline. He ignored
strategic issues in favor of quarterly numbers. "He pretended to be in
charge, and then would not acknowledge the reality that he was not,"
said a source close to Case who knew his thinking.

Some board members on the Time Warner side, including Dick
Parsons, found Case's effort to oust Levin appalling and resisted it—
despite growing reservations about Levin's leadership. Case thought
they agreed with him, but Parsons and others felt Case was ignoring
the process that such a large company required to consider such a
move. Case, they felt, had grown up in a wilder environment where

he controlled the AOL board, since it was seen as his company. But as soon as the merger was done, the combined entity ceased to be anybody's company.

But Case was aided by one key ally: Ted Turner, who was more than happy to join with him in impugning his old foe. Turner had attacked Levin throughout the later summer and into the fall over all sorts of issues, including his obstructing Turner's continued efforts to buy the NBC television network. By the end of the year, he took his anger public once again. At a widely covered cable event in November, Turner mocked Levin for having called him his "best friend" years before, during the Turner merger. Noting he had never been to Levin's home, Turner cracked: "I'm your best friend? If I'm your best friend, who's your second-best friend? Nick Nicholas?"

Now, Turner had an ally in Case, who gave him just the kind of credibility he needed, as well as an outlet for his longtime disgruntlement. At one November 2001 dinner of the board, Turner addressed Levin directly over the table for 20 minutes about what he considered was the CEO's incompetence and also his dishonesty. The AOL board members, who had not experienced the long-running battle between Levin and Turner before, were surprised by his candor. "We always heard he was always the madman, but he did not sound like a madman," said one board member. "This was not a two-week fix, and he made a good case that we needed to do something quickly."

With continued resistance from Parsons and other board members, however, Case couldn't muster the board votes to bounce Levin from his job. But he had done serious damage to Levin's ability to lead, and he began pressuring hard for a resolution. At a morning board meeting on December 5, he found one more ally in an unlikely source: Levin himself. Disgusted and tired, Levin had had enough of the struggle and decided to step down, since it was clear that Case had cobbled together enough board support to make his job impossible going forward.

Many sources close to the board told me that it would have been easy for Levin to delay any action or to fight, and that he might have prevailed against Case's coup attempt, since support for Levin's ouster was tepid. But Levin, weary of the machinations he'd had to employ over the years to retain his power, said he didn't have the heart. Now there would be no more politicking, no more sucking up, and no more war games. "People forget the merits," he said to me in 2003. "When something turns south, people turn on you, so I said, 'Forget it.'" In other words, there'd be no more Gerald Levin to kick around anymore.

Levin resigned without the board taking a vote. As a parting shot at Case, he'd already worked out the succession, naming Parsons—who was then seriously considering taking over the CEO position at Philip Morris Cos.—as CEO of AOL Time Warner. Pittman had already told Levin he didn't want the job, perhaps because he was acutely aware that the anger he'd engendered from the divisional executives would prove fatal. Besides, the board had also begun to sour on Pittman, for similar reasons, including Case. Levin told me he'd never felt Pittman was going to lead the company anyway, although it had been positioned that way by Levin many times. "I always considered Dick as my successor," he said, although that had not been true only a few years before, because Parsons was considered more of a lawyer than an operator.

When Levin announced he was stepping down, he gave a wide range of reasons for the decision—conspicuously leaving out the fighting with Case. In an email he sent to the company, he noted that he'd invoked a special provision in his employment agreement that allowed him to cut short his contract. "I felt that once my work was completed and I was satisfied with the company's direction and progress, I'd invoke that provision," Levin wrote. And his official statement implied his decision wasn't sudden: "Given that we are almost a full year into the merger and that an outstanding management team is now in place at the company, I am convinced that AOL Time Warner should begin an orderly transition to a new era of leadership."

But the most interesting spin was a typically lofty Levin literary reference that appeared in many news reports—one his detractors would mercilessly skewer. In the *Wall Street Journal,* he explained, "I'm my own person. I have strong moral convictions. I'm not just a suit. I want poetry back in my life."

Later, Levin told me he knew people didn't believe he meant that.

At the time, I certainly didn't. I assumed it was just some hokey declaration by a man who was desperately trying to justify a massive mistake that would surely outlive him. After all, in every reference to Gerald Levin from now until the end of time, the tarnish of the failed deal would be right at the top of the story.

But after he stepped down, Levin didn't seem to care about that anymore. He was finally free. And even though having sympathy for Levin is difficult thanks to his careless disregard for many who'd been loyal to him, his lack of leadership after the merger and his inability to say he was sorry or wrong—to say nothing of the money lost—I have to say I was pretty glad for him.

"What I want in my heart is not to be known as a CEO; I am a writer. A human being," Levin told me at our last meeting. "I can't believe any of this happened to me anyway." And neither could Steve Case, it seemed—since in ousting Levin he had unwittingly planted the seeds of not only his own destruction, but that of the company he had spent his life creating. In his aggressive efforts to move Levin out, he hurt his reputation with the board badly and also pushed himself to the forefront as the real rage began to build against the deal. Until then, Levin had been a shield for Case. Now that he was gone, Case no longer had that protection.

And though Case went along with it, he did not have a real choice in the selection of the new head of AOL Time Warner, Dick Parsons. Flicked aside like a flea in the initial months of the merger, the burly Parsons was generally perceived as someone on his way out. Even when he took over as CEO, I was struck by the assessment of one major investor, who characterized him as a "nonalcoholic beverage with greatness foisted upon him." In other words, Parsons was the only one bland enough to be agreeable to all the warring constituencies.

That was true enough. You couldn't find a more genial leader than Parsons, who was the polar opposite of Levin in his sociability and of Pittman in his ability to get all sorts of dislikable people to like him. The cliché about Parsons, which frankly got a little wearying after a while, was that he was "nice" and "decent" and "kind." Yeah, yeah, I wanted to say, he may be a sweetie pie, but can he deliver the goods?

One thing was certain: The choice of Parsons—someone who appeared clean despite intense involvement in the mess of the merger and its aftermath—was a coup for the Time Warner side.

This ability to move smoothly through life without making waves was a calling card of Parsons, who seemed to float from one successful endeavor to the next, trailing goodwill in his wake. His beginnings were unremarkable enough. Born in Brooklyn, New York, to working-class parents, he did not complete his undergraduate work at the University of Hawaii, but went on to finish at the top of his class at Union University's Albany Law School. He worked nights as a janitor during law school.

In 1971, the year he finished law school, Parsons became an adviser to then–New York Governor Nelson Rockefeller. He followed his boss to Washington when President Gerald Ford appointed Rockefeller as his vice president after Richard Nixon's 1974 resignation. Eventually, Parsons would become an adviser to President Ford himself. When his work at the White House ended, Parsons became a partner with Patterson, Belknap, Webb & Tyler, staying with the firm for nearly 12 years before making another career switch. In 1988, he became president and COO of Dime Savings Bank, and he rose to the chairman and CEO position within two years. In that position, Parsons was able to engineer the bank's turnaround, saving it from insolvency.

Following his success at Dime, Parsons was offered the position of Time Warner president in 1995, after having been on the board since 1991. Although he had no experience in media companies, Parsons had the qualities that Time Warner, struggling to make its recent merger a success, desperately needed: A conciliatory air; a commanding presence; and a diplomatic, approachable working style. In the five years he was at the company before the AOL merger, his reputation was steadily burnished—even as his style seemed to keep him mostly under the radar of the press and the world at large.

When he became co-COO with Pittman, with Case as chairman, many inside and outside the company scratched their heads trying to decide which side was really in charge now. Was Parsons just a placeholder before the final AOL coup, or the first sign of a Time Warner counterrevolution? At the time, AOLers were madly spinning the "sandwich" theory—Parsons would be squished between Pittman and Case and eventually squeezed out. Meanwhile, Time Warner executives relished the idea that Parsons's ascendancy signaled the end of the reign of their brutish conquerors.

Whoever had the upper hand, it was clear someone needed to take charge. By the first anniversary of the deal, in January 2002, AOL Time Warner's stock hit a 52-week low of just above $25 a share, giving the company a rapidly declining value of $147.2 billion. The company's earnings report that same month justified the drop, showing that the weak ad market and lack of synergy in getting any incremental revenues from joint company initiatives was taking its toll. The company reported revenue of $38.2 billion, up from the previous year's $36.2 billion, but nowhere near the $40 billion promised by Levin. Cash flow rose 18 percent to $9.9 billion from $8.4 billion—impressive enough, but not even close to the promised $11 billion.

The disappointment caused by that broken financial promise would soon pale in comparison to the calamities that would befall the company in 2002. Even though Jerry Levin was gone, a few of the company's major investors soon began to feel that not enough blood had been shed. Someone had to pay for the gargantuan mess they'd landed in—and soon enough, someone would.

It Sticks in My Craw(ford)

Gordon Crawford was very, very angry.

Even being simply angry was, in fact, unusual for the soft-spoken Crawford, a quiet man who looked as if he could have been a career accountant. He certainly didn't carry himself as what he was: One of the most powerful figures in the media world thanks to being one of its savviest and most influential investors for more than 30 years. As the media stock-picking guru for the Los Angeles–based Capital Research and Management, Crawford commanded billions of dollars of capital, and he wielded it with discrimination and force.

A close adviser to all major media moguls, Crawford used his financial heft to nudge them in directions he deemed correct. Despite his immense power, he was considered a gentleman who avoided the kind of overt confrontations or egomaniacal bluster that were typical of the executives he invested in. Usually, after intense study of financial documents, Crawford would communicate his views directly and calmly and follow through with his investments only after rigorous analysis. He prized loyalty above all else, and believed in long-term investing in companies he bet on.

In its various incarnations, Time Warner had been one of Capital Research and Management's longtime and large investments under Crawford. He had supported the merger with Warner and had been extremely influential in Ted Turner's decision to sell his company to them in the mid-1990s. Turner considered him a key voice and had consulted him frequently since then. And, over the years, Crawford had developed a close professional relationship with Levin, who also relied heavily on his advice. (The pair had another thing in common: Crawford, too, had lost a son—his in a tragic climbing accident.)

Right from the merger's announcement, Crawford, who understood that dealing with digital issues would be critical for Time Warner, had been supportive of the merger. While he'd long been wary of AOL's aggressive style, he had invested in the company many times and he didn't object to the deal, believing that Levin would control any possible excesses. But by the end of 2001, having suffered huge losses on his fund's stake of 113 million shares, he was starting to get ticked off.

Crawford's pique worsened when AOL Time Warner revealed its preliminary results for the 2001 fiscal year on January 7, 2002. In that report, Crawford found numbers that were much different from ones former CFO Mike Kelly had told him about in the fall of 2001, and he felt he had been lied to. The first surprise was hundreds of millions of dollars in additional losses from the online unit's joint venture with Bertelsmann in AOL Europe.

The second surprise was that substantial earnings were about to disappear thanks to the early termination of AOL's iPlanet business software alliance with Sun Microsystems—without adequate notice of the details to shareholders by company executives. The deal between AOL and Sun was dicey enough, a convoluted scheme cooked up as part of the Netscape acquisition. Simply put, AOL and Sun were involved in an I'll-scratch-your-back-if-you'll-scratch-mine transaction that appeared to have few real benefits other than to pretty up the bottom line of both companies.

In the complex deal, AOL had agreed to buy hundreds of millions of dollars' worth of Sun hardware and services at list prices—rather than at the discount the company doubtlessly would get in an arm's-length transaction. In turn, Sun agreed to spend hundreds of millions at AOL for licensing, marketing, and advertising services. Sun also guaranteed another almost $1 billion in other revenue commitments over time. In 2001 alone, the deal had added $400 million in revenue and $320 million in cash flow to AOL's bottom line, which Crawford felt AOL had not made clear. That deal was now ending, as described in confusing language that was buried deep in the company's arcane regulatory filings. Still, a more heavy Wall Street would figure it out, and Crawford knew it was a development that was sure to send the share price hurtling downward.

The day after the company unveiled the results and held a conference call to explain the changes, Bob Pittman delivered an address at an investment conference taking place at an Arizona luxury hotel. As he listened to Pittman, Crawford grew agitated, believing his address was too optimistic considering the dire circumstances. In the speech, Pittman apologized for missing expectations, but then continued to try to make things look rosier than ever. Speaking of silver linings in the ad recession that would only benefit AOL Time Warner, Pittman stressed the power of synergy and the company's great growth prospects.

"If you look at a company like AOL Time Warner, how do we, when you get to be this size, continue to be a growth company?" Pittman asked the gathering. "The only way you can do it is to continue to invent new businesses which have very high growth rates, and it's in our DNA." He continued talking up AOL Time Warner's future as a growth company, noting that all great innovations— including MTV—were considered failures before they later hit big.

And he particularly touted the online service, dangling visions of the unit's eventually garnering as much as $160 a month from each member from a suite of digital services, rather than the current $24 fee for simple dial-up access.

But Crawford had heard enough hype. After the speech, Crawford met AOL Time Warner's newly installed CFO Wayne Pace and investor relations head Richard Hanlon, as well as investor relations staffer Eileen Naughton, on the hotel's sunny terrace, and he unloaded. He expressed his contempt for what he considered questionable behavior, adding that AOL's top executives had misled him in earlier meetings about AOL Europe and other parts of the business. He railed against the lack of disclosure, the lack of transparency, and the unwillingness to be forthright under the new regime. Crawford noted that he "grew up" with Time Warner, and that there were certain standards that needed to be maintained. "Do not let AOL people pollute you," he warned Pace, pointedly not looking at Hanlon, who was from the AOL side.

"I knew right there it was over for anything to get better," recalled Hanlon, who left AOL Time Warner in March. "We had a long way to go to get back the faith and confidence of Wall Street."

Soon enough, Parsons and Pace tried to assuage Crawford and other outside investors that the company would change its style by disclosing more and promising less. They convinced Crawford to come visit the online service in March to get a better feel for the business. An internal document about Crawford's visit urged executives there to stop the spinning. "The essential mission tomorrow, therefore, is not to dazzle him with numbers," read the AOL Time Warner memo. "He has seen the numbers and that is what worries him."

Soothing the worried soon became Parsons's main job, and he decreed a new mantra to underpromise and overdeliver, rather than the other way around. His main messages were simpler and much less grand than before: A diversified business moving conservatively, but strongly, into the future. That was the internal message, too, as Parsons began to mend fences—including reaching out to Turner, whom he even went so far as to call "Uncle Ted" at a public event later in 2002.

To mend fences internally, the company's divisions were finally given permission in late March to use whichever email system they wanted—nullifying the company's earlier, wildly unpopular directive to try to use AOL email products. In an uncharacteristically sheepish statement, spokeswoman Tricia Primrose was forced to admit, "Unfortunately, it didn't work for everybody. So we decided to give everybody the choice that met their needs."

In early April, a similarly embarrassing policy change removed another major complaint for employees. To date, the company had offered matching funds for employees' retirement plans—but they could be invested only in AOL Time Warner shares. To help defuse the anger and frustration over the dismal stock performance, the company changed its policy. Henceforth, employees could put their matching funds in other stocks.

Bit by bit, management was trying to win back its frustrated employees—particularly those on the Time Warner side. But the one thing that would truly win back disgruntled workers was the thing the company seemed incapable of offering: A rebound in financial fortunes. That outlook became even more dismal at the end of March, when the company revealed in regulatory filings that it would adopt new accounting standards by taking an incredible $54 billion charge to reflect the depreciation of the company's stock value since the merger had been announced. While it was a noncash charge—and therefore had no impact on the bottom line—it was the largest write-down in corporate history. You couldn't find a more potent symbol for the failed marriage of AOL and Time Warner.

But soon enough, that huge charge would expand beyond anyone's wildest imaginations. Facing a slowdown in subscriber growth, declining ad sales, and difficulty in shifting its business over to high speed, AOL had finally—and very publicly—hit that cliff that had worried executives at the online unit as far back as 1998. Since the merger had been predicated on the power of the once mighty online service, the fate of all of AOL Time Warner now rose and fell with the unit that Levin had once bragged was the "crown jewel."

Now AOL was more like cubic zirconium. And it was left to the greatest salesman AOL had ever had to save the day again. Or, as I asked in a column when he headed back down to Dulles, Virginia, to try to fix what was clearly broken: "Can Bob 'Pitchman' toss another winning game?"

Hail the Conquering Zero

First, the ones who blew it—or who were to be blamed for blowing AOL's momentum, anyway—had to go. On April 9, 2002, the company announced that AOL CEO Barry Schuler would step down— shuffled off to head up a vague new purgatory called Digital Services Development Group. A software and gadgets geek, Schuler had been the wrong choice to head AOL, but it had taken nearly 15 months for his superiors to take action.

In a way, AOL's collapse wasn't only Schuler's fault, despite the fact that he turned out to be a polarizing figure after Pittman went to New York to become co-COO. It was, in fact, Pittman's departure to Manhattan after the merger that had signaled a dramatic shift in AOL's management. Ted Leonsis, who had been shunted aside under Pittman's reign, had watched those changes with trepidation. "The fact is, when AOL was in its heyday, we had a dream team, and here we were breaking up that team and letting the best head for New York," said Leonsis. "We should have been bringing the best from Time Warner [to Dulles] to make up the difference." Now, much of the executive ranks were dangerously thin at AOL.

And as AOL's wave of talent headed for Manhattan, Schuler inherited a troubled business well beyond his management capabilities at exactly the time the dot-com economy began to tank. Schuler had operated capably under Pittman's firm hand. But once in charge of things, he turned out to be a spectacularly bad choice, since he lacked his former boss's ability to keep everyone in line. Common complaints about Schuler included his short attention span, his lack of enthusiasm for selling ads, his excessive interest in tech trends that were not fully baked, his inability to get tough on weak staff members, and even the distractions created by his own vast wealth, which included an 83-foot yacht and a Napa Valley vineyard.

Schuler's fortune came out of a spectacular trade he'd made in the

1990s. Though not the highest-ranking executive at AOL, he was probably the wealthiest after Steve Case, after having sold his company to AOL for stock in a deal that was worth a fortune. Schuler's firm had been responsible for redesigning AOL's interface, an area Schuler was much more capable in than management. "I believe Barry took the [AOL CEO] job because Bob wanted him to," one high-ranking executive at AOL told me. "But when he got it, he did not want it." Schuler was, in his heart, a product guy.

Time Warner's Joe Ripp, who became the AOL unit's CFO after the merger, was even more cutting about the management problems that festered at AOL. "People like Schuler had always run small companies and in good times, but wealth made them think they were much smarter and could do anything," he said, underscoring AOL executives' inability to change with the times. "Schuler used to constantly tell me that I thought like an old media guy, and I said, 'Good, because all you new media guys are going bankrupt.'" He and others at the company began to complain to Pittman about Schuler's shortcomings as a leader, as the business weakened.

When he saw signs of trouble, Pittman appointed corporate CFO Mike Kelly to become AOL's COO in November of 2001 and sent him down to Dulles. It was a move encouraged by Schuler, who did not like to run day-to-day operations and preferred to focus on the products. It was also a perfect time for Kelly to make his own shift. He'd already rubbed raw the other AOL Time Warner divisional heads, and they all now despised him for his grinding and verbal abuse over the financial goals. And he'd also used up the goodwill of Wall Street. In one well-publicized instance, he had even cursed at powerful Merrill Lynch media analyst Jessica Reif Cohen in a conference call.

But Kelly's arrival didn't stop Pittman from getting further frustrated with Schuler, who couldn't seem to restore AOL's business to its former speed. "God could have been running AOL and it wouldn't have worked," said one AOL source. "The fighting with Pittman made it worse, since it didn't seem as if he was listening to what we were telling him about the falloff, since he had run it in the boom times." With growth down, Schuler now began to realize he should have spoken up sooner.

But Pittman felt Schuler was lagging, failing to bring out any new innovations in response to the changing times. Although AOL had a history of always managing to find a lucrative new business just before the old one disappeared and Pittman and others had promised that ad profits were sustainable, cross-company deals weren't coming through as fast as had been promised—due in equal parts to the weakening economy and noncooperation inside the company. More important, new incremental revenues simply weren't being funneled into the online company fast enough to keep up with AOL's formerly speedy growth. Pittman felt Schuler was incapable of making the kinds of cuts and changes the company needed to reignite AOL.

So Schuler had to go. And taking his place would be a returning savior: Bob Pittman. Pittman's reengagement seemed a good idea, since he also needed to restore the luster at the online service as his power base at AOL Time Warner began to erode. As AOL went, so, too, went his reputation in the rest of the company. Or as one Time Warner side executive put it to me: "Pittman was not going to tell me about running my business when his was tanking."

Dick Parsons was, as ever, more diplomatic. "Nobody understands AOL's operations and potential better than Bob Pittman, and no one is better qualified to manage this business," he said in a statement. With wonderful understatement, the quote went on: "Bob is taking on this role at a time of both opportunity and challenge."

To me, that translated as: Bob, you got us into this mess—now you get us out of it. When I first heard of the shift, I wasn't so surprised, since it was clear that Schuler wasn't the right kind of guy to make the changes AOL so desperately needed. But I wasn't so sure Pittman was the right guy anymore either, given the wholesale changes that had taken place in the market. Yahoo, under its new CEO Terry Semel, had already announced in November of 2001 that it was going to take comprehensive steps to fix its broken business, having recognized that the industry was now quite different. Over that fall, I had asked a string of AOL executives, including Pittman, when they were going to start admitting the obvious. But I heard only the same phrase echoed back from each of them: "AOL is different."

It wasn't, of course—but it was springtime in Dulles, and a whiff of hope was in the air. Bob Pittman was riding to the rescue, and the time was ripe for AOL to stage a comeback. This was a favored AOL scenario—a chance for the company to beat the odds and show up everyone. Over the next couple of months, the company undertook a few moves to try to make that happen, including making several executive shifts and bringing in some new faces. Only two days after the announcement of Pittman's return, the company named radio veteran Jimmy de Castro as the new president of AOL Interactive Services, to replace the retiring Jon Sacks. Creative and energetic, de Castro seemed like a good choice to inject some life into the moribund unit. A devotee of "spinning"—an exercise involving frenetic group pedaling on bike machines—de Castro ran his own spinning classes at the Dulles campus.

Spinning turned out to be a pretty good metaphor for the trouble AOL was in, since all key revenue metrics were declining fast. The company had predicted no growth for 2002, after a 7 percent decline in earnings for the AOL unit in the fourth quarter of 2001. But it was actually much worse than that, since AOL had gotten $138 million of advertising from other AOL Time Warner units. Without this critical inflow, ad revenue would have actually declined 27 percent for the division. There was a difference between order taking from eager dot-com prospects desperate to do a deal and actually selling in a weak ad environment. What was required was a culture change that Pittman was incapable of making, since he had created the one that needed to die.

Subscriber figures were also suffering: Now it took 75 days to sign up one million new members, more than double the time it had taken a year before. Overall growth—the key metric that had kept AOL's stock at a peak—had been slowing yearly as AOL ran out of likely prospects. To make matters worse, many more of the new dial-up service members joined through less lucrative offers via PC manufacturers, which cost AOL more to acquire since a big cut went to its partners.

And there was still no real broadband offering to speak of, even though this was clearly the area AOL needed to migrate its users to in the future. Development of a different kind of service based on broadband needs—more video, audio, and other robust graphics—was a costly endeavor compared to what was needed to satisfy dial-up users. And AOL got less money from each broadband customer, too, since it had to share much more of the monthly fee with cable and high-speed telephone suppliers. "Every time someone switched off of AOL and onto using AOL via broadband, it is a bad day for AOL," said one AOL executive. "High-speed blew apart what was a very lucrative business for us that we knew well." It is no surprise then that Pittman once again preferred to delay the inevitable as much as possible by attempting to persuade members to slow their broadband adoption.

But times had changed, and Pittman hadn't seen this particular movie before. "People always said, 'We can't,' and we did," said one executive who hoped Pittman could turn around the business. "But Bob underestimated the extent of the collapse, and so he thought he could fix it in the same way as he did before."

In my April 2002 column in the *Wall Street Journal,* I urged Pittman to focus on five key points—well beyond his old tricks of cost cutting and hypermarketing—as he tried to resuscitate his gasping patient. For one thing, I wrote, the company had lost its customer focus on simplicity and had become "a forest of annoying ad-laden billboards and marketing-fueled services. . . . Much of today's America Online looks like a brochure rack at a tourist rest stop. And its last two software upgrades have been lackluster, giving its service a feel of an era long past."

In addition, the brand had ceased to mean anything. "[F]or too long, America Online has operated like a real-estate mogul, collecting fat fees from companies like auction giant eBay Inc. for placement on the service," I wrote. "Instead of hosting sites like eBay, America Online should be owning businesses like these by now." Further, AOL had also fallen far behind in the all-important race to high-speed services like cable and DSL. And widespread morale problems at the company were threatening to bring the whole show down.

Finally, I suggested the most drastic option of all: "If all this doesn't work, AOL Time Warner Chief Executive Richard Parsons would not be wrong to consider a more drastic move, including spinning off the AOL unit. Sources at the top of the company call this option ridiculous. But is it? Right now, calculating the value of the corporation's assets at its current stock price, the AOL online service is valued at exactly nothing—so it's not as if this move would kill the company's value. The plus: It would allow America Online to become nimble again and rise and fall on its own, able to make alliances it needs outside the Time Warner family. While Mr. Pittman and others touted the magical abilities of the online unit to sell other Time Warner goods and services, it hasn't turned out quite that well yet, and such deals could still be done without the iron link on friendly terms. What's more, it's not as if any of the other slow-growth businesses of the company (magazines, for example) are helping AOL that much."

As Pittman got his hands dirty again in the minutiae of AOL's troubles, he'd soon find that nothing much was going to help—including himself.

There's No Business Like No Business

Despite the troubles, Pittman, Case, and Parsons grinned out from the June 2002 cover of AOL Time Warner's internal magazine, called *Keywords,* under the headline "Lift Off!" Actually, "Grounded!" would have been a more accurate headline, given the problems that would continue to mount over the summer.

That was especially true at AOL, where Pittman found that just about everything—from morale to ad sales to subscriber numbers—was trending downward at an accelerating pace. He had grown weary of the company infighting, exhausted from the traveling, and worn down by the prospect that turning around AOL would take more work than he had ever imagined. For three months, he'd been trying to revive AOL while still working as COO of the combined company, and was making slow progress. Pittman was stretched about as thin as he could go, and AOL was still sputtering. "He had been getting a pounding and he did not see a way to turn it around," said AOL marketing whiz Jan Brandt, whom Pittman had brought back into the top echelons of the company upon his return. "And there was no end in sight."

Indeed, for Pittman, there was no end in sight for the time it might take to fix AOL, especially because of how badly he and his team had alienated the entire Time Warner management. The *New York Post* even began running a regular "Pittman Meter," a graphic that offered assessments ranging from whether he was "toast" to "safe" on any given day. Mostly, Pittman was burnt to a crisp. With increasing skepticism that he could fix the problems at AOL, Pittman went to Parsons before the July 4 holiday weekend and told him he wanted out. "I can't do this anymore," said Pittman to Parsons, who urged him to think things through over the weekend.

But the weekend put him over the edge, when the *New York Times*—whose reporter David Kirkpatrick was deeply tapped into the growing rage of the Time Warner executives—ran a scathing piece, written with David Carr, detailing Pittman's failure to turn things around at AOL and suggesting there was a target on his back. "Executives and shareholders are united in more or less open revolt," wrote Kirkpatrick and Carr. While the story referred to discomfort with the departed Levin, too, it singled out Pittman explicitly. "Most of all, Time Warner executives have turned their ire specifically at one man— Mr. Pittman, a former America Online executive who became chief operating officer after the merger," it read. "He angered many Time Warner executives with what they called his brusque manner . . . he developed a reputation for brashness, ruthlessness and success at America Online, and he applied the same tactics at Time Warner on his return."

Chronicling in detail Time Warner's anger, the article summed up their message succinctly: "Now many executives from the former Time Warner wish the merger would go away, and, barring that, they wish that Mr. Pittman would." In the article, Parsons was quoted offering a rather tepid defense of Pittman: "People get angry and that anger has to be attached to something or someone," he was quoted as saying. "Some of it has been attached to Bob and I am not sure if it is entirely fair."

Well, not entirely, Parsons's quote seemed to indicate to me—but maybe it's a *little* fair! This deft response definitely did not look good for Pittman, and the long knives of Time Warner were drawn. And with Parsons firmly ensconced in the CEO position and no place higher up on the ladder for Pittman to go, what sense did it make for him to keep fighting what was, for the foreseeable future, a losing battle in which he would probably end up getting tossed out anyway? With the executive ranks blaming him and the board losing faith that he could turn around AOL, Pittman had no chance of regaining any credibility as COO. "Pittman left on his own steam, but he knew what was coming," said one board member, who actually admired Pittman. But others on the board felt his abilities were not up to managing such a complex operation. Case, never a true ally, all but abandoned Pittman.

Pittman wanted to announce he was leaving, but Parsons asked him to delay the news until the board could approve a new management structure in mid-July. His plan was to promote Time Inc.'s Don Logan and HBO's Jeff Bewkes to the top of the AOL Time Warner structure, effectively splitting Pittman's duties into two positions, both of which would report directly to Parsons. Logan would head the Media and Communications Group, the subscription and ad businesses that would include Time, Inc., Time Warner Cable, the Interactive Video Unit, Time Warner Books, and AOL. And Bewkes would run the Entertainment and Networks Group, made up of HBO, New Line Cinema, the WB, Turner Networks, Warner Bros., and Warner Music.

Getting the pair interested in the arrangement would be difficult, given the recalcitrance both had felt toward the merger in the first place. But it was critical for Parsons to pull this off, since Logan and Bewkes were considered the best and most successful operators in the company, though they were vastly different in personality and style.

Logan, who had been the CEO of Time, Inc. since 1994, was one of the most admired managers in the company, especially within his division, where he was openly revered for turning around the fortunes of the magazine publishing house. An Alabama native, he was the son of a housewife and a welder for the state highway department. Logan went to Auburn University as a math major and worked his way through school as a computer programmer for NASA in Huntsville. He continued his studies—specializing in abstract math—at Clemson University, and went on to pursue a doctorate part-time at the University of

Houston. While in Texas, he worked for Shell Oil, creating research tools in the search for oil, but he found big-company life too slow.

Answering an ad for a Birmingham, Alabama, publishing company called Progressive Farmer, later to be renamed Southern Progress, Logan worked first in data processing and fulfillment and later in direct marketing. Time Inc. bought Southern Progress in 1985, and Logan was running it by 1986. Admiring Logan's reputation for consistent results, Levin brought him to New York in 1992 as Time Inc.'s president and COO. Logan got the chairman and CEO spot two years later. Logan fulfilled Levin's expectations by goosing the magazine division's results dramatically, turning in 41 consecutive quarters of earnings growth and tripling its cash flow.

Logan managed all this while affecting a folksy southern image as a good old boy who just loved to go fishing. (He had even appeared on the cover of *Field & Stream* in a feature about jungle fish.) Pretty much everyone I asked about Logan felt the need to mention his fishing, as if it were a mysterious and complex part of his nature— imagine that, a fishing math major! In the company newsletter, Logan was quoted as noting that business was a lot like fishing, in that they both require "persistence and patience."

The burly Logan might have had true "down home" bona fides, but he was as smooth as any city slicker in leading the potentially divisive troops at Time Inc. His greatest strength appeared to be in leaving people alone yet demanding performance as a price for that independence. "He was a straight talker in a culture of bullshit and platitudes," said former Pathfinder executive Linda McCutcheon. "And he believed you grew incrementally to greatness."

The AOLers expected more rapport with Jeff Bewkes, the glib and good-looking head of HBO. Much as everyone mentioned Logan's interest in fishing, the expression Time Warner people invariably used to describe Bewkes was "a handsome man." And he was indeed good-looking, slim and tall with a curious mix of Hollywood glamour and vague preppiness that suited the more conservative elements of the company. "Golden boy" had long been a defining image for Bewkes, who was a graduate of Yale University and Stanford Business School (again, that heady mix of traditional East Coast and trendy California). The impact he made was a strong one—an executive comfortable with both Hollywood talent and New York deal makers alike.

When Bewkes first came to HBO, he worked in the finance and marketing departments. He was considered a winner even in his earliest days. "We all used to assume he would eventually be the boss," said former AOL executive Mark Walsh, who had worked with Bewkes at HBO. "He had this air of the inevitable about him that was very appealing." His star rose quickly and he eventually became the chairman and CEO of HBO, building a close-knit team around him that was responsible for burnishing the somewhat dull image of the pay-cable channel to an edgy sheen with such huge hits as *The Sopranos* and *Sex and the City.*

This conspicuous success quickly attracted AOLers, who identified with Bewkes's more outgoing style and considered his passionate, entrepreneurial nature akin to their own. They could not have been more wrong about his regard for AOL, though—Bewkes was one of the first executives to complain internally and loudly about the idiocy of the merger deal. He wasn't shy about challenging Steve Case's dreamy ideas of convergence in company meetings, and he could pull it off because his HBO success gave him such credibility. Bewkes's ability to move with comfort through all parts of the company made everyone assume that he was headed for bigger things. That included AOL, which Bewkes was asked to fix in early 2002. It was a position he'd quite smartly turned down, obviously aware that grabbing on to that sticky situation would hurt him.

Pittman had really had no choice in being the one to take on AOL—although I joked to him when he went back to Dulles that he'd just been handed a Tar Baby that he'd have a hard time pulling away from without damage. That was finally clear when the company announced his departure on July 18. As usual, his public statement had an odd mixture of spin and truth to it. "I've decided that after a new CEO is in place at AOL, I won't return to AOL Time Warner as chief operating officer," he said. "Having worked so hard to build the AOL service and brand, and after then going through the merger and the last 18 months, it's time to take a break." To his own staff, according to many sources, he was more honest. "Blame me for everything," he joked. "Because everyone else here will—it's a tried-and-true Time Warner tradition. No one leaves gracefully."

Pittman felt, said those close to him, that he had operated as best he could and in good faith. Others did not agree. Managers and staff at other company divisions greeted the news of Pittman's departure and the ascension of Logan and Bewkes with joy. "The Taliban have been routed," joked irrepressible Time Inc. editorial director John Huey. Finally, Time Warner had taken back the company from the horrible invaders. The gloating ran rampant.

Media pundit and *New York* magazine columnist Michael Wolff, who had worked with Time Warner on its various failed Internet efforts, took a dim view of the glee in his "This Media Life" column. Wolff correctly asked: What had Time Warner really won by purging Pittman—who walked away with a fortune—and where would that leave the company? "Of course, taking it out on the guy who out-smarted you does not, in turn, make you smart," he wrote in his slap-down style. "[Pittman] doesn't hang around a disaster area. This is show business. If the show flops, you close it. Onward and upward."

AOL's early CEO Jim Kimsey, who had long been enjoying his retirement, was even more direct, dialing Pittman up on the phone. "Is this the unemployed Mr. Pittman? Because this is the unemployed Mr. Kimsey," he greeted Pittman. "Congratulations—you moved Osama Bin Laden off the front page!"

But while Time Warnerites rejoiced in their hope that the merger turmoil was finally over, the company's troubles wouldn't leave the front pages for a long time to come.

A-O-Hell Redux

As major as it was, Pittman's departure was overshadowed by another development the same day it was announced—one that caused many to speculate that the two events were linked. They weren't, but they surely should have been. On that same Thursday, July 18, 2002, that Pittman said publicly that he was leaving, the *Washington Post* ran the first of two explosive articles detailing what its reporter Alec Klein called "unconventional deals" that AOL had made in an effort to prop up its advertising revenue both before and after the merger.

In fact, AOL's unusual ad practices had actually first come under the media spotlight after a revealing and award-winning article in the *Industry Standard* magazine the previous fall. In that article, writer Gary Rivlin had outlined in stunning detail what everyone knew about AOL's bad behavior and reputation in the industry. Rivlin had portrayed David Colburn and his team as "rough riders," branding everyone they could in a maniacal ride to the top of the heap. Although he had not zeroed in specifically on the questionable accounting for those deals, he did raise serious issues about a disturbing and unethical gestalt at the online company that was celebrated and rewarded.

Klein, the *Post*'s beat reporter on the company, took off from there, using internal documents, inside sources, outside accountants, and perhaps even government regulators eager to jack up the pressure on AOL, to scrutinize a series of AOL deals from 2000 and 2001, a time when things began to unhinge throughout the Web industry. His investigation represented exactly the kind of due diligence Time Warner should have done before the deal was sealed. Since a lot of AOL's behavior was disclosed in complex filings, as Klein chronicled clearly, these seemed like obvious things for Time Warner to have looked into.

Klein brought his first findings to AOL in mid-June. AOL hired an outside attorney, Thomas D. Yannucci, to handle the queries, hoping to dispute and upend many of the allegations Klein was pursuing, with a particular focus on those that might seem illegal but were not. The back-and-forth dragged on between AOL and Klein and his editors at the *Post* until the newspaper's publication of the series.

Titled "Unconventional Transactions Boosted Sales," the *Post*'s first front-page story described in detail several AOL deals that seemed to skirt the edges of propriety. As Klein succinctly put it, "AOL converted legal disputes into ad deals. It negotiated a shift in revenue from one division to another, bolstering its online business. It sold ads on behalf of online auction giant eBay Inc., booking the sale of eBay's ads as AOL's own revenue. AOL bartered ads for computer equipment in a deal with Sun Microsystems Inc. AOL counted stock rights as ad and commerce revenue in a deal with a Las Vegas firm called PurchasePro.com Inc." The bottom line was simple—in its quest to keep the momentum going, AOL had accepted less than quality revenues (if they were revenues at all) and had been extremely aggressive in accounting for them.

Some of the deals mentioned weren't surprising given AOL's push for synergy—including getting the Golf Channel to advertise on AOL in order to get carriage on Time Warner cable systems. Others seemed designed to book revenue as fast as possible, regardless of the business need, such as linking AOL users to a Spanish telecom site in order to use up ads in a certain quarter rather than booking the revenue over several quarters. Still others seemed like ways to make the finances seem fatter, such as booking overall revenues garnered from eBay rather than just the fees AOL got in the arrangement. Finally, others showed off a too-creative talent for creating ad revenues from stock sales—as AOL did with PurchasePro and also from legal disputes, such as one stemming from a lawsuit with an online gambling site.

Without these questionable revenues—however small they might have been in relation to the overall revenue number—the article surmised that AOL would have fallen short of Wall Street expectations in 2000. And that might have resulted in a termination of the merger, despite the lack of a collar and a possible fee that Time Warner would have had to pay to get out of the deal. While that outcome was hypothetical, the article deftly laid out the aggressive nature of AOL's deal making and its increasingly desperate efforts to delay the carnage that had decimated the rest of the Internet industry. The fact that Case, Pittman, and Kelly were giving Wall Street blue-sky assessments of AOL's prospects at the same time made the whole thing worse. Things that might have looked ambiguous in the boom now looked like malfeasance in the bust.

AOL defended itself in the piece, noting it had "maintained a strict and effective system of internal controls" and claiming the revenues in question were "truly microscopic," representing less than 2 percent of AOL's overall revenue, and therefore immaterial. It also defended its accounting, noting that it was "appropriate and in accordance with generally accepted accounting principles."

Maybe so, but it definitely looked bad. One AOL executive not involved in any of the deals called immediately and asked what I thought would happen. I said I thought that government regulators probably had no choice but to investigate the allegations, especially since the *Washington Post* was their hometown paper. Some of these same regulators may have even been a source in the series, since it was obviously going to lead to a massive investigation. While there had been no "smoking gun" in the paper's report—no explicit email, for example, where a high-ranking executive admitted to another that the deals were done to cheat Time Warner—the collective weight of the articles was undeniable.

My AOL source agreed, although he doubted AOL would become like Enron, the scandal-ridden Texas company. Still, his indictment was harsh. "There were some wild-assed assumptions that tomorrow would bring back the highly successful formula that they milked," said the same AOL executive. "But all they ended up doing was building a beautiful house on a faulty foundation."

Ted Leonsis, who was also not involved in the deals, agreed. "These ads turned out to be fool's gold," he said, noting he had gotten weary of meetings that were more about "burning off inventory fast" than about customers. "We stayed at the dance a little too long."

And, he might have added, got stuck there at the wrong time. As the AOL revelations hit the news, they got quickly sucked up into the maelstrom of Wall Street scandals over the prior nine months. From Enron's spectacular flameout to Martha Stewart's alleged insider trading to Tyco CEO Dennis Kozlowski's alleged improprieties, Wall Street ethics were under fire. Across the U.S., the white-collar executives who'd become heroes in the go-go 1990s were now widely seen as untrustworthy.

It was, in short, a bad time to be a big company, especially one with a brewing accounting scandal. And it was a worse time to be one with a history of accounting issues. AOL had already had trouble with the SEC before—and it was generally understood that the SEC tended to be less forgiving to repeat offenders. "The line between love and hate is very narrow," longtime AOL short-seller David Rocker told me in 2003. "The same behavior revered two years ago is now reviled."

The news about AOL's questionable accounting brought a new round of I-told-you-sos among its employees, who didn't give the online service any benefit of the doubt. To those at Time Warner, AOL was, at best, hugely aggressive in its accounting. At worst, it had used illegal means to dupe the media company into a merger.

Parsons would straddle the fence on that issue, since he had so little knowledge of any of the online service's deals. During AOL Time Warner's second-quarter earnings conference call on July 24, to the dismay of AOLers, he didn't launch straight into the better-than-expected numbers, which would have been immediately sent out over the business wires, giving the company an initial positive spin for the call. Instead, he started out praising the departed Bob Pittman, whom Parsons admired despite all, and the new executive structure, and then dropped something of a bombshell.

"I want also to say a few words about the importance of investor trust in our accounting and related financial disclosures," he began, mentioning the *Washington Post*'s two-part series. He offered assurances that outside auditor Ernst & Young had "confirmed in writing, without qualification, that the accounting for each and every one of the transactions mentioned in the *Post* articles, and the related financial statement disclosures for those transactions, were appropriate and in accordance with generally accepted accounting principles.

"In the circumstances," he went on, "I believe it is important to be proactive. Accordingly, I had our folks call the SEC and give them a heads up before the *Post* articles were published to assure the SEC that we would cooperate fully with any questions they may have after reading the articles." Then, he revealed the bad news. "After the articles came out, the SEC informed us that they are conducting a fact-finding inquiry."

Coming on the heels of Pittman's departure, as well as reports a few days earlier that the company was planning more layoffs in Dulles, the news of an SEC investigation made it look like AOL was falling to pieces. The *New York Post,* always eager to trumpet the company's troubles (real or imagined), put Porky Pig on its July 25 cover, next to the headline "That's AOL, Folks! Feds to Probe Media Giant's Books." AOL's stock plummeted, dropping below $10 a share, reaching an all-time low.

Less than a week later, as July staggered toward its end, word leaked out that the Department of Justice was launching an investigation as well. Unlike the SEC, which sought out civil violations of securities laws, the DOJ was focused on criminal violations. And the DOJ could issue subpoenas at will—a potentially serious distraction at AOL. As AOL marketer Jan Brandt later put it in an attempt to find some humor in the dire situation, being deposed was "sort of a part-time job when you're at AOL."

If you had a job at all, that is. Given all the attention, one executive seemed the most culpable and also the easiest to point the finger at: David Colburn, the godfather of the Business Affairs team responsible for the deals now in question. The company took immediate steps to distance itself from Colburn, although he had stayed in power through early 2002. But by the end of July, he had to give up oversight of the Business Affairs unit on a daily basis. And a little more than a week later, he was out completely just as a new CEO, Jonathan Miller, was confirmed as head of the online unit.

Colburn's ouster in mid-August came as a result of AOL Time Warner's own internal investigation, led by its law firm Cravath, Swaine & Moore. Soon enough, the investigation revealed more questionable deals—such as one with the tarnished telecom giant World-Com—related to the dubious practice of "round-tripping." This was the all-too-common dot-com era trick of making payments to a company for services, fully expecting to get them back in another form of revenue. Like many other companies, AOL had actively pursued round-tripping deals. While the practice was not illegal if done with disclosure, one AOL employee reportedly had brought emails to Cravath lawyers suggesting that Colburn might have kept some aspects of the deals from others at AOL.

AOL's lawyers had a heated confrontation with Colburn. "David, this doesn't look good," AOL Time Warner counsel Paul Cappuccio told him by phone. Colburn denied vehemently that he'd done anything wrong, insisting that all the deals had been signed off on by lawyers and accountants. Parsons called Colburn soon enough to deliver the bad news. In the atmosphere of distrust, he was out, and his office was sealed to search for evidence.

But despite news reports that Colburn had been fired, his contract forbade AOL Time Warner from terminating him without cause. When I asked a company spokeswoman in an email about the fact that Colburn was gone without being fired, she wrote back rather cryptically, "All the company has said is that David left the company." It was an odd purgatory, meaning Colburn was in a state of limbo— roundly considered guilty of something bad, but not convicted of anything at all. Colburn was to wait in atypical silence for his fate to play out.

Well, not convicted *yet,* given that more enemies would soon line up against him and other AOLers and more investigations and law-suits would pile up. As CNBC pundit and TheStreet.com online columnist James Cramer would put it, payback time had finally come for AOL, and deservedly so. "AOL had the finesse of Stalin, the sweet-ness of the KGB and the manners of the SS Druzhina and Kaminski Brigades when it came to dealing with partners," he wrote. "Some-times I would marvel to my fellow dot-commers that AOL better elect a president of the U.S., because it was making more enemies than Nixon at his savage worst."

Meanwhile, AOL's new Gromyko, Dick Parsons, had only a week after Colburn's departure to certify AOL Time Warner's financial statements to comply with a new federal law—the Sarbanes-Oxley Act of 2002. The law, the political reaction to the blame game that had gripped Wall Street in the wake of the many corporate scandals, required top executives of public companies to vouch for the accuracy of their reported results. This presented a problem for Parsons—who had little real visibility yet into the online unit's possible accounting problems—since the law also had stiff penalties of up to 20 years in prison and $5 million in fines for anyone who certified false reports.

Very quickly, and operating without much of a map, AOL Time Warner cobbled together a statement saying that the online unit might have improperly accounted for $49 million from three unspecified ad transactions spread out over six quarters. Noting that the company was still trying to determine if the accounting was appropriate, Parsons promised the investigation would continue.

Though only three months had passed, it must have seemed to

Parsons like much longer since he'd taken over the CEO job in May at the annual shareholders meeting. At that meeting, which was held at the legendary Apollo Theater in Harlem, the man who was leaving Parsons in charge had bade a moving farewell to the company. "Now I intend to just fade away," Gerald Levin had told the crowd in the theater, before offering shareholders and executives a final plea. "Have faith in this company."

If not in Gerald Levin, he probably hoped. But that was not likely to be for a long while, if ever, since Levin had become—and remains to this day—a deeply despised man in the company he helped build. Any credit he'd previously gotten for the company's successes was questioned, many of its problems were blamed on him, and his reputation had been irreparably damaged. Instead of being known as the great visionary he had hoped he would be remembered as, he was now forever to be known as the man who got suckered at the peak of the dot-com frenzy. When he struck the biggest deal of his life, Levin had likely thought it would be written, "He did this!" with glory and huzzahs. It would be said that "he did this," but instead with scorn and brickbats.

At a farewell party for Levin at Dick Parsons's apartment, there had been a revealing and amusing moment that summed it all up. Levin gave a speech that waxed poetic about many things, taking care to point out how critical Parsons's judgment and help had been to him over the years. From the back of the room, Parsons's deep voice rose up with the perfect retort: "Now don't go blaming me for things."

He needn't have worried. With Levin and Pittman gone, only one person was left who would get that blame: Steve Case.

> This is not the end. It is not even the beginning of the
> end. But it is, perhaps, the end of the beginning.
>
> WINSTON CHURCHILL

Chapter Seven

THE END OF THE BEGINNING

Case Closed?

It was weirdly appropriate, I suppose, that when Steve Case
bid his last farewell to AOL in May of 2003, he quoted
Winston Churchill, whose notoriously volatile career is now
widely seen in only the bravest and noblest of lights.

Paraphrasing the British wartime leader, as he had often
over the past year, Case noted in his speech to shareholders
gathered at a northern Virginia conference center for the
company's annual meeting, "This isn't the end, or even the
beginning of the end. It is merely the end of the beginning."

Actually, for Case and AOL, it was pretty much the end
of the end. He was stepping down as chairman of AOL
Time Warner after almost two decades of running the
online company. He had finally and correctly realized that
the rage of many Time Warner employees and major
investors would not abate until he was sacrificed in some
way. But he had also seemingly saved his head by having
willingly given up his title without losing his seat on the

board. It was one more clever move by the crafty Case to stave off losing it all.

Still, some angry shareholders—led by Capital Research and Management's stalwart Gordon Crawford—remained furious with Case even after his partial acquiescence, and fully 22 percent refused to vote to reinstate him to the board. The move added another layer of tarnish to Case's farewell, even though Time Warner's new chairman and CEO Dick Parsons had—with typical class—praised his predecessor as an important pioneer. Case had led "a revolution that introduced the Internet and connectivity to this country and the world," said Parsons generously. "This is a legacy that will be with you for the rest of your days."

Well, Case could hope so, given that his personal reputation was now in tatters at the company, in the media, and on Wall Street. The word "beleaguered" had been attached to him almost as soon as Gerald Levin had announced that he was stepping down in December of 2001. And after Bob Pittman had also cleared out in July of 2002—I think the media-savvy Pittman must have anticipated the hurricane of fury that was coming—Case had become the target of the unending anger over the deal's failure.

This was to be expected, given that this was a disaster so huge that everyone had to pay, and pay big. And, naturally, that meant Case most of all, as the man who'd been most responsible for the merger's creation, and who'd also steadfastly refused to go until the calls for his ouster as chairman had become almost deafening.

The drumbeat was constant, especially in newspaper and magazine accounts that began to pop up regularly in mid-2002. They started with simple questions about Case's role and degenerated into flat-out demands for his removal. In his July 2002 column about Pittman's departure, for example, *New York* magazine's Michael Wolff summed up the widespread bafflement about Case's position. "Case is a strange, even eerie figure," wrote Wolff. "[N]o one quite knows what to make of him. It's bewildering, and embarrassing, if you're a student of power, which almost everyone at AOL Time Warner is, not to know if someone is all-powerful, or if someone is of no consequence at all."

Soon enough, the pondering about Case's power turned to out-right analyses of when and how he would be gone. The *Wall Street Journal's* Martin Peers soon wrote a story in September 2002 titled, "Will Steve Case Leave AOL?" Calling Case a "lightning rod for intense anger at AOL," Peers detailed all the reasons why investors and employees wanted him out. Employees had "lost small fortunes when the value of their stock options was wiped out because of the collapse of the company's stock price. . . . Some staff members believe Mr. Case should take responsibility for the merger's failure, as well as for the aggressive business culture at America Online that led to questionable deals now under investigation by government authorities."

The anger was intensified by revelations that Case had sold massive amounts of company stock just before and during the merger, netting almost $400 million before taxes from 1999 to 2001, according to Thomson Financial. While he had also bought a lot of shares—some $36 million worth—in early 2002 and still held one of the largest individual stock positions at AOL Time Warner, that mattered little. And he was not alone among AOL Time Warner executives in reaping big gains—Pittman and Parsons, for example, did so as well. But for employees whose jobs had been cut, savings had been lost, and stock had tanked, the image of Case socking away a fortune while spinning his grand visions was too much to bear.

Worst of all was Case's refusal to take blame for the sorry situation in both public appearances and private sessions with employees and investors. Espousing a firm conviction that the idea of the merger was still valid, Case acted as if the obvious troubles were just another bump in the road. Even as he gave up his chairman's post in May 2003, he remained defiant. "As I step down as chairman, you might expect that I would be inclined to reflect back on the company and its achievements over the years, or use the time to set the record straight about recent events," he said. "If so, you'd be right. The temptation is great."

But while he didn't set the record straight at that meeting, Case still refused to back off his visions of what could have been—and what still could be—from the union of AOL and Time Warner. "Brighter days are ahead," he promised the shareholders. This sentiment got Case a standing ovation before he left the stage, since the audience at the annual meeting was stuffed full of AOL employees who'd driven over from its headquarters in nearby Dulles, Virginia, where Case remained an icon, admired as the greatest leader of the digital era.

Case's AOL fans also had financial reasons to revere their boss—his perfectly timed trade for Time Warner in 2000 had sheltered the company's stock from the harshness of the Web bust. Columnist Allan Sloan first made this salient point in his "Deals" column for the *Washington Post,* and others soon picked up on it.

"[Case] actually took wonderful care of his old America Online shareholders by snookering Time Warner into taking bubble-inflated AOL stock without any safeguards against price declines during the year it took the deal to close," Sloan wrote. "AOL stock is probably selling for about twice what it would be fetching without the deal." Internet stocks, as Sloan noted, were mostly down 95 percent, and if AOL hadn't merged it might have gotten as low as $6 a share, rather than languishing in the mid-teens as AOL Time Warner stock.

Even a major Time Warner shareholder who lost billions on his stock couldn't help but agree with this alternative take on Case. "Steve was fabulous for his shareholders," John Malone, the cable baron, admitted to me, even though the value of his stake in AOL Time Warner had plummeted. "They should build a statue to this guy."

But knocking down any statues of Steve Case was more the mood on the Time Warner side as Case departed the scene. Many employees remained so angry at him that it seemed nothing he could do—short of jumping off the top of the future AOL Time Warner headquarters under construction at Columbus Circle in Manhattan—would suffice. In one encounter I had with a former Time Warner employee after Case had stepped down, the wrath and hatred of Case was still so strong that I worried the employee would pop a blood vessel. This person talked eloquently, if a bit too fervently, about the "little people" at the company who had lost jobs and savings because of Case's false dreams, even as he had lined his own pockets.

While I tried to make the point that this was a complex situation, and that it was hard to boil the merger's failure down to one or two black-and-white reasons, this employee, like many, wasn't having any of it. Steve Case was, in many eyes, evil, pure and simple. And I, having spent too much time with Case and in the heady Internet sector, was too stoked up on the fumes of the Web mania to see that.

Maybe so. But I was still not certain what the true legacy of Steve Case and the entire Internet era would be. I couldn't disagree that much had been lost. But I wondered too, was there still something to salvage for both AOL and the digital future it had once led? Before I got to that, though, I had to find out how the story ended.

It Sticks in My Craw(ford), Part II

Gordon Crawford was still very, very angry.

Still piqued over the deteriorating situation at AOL Time Warner, he was now annoyed at himself too. After laying into AOL Time Warner CFO Wayne Pace in early 2002 over what he perceived as hyping by COO Bob Pittman and dissembling by former CFO Mike Kelly in 2001, the powerful media investor from Capital Research and Management in Los Angeles had decided over the spring to continue investing in the company.

He visited AOL and was heartened that executives were hard at work on a solution, even as the other divisions of the company were excelling and new CEO Dick Parsons had boosted morale. Crawford calculated that the stock price had fallen well below the potential breakup value of the various parts of the company, and he'd decided AOL Time Warner stock was being beaten down unnecessarily. It now seemed a good buy. After all, how much worse could things get?

A lot, actually, as the online unit continued its downward spiral as new accounting allegations were revealed over the summer and more signs appeared that both subscriber numbers and ad revenue were in trouble. Crawford would later kick himself for ignoring the signs he had flagged earlier.

"When there is one cockroach, one should always assume there are others," said Crawford to me in 2003. "It was a stupid mistake."

And Crawford wasn't going to make another one, especially after he began hearing more and more angry voices from his network of sources across the divisions of AOL Time Warner. Almost all the complaints were now centered on one person: Steve Case.

After Levin and Pittman had left, Case had begun to reassert himself at the company, visiting various divisions and doling out guidance on how to better achieve synergies. But few divisional executives welcomed the advice, especially coming from the man they held most responsible for the huge decline in the company fortunes, who was also a constant reminder of how Time Warner had been tricked. "To have to sit there and listen to him was extremely aggravating for them," said Crawford. "His continued presence was taking a terrible toll on morale."

As the protests mounted, Crawford took it upon himself to gather key allies among the big shareholders—beginning with Ted Turner, who had now soured on Case much in the same way he had on Levin. Crawford then contacted Malone, who had wanted to stay neutral, but agreed to hear them out in an August visit to Denver. There, Crawford and Turner made their argument to Malone.

"Their view was that it was a disaster and no one could stand to have Case around," recalled Malone. "The numbers lost were just too big, so he had to go." Lingering in the background, noted Malone, was the sense that Case had outsmarted everyone at Time Warner, a fact that further grated on them.

Since Crawford was headed east to New York for a series of meetings at various media concerns, including AOL Time Warner, the trio decided that he would be the one to deliver the news that Case should go. Crawford first met with Dick Parsons and Wayne Pace on other topics at the company's Rockefeller Center headquarters. During the meeting, Case joined the group and invited Crawford to his office when the meeting was done for a private talk.

Case might have reconsidered the invitation when he heard Crawford's definitive message: Resign. Outlining his feedback from employees, Crawford explained that neither he nor other major shareholders thought Case could be an effective chairman any longer. Case, sources familiar with the conversation said, was shocked by Crawford's frank assessment and immediately began to argue with him. Crawford was stunned when Case told him AOL was fine before the merger announcement and that he had no responsibility at the company after the deal was done. It was not his fault that the economy had tanked. It was not his fault that both Levin and Pittman had proved to be unsuccessful leaders. It was not his fault that the Internet boom had turned to bust. Case flatly informed Crawford he was not leaving.

The meeting ended with Crawford deeply troubled over Case's finger pointing at everyone but himself, and the casting of himself as a victim. The gall of it rankled the longtime investor, who expected people to take responsibility for their errors, especially if you had been CEO. Yet Case hadn't made even a slight effort at any kind of apology, claiming he was either not in control or not responsible.

What Crawford couldn't grasp was that Case had no intention of saying he was sorry when he was not. To Case, offering a mea culpa would have been dishonest. In addition, he felt it was more useful to figure out what to do next rather than wallow in blame. This was vintage Case, a behavior of moving on and compartmentalizing failure that had served him well for so long. Case felt he had little authority to do anything but a lot of responsibility to get it right.

Case called Crawford soon after he returned to his California office. "How can we patch things up?" asked Case. But Crawford's message was the same: "We can't."

Still, in the same conversation, Case asked Crawford to discuss the situation further in person when he'd be in Los Angeles on a visit to Warner Bros. in September. He and Crawford, along with AOL's Donn Davis and Capital Research and Management's David Siminoff, decided to have lunch at a private executive dining room at the film studio in Burbank. Case was nervous as they sat down, and he quickly said that he wanted to find a way to return to a productive relationship with Crawford.

"What do I have to do to become friends again?" Case joked. He noted that he cared deeply about AOL Time Warner and wanted to help rebuild value. But then he again asserted that the blame for the failed merger was not his, since Case wasn't the one running the show at either AOL or AOL Time Warner. To Case, this made sense—there were a lot of mistakes to go around, but all that mattered was where the company was now and what it should do to fix matters.

Case had no idea how badly he'd misread Crawford, who wanted neither a friend nor excuses about leadership deficiencies nor lessons about the here and now. Crawford understood that executives made mistakes, and he even thought it was okay to miss numbers—as long as you had the guts to admit that it was your fault and you didn't point fingers. Crawford told Case that he didn't hate him and didn't want to be accused of going behind Case's back to get what he wanted as a major investor, as he began to talk to AOL Time Warner board members and shareholders about his concerns. While they parted on friendly terms, Crawford didn't have a whole lot to add to what he had previously said.

And that was: Resign.

Case didn't have much to add to his prior response, either: He would not.

Meanwhile, Back at the Ranch

With the August 6 announcement of Jon Miller's selection as AOL's new chairman and CEO, the company hoped to shift the dialogue away from the stench of scandal and onto a fresh start. For a few days, at least, the tactic worked.

The 45-year-old Miller was a veteran of several media jobs. He'd worked for Barry Diller as a top executive at USA Interactive, he'd been managing director of Nickelodeon International, he was a vice president of NBA entertainment, and he'd even been in public television at Boston's WGBH. Most of all, his low-key, no-frills demeanor, so different from Pittman's glamour, made him a safe choice for AOL. And given that this was clearly a big step up for him from his former jobs, it was obvious that Miller would follow the directives of the AOL Time Warner bosses who had hired him, notably Dick Parsons and Don Logan. When I first interviewed the uncharismatic Miller, he admitted to me that he was surprised—and pleased, of course—that he had been the one selected.

If it had been up to Case, he would not have been. While Case had eventually agreed to Miller's selection, he had lobbied for the company to consider his old friend and fellow convergence believer, Thomas Middelhoff, who had left Bertelsmann in July after many disagreements with the family who controlled the private company. The energetic and aggressive Middelhoff—who was responsible for Bertelsmann making a fortune as an early AOL investor—cut a wide swath in the new-media world, even going as far as buying a stake in the controversial music-swapping service Napster.

But there would be no more such dreamers at AOL, only executives like Miller who were sure to behave and who steered clear of all controversy. In an AOL Time Warner press release, Dick Parsons emphasized Miller's squeaky-clean qualities. Miller was, he said, "absolutely the right person to lead America Online into its next stage of growth . . . He is, moreover, a person of unquestioned integrity and character, and a great team player, to boot."

Boring and well-behaved was obviously in, with one AOLer noting that "if we could have linked him to the Boy Scouts we would have." Thank god then for Ted Leonsis, who had remarkably remained at AOL even though both Case and Pittman had frozen him out of operations over the years. Leonsis was still widely admired for his bold ideas and ebullient personality, as well as his advocacy for subscribers—which is probably why he never left and why no one ever asked him to. But his long exile had rankled him, and he felt that Case had turned his back on AOL's roots by backing Pittman's moneymaking machine. Nonetheless, Leonsis still had great admiration for Case, whom he felt had only lost his way and needed to be forgiven.

Leonsis told me as much later that month, just after I started working on this book, in a short IM session. He was in high spirits about the company's new mission to rescue AOL from itself.

leonsis: [The] pendulum went too far. 2 glasses of wine is good. 5 bottles is bad . . . we have refound our north star and inner self, like a person who self-actualizes, and has a reckoning, and comes home . . .

swishk: And you are the one who survived.

leonsis: I am centered, and in love . . . it is like a wife. Even if she had an affair, u couldn't leave her . . .

And Leonsis had shown that he could not, even turning down a chance to run Time Warner's Road Runner in 1999 after Case thwarted him. After having been sidelined for several years, when he turned his attention almost fully to his sports teams, his "members first" philosophy had swung back into vogue in Dulles. On September 12, 2002, a reorganization of AOL's top ranks made it clear that his comeback was total. Leonsis, who had remained AOL's vice chairman, would now head new committees overseeing brand, product, and technology strategy.

The September restructuring radically streamlined AOL, eliminating the positions of COO and president so that Jon Miller had clear dominance. The controversial Mike Kelly, who had most recently been the COO, was named chairman and CEO of AOL International—a move that gave him a much less visible role just as the accounting scandals he soon became linked to as former CFO began receiving more attention. AOL President Ray Oglethorpe was also slated to retire. Most "friends of Bob" Pittman, or FOBs, were soon on their way out, if they had not gone already.

When I came to visit AOL in August 2002, I commented to Leonsis that it looked pretty lonely up on the fifth floor of AOL's headquarters, since just about everyone who had built the company was gone. "I am the 'Last of the Mohicans,'" joked Leonsis.

Indeed, AOL was being gutted and re-formed mostly through the dictates of Logan, who now visited weekly and took real charge of turning AOL around. Sources involved in conversations with him noted that he was deeply critical of all that came before. He questioned the poor quality of AOL's ad base, the weakness of its customer service, and—something especially irksome to the longtime mathematician—the existence of "too many metrics" to judge success.

Under Logan, the initial formula to steady the ship would be drastically simplified to one main metric: Increasing profitability per subscriber, or raising a member's lifetime value. Instead of the go-go growth of the Pittman era, which was all about slamming big numbers on the board in all areas, Logan would be all about preserving and growing the business that AOL already had. This kind of success through incremental gains was a Logan calling card. "The company had no process. It was a one-trick pony whose growth had crested," said a person familiar with Logan's thinking. "First, we needed process."

Such steadiness, as dull as it seemed, was probably just what the company needed as AOL's problems continued to mount. In September, the company lowered its revenue guidance for the online unit due to the weak online ad market. And at the end of the month, three former executives at Homestore.com pled guilty to criminal fraud charges, agreeing to cooperate with investigators who were probing AOL. Other ad deals were cratering too, including AOL's much touted but also questionable deal with WorldCom, which was canceled by the long-distance company's bankruptcy judge—lopping $180 million off of AOL's backlog of expected revenues.

With questions about Case swirling unabated and the government investigations continuing, AOL attempted to remain focused on its mission. And as it had done so many times in the past, it would turn to the Evil Empire from Redmond—Microsoft—to help goad its employees to focus.

Battling the Butterfly

On October 15, 2002, in the midst of the sniper spree that was terrorizing the Washington, D.C., metropolitan area, dozens of mid-level AOL employees caught the train from Washington's Union Station to New York City for the launch of AOL 8.0. Plugged as the beginning of the turnaround, the official program for the day included speeches, videos, celebrity appearances, and a demonstration of the new product. On the unofficial program: Corporate self-flagellation, lots of cheerleading, and some old-time redemption.

Employees, specially invited AOL members, and the press filed into Lincoln Center's Avery Fisher Hall, where they were handed giant foam hands to wave. A few Elvis impersonators milled about, while perched above a bank of computers, an artist spray-painted a live model wearing a white jumpsuit as part of some incongruous performance art piece. Inside the hall, the first 20 rows were abuzz. These were the true believers, the men and women who had watched AOL being pilloried over the past two years, and who would be the vanguard of the supposed comeback. As the lights dimmed, an air of expectation hung in the hall.

The launch was, in fact, a case study in corporate culture. Apart from the caustic musings of emcee and comic Dana Carvey, who gleefully skewered the AOL service in a short monologue, it was an absolute cheer-fest, with its share of strange moments. Who could explain, for example, the choice of having one musical guest, an unknown Italian pop star, sing a song with the repetitive refrain "I surrender"? Or Dick Parsons's introduction of "Uncle Ted," followed by Ted Turner's approximately four-second appearance on stage, where he blurted, "Watch out, Bill Gates and Microsoft! Here we come!" before immediately spinning around and retreating behind the curtain? Or Steve Case shaking his rear end at the crowd while Dana Carvey screamed "This is a TOS [terms of service] violation! Right here on stage!"?

But of all the odd moments, none topped the story Case told in the midst of a saccharine segment featuring people whose "lives have been changed" by AOL. After describing the travails of Mary and Peter, a couple who had adopted two Bulgarian sons after consulting AOL's adoptions message board, Case offered up an anecdote about meeting the boys, John and Matthew. (Case pointedly ignored Carvey as he shouted, "What happened to Luke and Mark?")

He had been talking to John and Matthew outside, Case said, when "[John] looked at me and asked, 'Are you the boss?'" After brief laughter, the auditorium went silent, and in the split second before Case spoke again, one could almost hear people's thoughts churning: Well, was he anymore? Then Case mercifully continued. "And I said, 'No, I'm not the boss,'" he said. "'The mom and the dad, they're the bigger boss.'" The crowd giggled with relief.

Toward the end of his presentation, Case grew serious. "We looked all around the world" for the perfect CEO, Case intoned. "Please welcome a champion of the members, Jon Miller!" The rows of AOL employees, most dressed in black T-shirts bearing the logo "AOL 8.0 Express. We're On Track," erupted eagerly into applause.

Here was the man who would lead the company out of the wilderness. Here was the anti-Pittman, the back-to-basics outsider who could set them back on the proper course.

Miller looked pale—perhaps fitting, in that he'd spent the previous two months holed up in Dulles for hours on end, trying to assimilate every possible fact about AOL and the Internet in record time. His remarks were as bland as his wan face, but he did offer up the marquee news of the day: AOL would no longer sell third-party pop-up ads on its service. It was a welcome change, although AOL would still continue to deliver its internally generated pop-ups. But was it all too little, too late?

One week later, Microsoft attempted to answer that question. In a bubble tent erected over Central Park's Wollman ice rink, Bill Gates introduced MSN 8.0—never mind the fact that the service had only had five versions up to that point. In every way, the tone of this launch was different from that of the AOL 8.0 launch. If AOL's was a frat-party feel-good event, the MSN launch was a very grown-up affair, starring Bill Gates, champagne, and canapés.

Gates, dressed casually in a blue open-necked shirt and olive pants, formed his trademark 10-fingered globe with his hands as he spoke. "Our commitment is to keep investing in this year after year as it moves to the mainstream," he told the crowd. Later, he added that "Microsoft is not a media company. We use channels with content that partners create, managed by software that Microsoft creates," before introducing Disney head Michael Eisner in heralding a new partnership called "Disney on MSN"—a new dial-up service aimed at Disney's core audience of families with children. (Gates glossed over a previous MSN-Disney effort to sell a premium kids' service that had been a bust.)

Though the tone of the MSN launch was quieter—practically reverent, in fact, compared to AOL's—it did have its moments of hilarity. Gates and Microsoft CEO Steve Ballmer appeared in one video dressed up as butterflies, handing out MSN CDs to bored urbanites. And in a presentation on fighting spam, Gates flashed slides of a few of his unwanted emails on the giant screen behind him. One read: "Get out of debt today!" to which the richest man in the world noted, "I didn't respond to that one. I don't think they had me profiled quite properly." Another, "Are You Frustrated About Legal Concerns?" drew this comment: "I might have been interested in this if I'd gotten it a few years ago."

Watching the two events, one couldn't help but think that AOL was the underdog of the two—even though it had three times as many paying customers as MSN. But the David-vs.-Goliath scenario had worked for AOL in the past, so somebody had obviously decided this "back to the future" tack was the right one for the times. At AOL headquarters in Dulles, cheap photocopies of anti-MSN slogans had been taped up all over the walls, with faux insights such as "Did You Know? In many parts of the world, The Butterfly has failed to evolve and is facing extinction." And, "Did You Know? The Butterfly stinks and gives off an extremely unpleasant odor when disturbed."

But despite the temporary lift in spirits that the AOL 8.0 launch brought, the bad news kept coming through the rest of the fall. Recognizing how little had been done with the new version of AOL, *Time* magazine and many others reported that MSN 8.0 was just as easy to use as AOL 8.0, had better features, and was also cheaper. In November, Jon Miller would announce that the division's traditional holiday parties would be canceled in 2002. Most disturbing, the *Wall Street Journal* warned that another massive write-off might be on the way for the company, due in large part to the declining value of the online unit.

And on October 23, AOL Time Warner's Parsons announced that the company would again revise its financial results following its own internal investigation of the ad deals that had drawn government scrutiny. On August 15, Parsons had pegged $49 million as the amount of questionable revenue related to three deals. But Parsons had spoken too soon—before CFO Wayne Pace could properly complete his internal audit of the online unit. The reduction in revenue was now $190 million, which would result in slicing a whopping $97 million off EBITDA. Parsons would also report flat earnings for the quarter, despite large gains at other company divisions, because of the continued poor performance at AOL.

At the time, Parsons promised no further restatements or surprises. In fact, he noted, with some hope, that big changes were ahead, with a public strategic overview of the roadmap to fix the online division slated for December.

The Sins of Our Fathers

To soften up the hard ground, Dick Parsons made a speech a month later at a Variety conference in Manhattan, in which he finally said it was time to stop the bloodletting inside AOL Time Warner. In an on-stage interview with *New Yorker* writer Ken Auletta on November 22, 2002, Parsons said that it was time to move on, and that those at the company who could not should then move on from AOL Time Warner. To those who continued complaining about their decimated port-folios, Parsons offered a crisp bit of advice. "I'd say, 'Look, you've got to get over that.'" AOL Time Warner couldn't, Parsons added, "go back and undo the past."

Well, I thought, when I heard he'd declared peace: *That solves that, Dick!* The remark was a year late, but it was still necessary, since AOL needed all the help it could get from the rest of the company if it wanted to right itself and keep from dragging everyone else down with it. And on December 3, the company unveiled its strategy for how that would happen at a presentation to analysts at a Sheraton hotel in midtown Manhattan.

As several hundred analysts, investors, and reporters sat in the hotel's darkened ballroom, Dick Parsons and Don Logan took turns offering up general platitudes about "working together" and having a "new start." Then Logan introduced AOL CEO Jon Miller with a joking nod to the additional hours he'd been spending holed up in Dulles. "He's been working between 80 and 200 hours a week," declared Logan in his warm Southern drawl, adding that the company had gotten "a year in four months of work, or, conversely, he's been working for minimum wage."

Spouting numbers and facts in a stiff, robotic manner, Miller looked like a schoolkid who'd been drilled all summer on spelling words and was now operating on autopilot at the big spelling bee. His prepared shtick was a recitation of each thing AOL had been doing wrong, followed by the phrase: "That . . . ends . . . NOW!"

In a tense monotone, Miller declared: "For many years, we've thought about our business in one way—how many people we brought in the front door. That . . . ends . . . NOW! We missed the first wave of broadband because we were too focused on connectivity, and too timid about pushing our product. That . . . ends . . . NOW!" And so on, through a list of about 10 sins AOL had been committing. Miller's main message was to be contrite about the past, insisting that kind of behavior was all over now, in favor of the more promising future.

The rest of the presentation laid out how AOL was going to achieve its new goals. Ted Leonsis took the stage and waxed poetic on his favorite topics: The love affair with members and AOL content. "We want our members to love us and need us once again," he said. "We want to delight them. . . . We are putting a much greater emphasis than ever on content, programming, and navigation."

That was all well and good, but it was debatable whether great content would really lure anyone new to AOL. The real issue was that legions of Internet users were switching to broadband connections—a race in which AOL had fallen far behind in the last three years. New AOL President of Broadband Lisa Hook, a Time Warner veteran, took the stage to describe AOL's new efforts in that arena. The major initiative was a "Bring Your Own Access" offering. AOL hoped to lure users who were already paying $40 or $50 per month for high-speed connections to pay an extra $14.95 per month for AOL's supposed cornucopia of valuable fare.

And AOL presumably hoped to accomplish all this with AOL Time Warner teamwork. Parsons made sure he had the right visual for the occasion, with all the division heads in the front row at the presentation—everyone across the united company now ready to lend a hand. He'd need that happy family picture, since any plans for the future seemed destined to be quickly overwhelmed by concerns of the present.

Along with the new strategies, the company announced more surprises that day—including expectations for even larger declines at the online division. Ad and commerce revenues for 2003 were expected to dive 42 percent, while cash flow would plummet up to 25 percent for the year. Miller noted that this was the year AOL would "bottom out," and he predicted double-digit growth for 2004.

So instead of focusing on AOL's new plan, most news accounts the next day dwelled on the online ad fallout that was still dragging the online division—and AOL Time Warner along with it. Attempting to look to the future, the quiet and diffident new AOL CEO, Jon Miller, had been roundly upstaged by the past.

Good-Bye to All That

And it was the past that would finally catch up with Steve Case, too, as hard as he tried to outrun it.

After his disastrous meeting with Crawford, Case reinserted himself in the process of trying to fix AOL, a process that went on through the late summer and early fall of 2002. Case started coming in more regularly to the Dulles headquarters, freely adding his typically provocative opinions about the direction of the service via emails and in meetings.

Case reached out to Dick Parsons, as well as to Don Logan and Jeff Bewkes, in an attempt to create stronger ties with the new executives running the company. In doing so, he hoped to position himself as the one who looked out for the longer-term interests of AOL Time Warner. To Case, the combined company was still operating like Europe, tugging back and forth with no central idea to inspire it. He still hoped to play the role of the strategic visionary who hovered placidly over the scene.

But there'd be only more turbulence for Case, as his critics soon grew louder. This critical free-for-all had really gotten its start back in the springtime of 2002, during a now-legendary management meeting. At that meeting, Jeff Bewkes, who was then head of HBO, questioned Case in front of everyone, expressing disdain for Case's constant harping on convergence while AOL was suffering.

Bewkes had, in fact, been conducting a long-running and friendly intellectual debate with Case for a while before the spring meeting, where strategies about how to run the company were being discussed.

There, Bewkes pushed for more recognition that AOL Time Warner was a business that straddled multiple industries, instead of harping on the fact that it was one company. In Bewkes's assessment, some of the businesses were closely related, while others were not. But Case had a different take, noting that everything should be considered through the prism of convergence. He thought each piece should be subservient to the needs of the whole, much as AOL had been run. But, Bewkes correctly countered, AOL was actually the one with the major problems and so he was not sure why they should use its ideas, since it had the most screwed-up situation. While Bewkes had been polite in his arguments, once the account of the clash got play in a *Wall Street Journal* article by Martin Peers, it was open season on Case.

As the September board meeting approached, the press began to predict that Case would be thrown out as chairman. These reports were inexplicable, since, according to the terms of the merger, Case couldn't be removed before the end of 2003 without a supermajority vote—three-quarters of the board. Case clearly had more than enough votes to stay on, including those of his close and deeply loyal associates, AOL's Miles Gilburne and Ken Novack.

And, as he'd shown in stubbornly refusing Crawford's request to resign, Case had no intention of going gently. "We're going to shame him into quitting," one big AOL investor told me at the time. Clearly, this person didn't know much about Steve Case, who had always been notoriously indifferent to any kind of external judgment. Case was a man who was difficult—if not impossible—to shame.

Meanwhile, amid the speculation, Case's position got even more complicated. The *Wall Street Journal* ran another story in late October outlining his growing frustration for AOL under the new Time Warner leadership, which Case felt might be "managed into oblivion." Case, as was typical for him, had begun goading his Time Warner critics in meetings, telling them if they didn't like what was happening with the AOL unit, they might consider spinning it off to him (or whomever). Ted Turner was apparently also advocating this idea. So while this kind of needling was merely Case's usual method for provoking debate, many took him seriously. And they were furious at his presumption.

But Case wasn't the only one floating spin-off scenarios. Possible buyout players such as Kohlberg Kravis Roberts, the Blackstone Group, and James Lee now seemed to be circling around AOL. Other big Internet players such as Barry Diller also hovered in the background, contemplating options for gaining control of AOL—which was still, despite its troubles, the biggest online service by far and worthy prey.

Case didn't actually want to unwind the deal, as he still held fast to the dream of AOL Time Warner as one powerful entity. He continued trying to build support with Turner—who by now was publicly and loudly critical of Case—and even traveled down to Georgia to have dinner with Turner at one of his buffalo-meat restaurants to listen to his gripes.

But Case's efforts lost steam with a series of setbacks both large and small. With the ascent of Parsons's Time Warner team, some began raising the question about excising the despised AOL from the company name, changing it back to simply Time Warner. And in November, attorneys filed more shareholder lawsuits against the company over AOL's accounting issues, alleging illegal insider trading, revenue and income overstatements, fraudulent business deals, and sham transactions. It was also revealed in news reports that federal regulators were investigating the activities of David Colburn and other AOL Business Affairs staffers.

A few slights seemed silly, but they intensified the overall headache anyway. At the glittery September 2002 season premiere of HBO's *The Sopranos* in Manhattan, Case was left sitting alone, with empty seats on either side of him—a supposed ticket snafu that many on his staff considered a purposeful snub. "What can I say?" said one Time Warner staffer in attendance. "No one wanted to sit next to him."

Or acknowledge his existence, either. In November, the *Washington Post* reported that at a dinner thrown by *Fortune* magazine in Washington, D.C., Case's hometown, Time Inc.'s new head, Ann Moore, accidentally introduced Dick Parsons as the chairman of AOL Time Warner. While Parsons suavely corrected her, according to the newspaper account, thanking her for the "promotion" and pointing out Case sitting nearby, it was a telling Freudian slip.

Still, Case pressed on, taking pains to link himself publicly with the changes taking place at AOL. At the December 3 strategic overview presentation, he was the final speaker, in an attempt to underscore his importance to the process. And he posted one of his old-style "Steve" letters to AOL members on the service's welcome screen that day too—but it unfortunately came off like a ghostly reminder of a time gone by.

Case seemed determined to revive the old AOL spirit. But his efforts weren't welcome, a fact that became publicly apparent on January 6, 2003, when the *New York Times*'s David Kirkpatrick took the temperature of the still hotheaded Time Warner troops, adding in new reporting on the growing displeasure with Case at AOL itself. The article painted a picture of discord between Logan and Case, noting that poor Jon Miller was now playing "a role something like that of a precocious child trying to salvage his parents' strained marriage. . . . Both men meet frequently with Mr. Miller but as little as possible with each other, leaving Mr. Miller to shuttle between them."

Noting that they had a "difference in style," the normally press-shy Don Logan was practically garrulous in talking about his frustration with Case for the article. "I am a big believer that when you give someone responsibility, you have to give them authority and let them see if they can succeed," Logan, in his typical blunt manner, told the *Times* about Miller. "That is not to say that we don't listen to Steve— we value his opinion—but it is Jon who is calling the shots and he reports to me."

In a devastating parting shot, Logan noted, "AOL has had enough, I think, of the high-profile visionary CEOs who were building the company." Ouch. Except for Jim Kimsey's early tenure before the company took off, Steve Case had been AOL's CEO for the bulk of its history.

Logan's problem with Case, in fact, was almost opposite the one he had with Bob Pittman. "If the issue with Pittman was that he could only focus on the next 30 seconds, the issue with Steve was that he only looked at the next 30 years. But at AOL, you have to think about today, tomorrow, and next year," said a person familiar with Logan's thinking. "When you boiled it down, he did not realize what the problems were. So he was not always helpful since there was no silver bullet and he had a very vocal style."

Within three days, another public smacking of Case was cued up: A CNBC show called *The Big Heist: How AOL Took Time Warner.* The cable network hyped its first primetime business documentary special as "a story of corporate intrigue, visions of grandeur, and ultimately personal failure. It's the inside story of one of the most infamous mergers in modern American business." Full of interviews with AOL Time Warner competitors gleeful at the chance to make fun of the merger, the program, not surprisingly, did not flatter Case, although Levin came off much more poignantly.

As more rounds of cuts and layoffs descended on the AOL unit, it was clear that the third anniversary of the merger's announcement, on January 10, 2003, wouldn't be quite the party Case might have imagined back at the turn of the new century. Case began to hear through backchannels that Crawford and other major investors planned to attack him publicly, both before and at the May annual meeting, by gathering a large parcel of shares in opposition to him. With enough momentum—helped in part by constant press attacks—this effort might just finish Case off. At the very least, it would be a huge embarrassment.

Crawford had been calling major investors since the late summer. Already, Crawford had Turner, Malone, and many others on his side, including some AOL Time Warner board members. He was not going away in his quest to unseat Case, and he probably held sway of at least one-third of AOL Time Warner shareholders. "Case was an irritant, especially in a managerial role," Crawford said to me. "He hurt the esprit de corps—you can't be the general when your troops want to shoot you in the back."

Another person close to Crawford offered a more descriptive take on the media investor's motivations. "He did not do it to embarrass Steve," this source told me. "Steve was just a festering boil at AOL that needed to be cauterized and removed."

But before Crawford could further push toward an ouster, Case took matters into his own hands. Over the second weekend of January, he went to his home in Virginia to decide what to do. He still felt he'd had very little authority in the combined company, but he knew he'd be held responsible for the merger's failure anyway. And it was clear that no one at the company would allow him to have any influence anymore. Case knew he had become ineffective and that he had done his best to make his points. But no one was listening any longer. "At the time of the merger he went from being a genius to almost overnight becoming a fool," said one person close to Case. "But Steve was not an idiot—it was time to go."

After talking to his wife and longtime confidant Jean, Case called Parsons and others on the board on Saturday and told them he would step down. The next day, Sunday, January 12, he announced his decision to go—a move that surprised many. For a moment, at least, Steve Case had the upper hand, since he retained his board seat. For the moment, Crawford's efforts to remove him totally from the company had been thwarted.

"Given that some shareholders continue to focus their disappointment with the company's post-merger performance on me personally," Case said in a statement, "I have now concluded that we should take steps now to avoid the possibility of that effort hindering our ability to pull together as a team and focus fully on our businesses."

Steve Case had finally ended his battle. And, given his nature, I'd bet he'll step down from the AOL Time Warner board within a year. Because amid the circus of analysis and coverage that followed, one fact stood out for those who cared to notice, which Case had downplayed. During 2002, while Case had waged his tumultuous business war, his older brother Dan had finally succumbed at age 44 after his long battle with brain cancer.

Ted Leonsis, for one, thought Case's move was a good one in light of the more important personal issue. "His brother's passing was sobering and certainly put any business losses into perspective," said Leonsis. "I think he thought, 'Who needs it?' And anyway, who knows how the story ends?"

Who Robbed Ted Turner

For Dick Parsons, the story just kept going. Within days of Case's announcement, the board voted unanimously for Parsons to succeed him as chairman. While some thought the chairman and CEO jobs should be filled by two people—a product of widespread concerns over corporate governance—most agreed that Parsons was a good salve for the wounded egos scattered throughout a company that remained in deep internal pain.

Yet new stories questioning Parsons's leadership ability popped up almost immediately, along with unfounded Wall Street rumors that Viacom's pugnacious president and COO, Mel Karmazin, was being courted for his job. And now that Parsons was the only major executive left from the original deal team, some openly wondered what culpability he should shoulder for the merger debacle.

I had expected Parsons to be next into the frying pan for this, but it was hard to make a case that he was responsible for the merger mess, considering his status as a clear subordinate to Levin. But while he was arguably not directly responsible, it was still true that he had done nothing to stop the merger. To me, that made him complicit, but probably not to blame.

In any case, Parsons, with his deep reserves of political goodwill and an amiable manner that would help calm the rage still coursing through the company, was the right kind of executive for this moment, at least—and perhaps for the longer run. After all, Time Inc. Editor-in-Chief Norm Pearlstine had pointed out to me in 2003, he'd already managed to unite the company more than Levin ever had. "I am a huge Dick Parsons fan. First of all, he knows what he does not know and relies on others who can help him figure it all out," said Pearlstine. "In a lot of ways, Parsons has really brought together the company as never before and gotten a lot more done in a very short time and under difficult circumstances—settling the TWE ownership, readying the cable for an IPO, putting the two best division heads in charge of a much more centrally run operation."

But if anyone thought Case's departure would leaven the company's stock, they needed to think again. Neither of these moves—Case out, Parsons in—really helped move AOL Time Warner shares in early 2003. In fact, the stock would soon take a new plunge downward with the incredible announcement that came at the end of January.

In yet another "surprise" of the kind that seemed to have become his signature, Parsons revealed that the company would add $45.5 billion in the fourth quarter to the already giant $54 billion charge it had announced in the first quarter. All told, the company would declare an almost $99 billion net loss for 2002—the largest in corporate history. At the same time, the company revealed that the AOL unit had suffered its first quarterly decline ever—a drop of 170,000—in its base of U.S. dial-up subscribers, which would only get worse as 2003 progressed. AOL Time Warner stock declined 14 percent on the news of the change, dragging down the whole market.

In another surprise the same day, Ted Turner announced that he would resign as vice chairman of the company. Turner had grown increasingly exasperated that he could do nothing to restore either his power or his vanished stock wealth. He was also irritated that he wasn't even considered for the chairman position, and his fortune— still mostly in AOL Time Warner stock—was dwindling by the day, with little hope of a rebound.

In typical Turner style, he publicly flagellated himself and others about the situation, while bemoaning the fact that he had little purpose at AOL Time Warner. On the weekly TV news program *60 Minutes,* Turner colorfully noted that he held a "title without portfolio, like the emperor of Japan."

I laughed when I heard that comparison, but I wasn't sure why Turner had expected much else, since he had ceded control long ago when he sold his company to Time Warner. As Barry Diller, well known for holding tight control over his assets, had noted about Turner's woes in 2002, "When you sell, you sell." To me that meant one thing: Let the seller beware.

The $99 billion charge and Turner's resignation were bombshells, but because this is AOL Time Warner, the drama had yet to end. More accounting woes were soon unveiled, followed by the inevitable herd of shareholder lawsuits with their allegations of insider trading by the company principals. In March, for example, Parsons revealed that the company was in a dispute with regulators over $400 million in advertising revenues relating to another deal with the German media giant Bertelsmann.

In a complicated deal led by Mike Kelly and based on longtime agreements, AOL Time Warner had agreed to buy back Bertelsmann's

49 percent stake in their joint subsidiary, AOL Europe, over time for $6.75 billion in cash rather than the $8 billion that had previously been agreed to. Bertelsmann obviously preferred cash, although AOL had the option of using stock.

One of the enticements for AOL to use cash was the price discount—but there was also a simultaneous deal for Bertelsmann to buy $400 million worth of ads on the online service. Regulators contended that the revenues were actually a "forced purchase" and should have been accounted for as a reduction in price, an interpretation AOL Time Warner disputed. Unlike some of the other questionable ad deals, this one was made after the merger, when it was harder to target only AOL executives as the bad actors. Later, the company noted it might have to cave to government demands on the issue to move forward with its cable IPO.

Other troubles hung over Parsons's team too, including the need to sell assets in a down market in order to cut AOL Time Warner's giant $27.5 billion in debt; the difficulty of completing a much-needed IPO of its cable division while government investigations loomed over the company; and the complexity of moving into its spanking new headquarters at Columbus Circle, which was costing the company billions. And, even AOL's once-vaunted ability to attract subscribers took serious hits, as practices to goose numbers—such as selling accounts in bulk to marketing partners—were suspended.

"Heavy hangs the head that wears the crown," Parsons joked at the annual meeting in May, when asked about how he felt regarding the tough tasks ahead of him. As Case had paraphrased Churchill's famous quote, Parsons had changed Shakespeare's well-known line from *Henry IV, Part II*, which actually reads, "Uneasy lies the head that wears the crown." Parsons's version was surely kinder to himself, since the latter version, of course, suggests a scenario where one might actually lose one's head.

That would be the fate left for Ted Turner, who became more erratic as 2003 went on, giving some funny but ultimately sad interviews about his many losses and disappointments. In one *Fortune* piece in May, appropriately titled "Gone With the Wind," he waxed on about his troubles—financial, personal, emotional, and even planetary. "I think the chances are 50-50 that humanity will be extinct in 50 years," he declared in the article, in which he somehow also compared longtime media mogul foe Rupert Murdoch of News Corp. to Adolf Hitler.

While Turner ended up staying on the board, he ended his reign as a huge shareholder at the same time he stepped down as vice chairman. On May 5, 2003, he sold almost half his AOL Time Warner shares—50 million shares of his own and 10 million he had transferred to a charitable trust—in order to "diversify his financial holdings." At a price of about $13.38 a share the day of the transaction, Turner would soon end up on the short end of the stick—um, stock—again. By the time of the May 16 annual meeting, AOL Time Warner stock had risen by $1 and by the end of the month by $2 from when he sold. That meant, within one month, Turner lost an upside potential of $120 million.

Perhaps I had found my answer to who had really robbed Ted Turner. There were many culprits, along with some bad ideas, an economic boom and a bust, poor business decisions, and questionable accounting.

But most of all, I would have to finally conclude, it was Ted Turner himself who had actually robbed Ted Turner.

It Never Rains in California

It was, improbably for the middle of winter, a perfect night in Silicon Valley.

The rain that had been dribbling in off the coast had cleared, and the fog was gone. It was February of 2003, and the exceptional weather was just right for the Valentine's Day party I'd been invited to. The host was that very same venture capitalist who had offered me the $10 million napkin back in the salad days of 1999.

I walked toward his lovely home, with its pool and wine cellar and big sparkling windows that looked out onto lush lawns. The faintest scent of wet eucalyptus hung in the night air. Just beyond the house, I could see a softly lit, transparent tent that glowed with the kind of bonhomie I hadn't witnessed in years.

Inside, the crowd was full of tech players such as Yahoo's Jerry Yang, telecom pioneer Craig McCaw, and a passel of venture capitalists and entrepreneurs who had survived the vicious bust. But rather than looking defeated, as I'd expected them to, they were animated, they were enthusiastic—they were happy.

I was a bit surprised that everyone was in such a good mood, since the last several years had been about as kind to those gathered here as it had been to Steve Case, who had stepped down as chairman of AOL Time Warner a month before with his dreams of digital dominance dashed. It had been a very tough time to be in tech after so many up years. And no one here had much to look forward to, since little energy—or money—was flowing through the tech scene even after the years of drought. Investments in tech startups, for example, were just then hitting a five-year low from their peak—which happened to have been the first quarter of 2000, or the exact moment of the AOL Time Warner merger. In that golden quarter, a record $28.6 billion was pumped into 2,169 companies.

That time seemed a long way away for this group, but it seemed even further away for another gathering taking place at the very same moment across the country, in frigid Manhattan. There, in the Ritz-Carlton hotel in Battery Park, AOL Time Warner was holding an offsite management confab for a couple hundred senior executives. The choice of location—not far from the empty hole where the World Trade Center towers once soared—was unfortunate, and the mood inside the room was tense, especially for the group from AOL.

With Time Warner now in ascendance, it was clearly payback time. The morning started off badly, with a few Wall Street analysts giving their take on the company's prospects. Right away, Ray Katz of Bear Stearns came out with a line that set the tone for the day: In describing the AOL unit and uncertainty over its broadband efforts, he compared it to "the pimple on the face of a beautiful lady . . . you can't keep your eyes off of it."

Next up, there was an interview session led by Time Inc.'s acerbic editorial director John Huey—the same man who had jokingly likened AOLers to the Taliban when Bob Pittman left the company—where Jeff Bewkes and Don Logan talked about the future of AOL Time Warner. The trio, assessing the company's prospects, made a number of cracks about AOL. Bewkes also offered up a zinger about Gerald Levin's new love life, noting with mock astonishment that the austere former CEO was getting "more action than me." It was a bit of a surreal moment for those in attendance, who did not often link Levin with sex.

"It was not a nice morning," recalled Joe Ripp, the former Time Warner CFO who was now working at AOL. Other AOLers were similarly upset. So Ripp decided to try to change the tone in an afternoon question-and-answer session.

After checking with Parsons beforehand, Ripp stood up in the session and asked him how he felt about AOL. Ripp attempted to smooth things over, telling his former Time Warner colleagues, "I'm now [at AOL], and I see 19,000 people working hard every day . . . and I was from Time Warner and I know you all have pimples on your butts." The ever-diplomatic Parsons gave a positive answer, and he offered an honest yet logical appraisal of the bad feelings many in the room had toward AOL. It wasn't that Time Warner people didn't like AOL employees, Parsons suggested, but that they were angry with them. And it was easier to direct anger at people than at an institution.

Parsons's assessment couldn't have been more wrong: The Time Warnerites still couldn't stand AOL. The group got even bolder, especially after Parsons soon miscalculated and took a question from Warner Bros. executive Alan Horn, who expressed a desire to lop the AOL clean off the company name. In a kinder suggestion, Warner marketing honcho Brad Ball suggested a name change might actually help AOL recover its tarnished brand name.

Before Parsons had a chance to close down this line of discussion, others jumped in, and Horn was soon enough lecturing the group on how it should be an honor to have your name on a corporation, and how he didn't think AOL's name was appropriate. This struck many present as absurd, considering the thuggish and excessive reputations of many in Hollywood. As Ted Leonsis put it, "I found it ironic to have a movie studio executive talking to me about integrity, honesty, and lifestyle."

Mercifully, when Horn asked to put the name change question to a vote, Parsons cut him off. Despite Parsons's efforts, the AOL group was shell-shocked at the continuing acrimony. AOL head Jon Miller was particularly dispirited, and later described to me the AOLers' desperation to get away from the event and the dinner scheduled for that night: "We're all looking at each other and thinking, 'So, what restaurant do you want to go to?'"

The AOLers did end up staying for the group dinner—only to get ribbed some more by comedian Wanda Sykes, who noted that AOL's table behind the small WB network was a very bad sign. She compared Steve Case to Joe Millionaire: "He's good-looking and nice, but he ain't got no money!" Sykes joked. She also noted that Case was not there, but if he were, the group could come up on stage and "kick his ass." Sykes also got a good one off on Parsons, noting that there was no need for affirmative action "when a black man loses $98 billion and he doesn't lose his job."

Despite the comedy, Leonsis and others were still disgusted, even after a few Time Warner executives came over to the AOL table to apologize. "Well, that was certainly motivating," Leonsis noted dryly, before warning the executives that they should be careful what they wish for. "What if we all go home and quit, and say, 'If you guys are so smart, why don't you run it?'"

The AOL group being harassed in Manhattan would surely have gotten a much better reception at the party going on in Silicon Valley. While the tech industry had always disdained AOL for its simplistic technology, many at that party and throughout the sector still wouldn't think of slapping around AOL in such a manner. After all, AOL had managed to do what no one else had done: Bring tens of millions of mainstream customers online. By popularizing the online experience, AOL had solidified its place in tech history.

And without AOL, the entrepreneurs and investors of Silicon Valley knew that many businesses that had survived the bust—Yahoo, eBay, Amazon, and others—would never have been as powerful as it looked like they would surely become in the future. And they couldn't help but admire the money AOL had made for so many in the market. Even taking into account the downturn and all the stock declines, $1,000 invested in AOL at the end of 1992 was now worth almost $58,000. Of course, if you had put your money in during 2000, you'd be down almost 50 percent, so it was easy to understand the Time Warner rancor.

But this group didn't seem to care about that, or about the blame being heaped on Steve Case. Yes, Case might have failed—but failure was a familiar part of the tech scene, and it was more often celebrated than maligned. I often found myself amused at the constant rewriting of history that took place in Silicon Valley, and at the way techies always managed to make utter disaster seem like nothing more than a learning experience.

Failure was arguably seen as admirable, since only those who had lost something were of value to the next phase of innovation. No one was better equipped to handle problems than someone who had been burned once. At the party that February night, numerous guests told me they intended to ask Case and other seemingly disgraced AOLers to serve on the boards of the various startups they were cooking up. They wondered what Case would do next, and compared him to another tech phoenix, Apple's Steve Jobs, who had returned in triumph long after many had counted him out. Most of all, it was clear the group at the party had a high regard for Case's chutzpah—even if it hadn't helped him much at AOL Time Warner. For these risk-takers—or, more accurately, these people who considered themselves risk-takers—Case's catastrophe was just another bump in the road.

Even so, not everyone at the party felt that way. I ran into one old-style venture capitalist who hadn't much liked the whole wacky dot-com explosion even when it was happening. I'd first met him when I was working on *aol.com,* and he had been grumpy about AOL then too. He didn't like the company from the start, because of its aggressive accounting, shifting business plans, and overblown stock.

"I just don't get it," he'd told me in 1997, just as AOL was really soaring into the market stratosphere. Now, with AOL in ruins, he pointed his finger at me and teased: "See, I was right! It was all craziness." He left out, of course, the fact that his firm and many others had made a mint on that very craziness before everyone had wised up.

But he was, I guess, echoing a now-common sentiment that another legendary tech financier named Don Valentine had offered up at a public forum on the pioneers of the venture business at a computer history museum in Silicon Valley in October 2002. Speaking about the bust and the insanities of certain digital investments, Valentine was quoted by the *Boston Globe* as having said that aliens had come to the tech industry and drugged everyone. "We all took stupid pills and now we're all better," he joked.

"All better," of course, is a relative term. Ted Turner had still been robbed. Beverly Sills was presumably still confused. The once admired architects of the AOL Time Warner merger were still dogs. And I was still flummoxed.

When I first started to search for answers to the ultimate legacy of AOL, I asked media columnist Michael Wolff for his take. He and I had long disagreed about AOL, but I always admired his sharp analysis and point of view. "We can go on arguing this point," he emailed me flatly. "[But AOL] was always more an illusion of a company than a real company."

Part of me, I had to admit, knew he was right. But at that Silicon Valley party, looking back on the clear proof that so many lives have already been changed in profound ways by email, the Web, cell phones, and a plethora of interactive devices, and with the excitement and new ideas about the digital future still swirling around in the warm night air, I had to admit I was still a believer. And no matter the cost of its failure, AOL might still be an important factor in shaping the future—a future that will continue to be profoundly changed by technology.

Yes, a lot of what AOL and Steve Case had promised was bunk, and they had been found out and punished. And a lot of what the people at the party were so excited about—wireless networks, fully electronic markets, boundless pools of interactive information available everywhere—might turn out to be more of the same.

But I also believed that these kinds of idealistic visions were achingly American, and something that no amount of naysaying would ever stop. They're hope and hype and lies and truths, all rolled into one— so much so that it's simply impossible to separate them.

Because no matter the regrets, the rage, and the recriminations, on a lovely night such as this in Silicon Valley, it was just too easy to take stupid pills again and dream all new dreams.

Epilogue

A PORTFOLIO OF PERSPECTIVE

Watching the Signs

For months, whenever I went to do interviews at Time Inc. headquarters, in the Time-Life building on the Avenue of the Americas, I walked right by one particular sign in the lobby without paying any attention.

But on one of my last visits I finally noticed it—a window ad with a motto that all these people, so battered by the AOL Time Warner merger debacle, had had to put up with all this time. Plastered in front of a walk-in Fidelity brokerage was a huge poster with this advice: *"The most valuable thing you can put in your portfolio right now is perspective."*

The thing is, I'm not sure there is enough perspective in the world to assuage those who had suffered under the disastrous marriage with AOL. After talking to many people for many months about the merger and its aftermath, I'd concluded that any reflection on the benefits AOL might bring to the company would still be a long time in coming. This was especially true for the Time Warner side of the company, which remained paralyzed by anger and decidedly unable to embrace the digital future. An "imposed narrative"—a phrase I had heard writer Joan Didion use to describe a story that had become cast in the cement of conventional wisdom—had been set concerning Time Warner's forays into cyberspace: They were all a terrible mistake, most especially its union with AOL.

And yet, this was not so. While I hate to agree with a come-on for a stock-selling firm, I must invoke Dick Parsons here: It is time for AOL Time Warner to get over it. Because no matter the employees' feelings about AOL, the future of the company—and of many others like it—will be deeply impacted by the changes technology will continue to bring. Two important and intertwined truths lie at the heart of finding out where the digital world is going. The first truth: The tidal wave of technological change continues to advance. And the second truth: Tough times are often the best times in which to lay foundations for the next phase of digitization.

And so, now that the hype and agonizing have almost worked its way through the system—an uncomfortable journey that has always been part of major technological leaps—it's time to take measure of the landscape. Why? Because post-boom, post-bust, the moment has arrived to figure out what this flood of digital innovations will do to AOL Time Warner in the decades ahead.

I know it's easy to sneer at this kind of dreamy hopefulness. Not having lost my savings, my job, or my belief in some company I'd spent my life building, I probably have no right to urge a company like AOL Time Warner forward. But, even surveying the carnage of the merger, I firmly believe that all things will be touched and transformed and improved by what the next digital era will bring, especially for huge media companies like AOL Time Warner. And while you can't go back and repair all the stumbles and missteps that have been made along the way, there really is no other way but to press on. Everyone may be limping now, but things are moving forward nonetheless, especially since young people, the next generation of media consumers, are.

One need only recall an on-target prediction made by Marshall McLuhan in his 1960s landmark book, *The Medium Is the Massage,* which applies even more today. "Innumerable confusions and a profound feeling of despair invariably emerge in periods of great technological and cultural transition," he wrote, although he was referring to very different technologies than interactive ones. "Our 'Age of Anxiety' is, in great part, the result of trying to do today's job with yesterday's tools—with yesterday's concepts. Youth instinctively understands the present environment—the electric drama."

Dreaming new dreams was what AOL Time Warner's other Ted—Ted Leonsis—was trying to do when I last visited him at his office in Dulles, Virginia, in the spring of 2003. Now the head of AOL's flagship online service, Leonsis was sassy and defiant, as usual, trying to figure a way out of the mess. As usual too, he had a million ideas—some of them good, others not so good, but all of them interesting.

He joked about the sorry state of the AOL division and about his wife, who had, he related, told him it was time to "get off the stage." She'd made him write up a list of friends who had retired and were enjoying life. But rolling and twirling his chair across his small office (quite nimbly, in spite of his girth), he tried to approximate with his meaty hands what it was like now trying to turn the rudder on the business. And, as was his style, he randomly dispensed a series of sound-bite insights about the disaster, even as he spewed ideas about the digital future.

"We are a division of a group of a corporation, and I am a middle manager working to get my gold watch," he joked.

And also, "We have clarity now, but no hero."

And also, describing a recent meeting with *Sports Illustrated* magazine over the cost of licensing exclusive content for AOL users, he told me, "Now they are shaking us down like the Mafia, which they used to accuse us of being . . . it's all in the eye of the beholder."

Leonsis made me laugh, even though there didn't seem to be a whole lot that was funny at AOL, which Time Warner was still treating like a leper. Despite Parsons's admonitions in late 2002, internal bashing was still going on, although many insisted it was not. By now, this was just bad business, as another longtime and well-respected AOL product executive, David Gang, pointed out in a 2003 interview with me. Fretting about the anger he still felt from the Time Warner side, he asked, "Do they really want to say, 'I killed you, but in the process I cut off my arm and lost my eye'?"

Leonsis had his own prescription for that particular attitude. "The

Time Warner anger is just noise . . . and we have to remove the rear view mirror to move ahead," he told me. "The only way to reclaim the moral high ground is to make AOL great again."

Oh, is that all? Because by then, I was beginning to feel that it might just be too late for AOL, which seems to have paid for its many sins by becoming irrelevant. I felt sorry to think this way, after all the time I'd spent believing in the company's prospects while others had made fun of it. Now, almost 10 years later, had I finally reached the point where I thought it was curtains for AOL? Things certainly look bad for the company that made history by casting itself as the lead character in a digital *Perils of Pauline*. This time, it finally seemed that AOL, strapped to the railroad track, might not be rescued in time.

The first problem was time itself. Internally, AOL had only 18 months from the fall of 2002 to turn things around—meaning that things had to start looking good by the end of 2003. "Parsons told me, 'Deliver what you say and I am your greatest fan,'" AOL CEO Jon Miller recounted. "If not, who knows?" Indeed, to Wall Street and reporters, Parsons seemed to be drawing a line in the sand, making a promise that he would be able to fix AOL's problems pretty fast.

There had been some precedent already for Wall Street to accept such a story. By May of 2003, Yahoo's Terry Semel was being praised on the cover of *Business Week* for reinvigorating the troubled online company, for example. Wall Street was impressed, too, as Yahoo was showing strong progress in both online ad sales and expansion of paid premium services, a feat that had given a $20 billion valuation to Yahoo. With AOL's many more assets and stronger brand, and despite its higher costs, surely AOL's executives could at least keep up.

But there was also a devastating morale problem at AOL, stoked by cost cuts, layoffs, press attacks, and that persistent feeling that AOL was now—as David Gang had quipped to me—the "ugly stepchild" of Time Warner. The formerly vibrant culture had badly degenerated with all the changes that whipped through on a daily basis.

Cost cuts would doubtless remain a fact of life, but Jon Miller told me he was desperately trying to turn around the dysfunctional situation at AOL by turning its employees into "buyers and sellers"—

meaning everyone would better understand his or her role. By formalizing job descriptions and making responsibilities clearer, he hoped to limit the endless email debates that cluttered up employees' workdays. Yet he didn't pretend that things would change overnight. "My message: It ain't perfect here and it ain't gonna be," Miller said he told employees. "Let's just go to work."

Miller had recently spent some time visiting the company's other divisions, and he related an anecdote he'd told them to try to help move the relationships forward. "Have you ever had your car towed in New York?" he said he'd ask executives in other divisions. "When your car gets towed, there's a sign at the place where you go to pick it up that says, 'The person behind this window did not tow your car. If you cooperate with them, you will get your car back quicker.'"

But the question I'm sure many of them were thinking was: Would Miller be returning the car intact, or would it be the wreck that everyone was expecting?

The Inevitable Future

That, of course, depends on a lot of things that have to do with the past. Because if it is any guide, the Internet will be an even bigger deal in the future than it was when it first burst onto the scene.

The history of technological evolution is proof of that: Innovations first cause a frenzy, and then flame out and are sometimes widely discounted before they ultimately reveal their true power. I'm always reminded of this truth with a quote, from an 1876 Western Union internal memo, that I keep pasted to the side of my computer screen. "The 'telephone' has too many shortcomings to be seriously considered as a means of communication," some doubtlessly intelligent Western Union executive wrote then. "The device is of no value to us."

I keep that quote with a bunch of others I've saved that deliver the same message. Ken Olson, president, chairman, and founder of Digital Equipment Corporation, 1977: "There is no reason anyone would want a computer in their home." Thomas Watson, chairman of IBM Corporation, 1943: "I think there is a world market for maybe five computers." And, of course, Bill Gates, chairman and co-founder of Microsoft Corporation: "640K ought to be enough for anybody."

Bill Gates certainly wouldn't have been celebrating the 20th anniversary of the personal computer in 2001 as the richest man on the planet if that particular prediction had come true. The PC most definitely underwent a vicious shakeout after its introduction. And the same thing happened to the Internet, which celebrated the 10th anniversary of the famed Mosaic browser in 2003. As the first commercial Internet decade comes to an end, the froth has finally worked itself out of the system, with 5,000 companies having gone bust since the high point in 1999. Now, with the anger at the popping dot-com bubble (writer Mike Kinsley astutely noted that "no one minded the bubble itself") as the result, it makes it a good time to take stock.

First, and please don't scream, I believe that the Internet is still under-hyped. Venture capitalist John Doerr first made that startling remark in 1995 and was forced to apologize for it in the bust. He shouldn't have—unless he was referring simply to the stock market and then there should be I'm-sorrys into eternity. But the medium remains the fastest-growing in history, becoming widespread quicker than telephones, radio, and televisions. And it still has yet to penetrate the global market as significantly as it will. With the twin prospects of even more new features and improvements in ease of use still ahead, the interactive space is obviously in the very early stages of the game.

And the growth will only continue, as the Internet quickly becomes akin to electricity in homes and businesses. A recent Pew Internet and American Life Project survey reported that more than 60 percent of respondents said they used the Internet routinely, and that two-thirds had been using the Web for several years. Studies like this have become commonplace, and all have the same theme: Internet usage is no longer special, but a regular part of daily life. Like electricity, the telephone, or the television, the Internet is on its way to becoming invisible—you only notice it when it's *not* there.

Now, a decade into it, the interactive arena has matured. It has achieved growth on an unprecedented scale, and has changed the way we work and play. It is also now a pillar of our economy, rather than a quirky little sector consisting of a few small companies. Yet, I wish sometimes that I could go back to those very first days when I started covering the Internet. When the money didn't matter. When the whiff of ideas was fresh. When words like "multiple revenue streams" and "network effect" didn't exist. When there were no Jeff Bezoses and their goofy grins gazing out from national magazine covers.

I realize, of course, that this kind of the-past-was-pure sighing makes me sound like a bit of a dope. But I am a bit of a dope when it comes to watching what kind of mutations have developed around the Internet. It's a place that still amazes me, with its ability to resist the pressures that have made most forms of media a kind of dead zone of ever-diminishing expectations and little dynamic growth. Today, most traditional newspapers, magazines, networks, and radio are sadly predictable and severely boring.

Not the Internet. As online pundit and columnist Scott Rosenberg pointed out about the Web in a spot-on piece in the *Salon* online magazine: "It just sits there, center stage, after the curtain has dropped behind it, thumbing its nose at the booing crowd: The Internet itself hasn't gone away. Hundreds of millions of people around the world continue to bend it to their own ends, in chaotic, unstable and unpredictable ways. As a generator of instant wealth, the Net may now be a big bust; as a generator of instant ideas, it keeps thrumming along."

But, even though it is clear that the Internet market will continue to grow, what does that mean for AOL? AOL—and here I'm talking solely about the online service—certainly faces numerous problems as it attempts to go forward. As everybody knows by now, it suffers from rapidly declining subscriber growth, weakened ad revenues, a need to switch to broadband for its dial-up subscribers, a loss of experience at top-level positions, the shadow of government investigations and shareholder lawsuits, and a loss of confidence from the investment community.

With all that, will AOL, as powerful as it has been, even manage to make it to the next phase of the Internet? Or was the first part of the Internet ramp AOL's one great moment to shine? Will it now sputter out, having outlived its usefulness? And, will Time Warner's anger, even as it cools, allow AOL to thrive?

That is perhaps the most critical question, especially since speculating any longer on what could have been or wishing that the merger had never come to pass seems pointless now, even though the inclination to do so seems entirely justified. But such recriminations may end up hindering forward progress that everyone at both AOL and Time Warner wants to make now. Former AOL executive Richard Hanlon wrote me an eloquent and sad email right after Steve Case resigned that illustrated the cost of such regrets.

"What worries me is that the story is about so much more than failure and punishment. Steve's resignation absolutely brings that home to me. To the extent that it is greeted with gloating, it seems to dismiss the fact that an enormous amount of work was done to produce something other than failure, and to discount the larger fact that a vast amount remains to be done," he wrote. "I fear that the bitterness at much of Time Warner may blind them all to this. If so, this will be a lot more than the only war that began with the declaration of a truce: The departure of Steve Case and many at AOL will guarantee their adversaries the greatest Pyrrhic victory in business history."

How to Fix AOL in 13 Easy Steps

One thing is certain: At this moment, in terms of subscriber growth, ad revenues, momentum and innovation, as well as reputation, AOL is in decline. Stuck in what seems to be an unpredictable and slow growth cycle, it's skittering along while executives search for ways to reinvigorate it. One competitor recently likened it to a "jalopy."

But to begin, let's not act as if all hell is breaking loose—AOL is still a very reliable cash machine for the larger company, spewing out $1.5 billion in cash flow annually. This is a major plus for AOL as it moves forward. While it's a dangerously declining number—down from $2.3 billion in 2001—it allows AOL some flexibility in its choices going forward. Still, the online unit is valued negatively, while smaller competitors garner multibillion-dollar valuations.

The question then—which is being asked over and over again at AOL Time Warner—is this: How do you get full value of the assets?

Three main scenarios have taken root among those both inside and outside the company:

1. Milk it by cutting costs and employees, limiting new investments in technology or offerings, and continuing to make money on its dwindling dial-up user base.
2. Leverage its massive member base and brand name into more promising businesses, spending on software and other improvements, and take the risk that it might not pay off.
3. Sell it off, in parts or whole, to companies better able to take advantage of the assets and more open-minded to the possibilities.

This may be simplifying it, but I think the answer to repairing AOL resides in a weird combination of all three, especially as you list the various facets of the online company that are key to its success or, alternatively, its failure. Here's a list of current problems and their possible solutions.

Problem: Lack of Passion

Passion was a longtime strength in AOL's early history—the problem was that it turned too much into lust for a high stock price. Yet the necessity of renewed passion cannot be underscored if AOL is going to reassert itself. While AOL—located on the East Coast rather than in the red hot center of Silicon Valley—has never been a font of techie energy, or talent, it always had an employee base that was missionary in its goals. That energy is clearly still present at fast-growing Internet companies like eBay, Amazon, and Google, and it's an important part of their ability to attract and keep top employees.

Even longtime companies like Microsoft still have that hard-charging feeling, as exemplified by the fact that the world's richest man, company co-founder Bill Gates, comes to work daily and says he still sees his mission as unfinished. Although they must move out of start-up mode as they mature, very few tech companies can operate on autopilot or become complacent if they want to stay competitive. But with poor morale and a mood of being cut to pieces rather than on the cutting edge, AOL's energy seems sapped.

Solution: This is a tough one, since you can't just order people to get passionate about their jobs. Given the constant belittling of AOL in the press and from the other divisions of AOL Time Warner that is only now waning, I think it'll be pretty hard for management to find a way to excite employees. The departure of Steve Case, an icon at the company, probably didn't help, but the continued presence of cheerleaders like Ted Leonsis is a good thing. I suspect the only thing that will return passion to this company is a measure of success. But one thing is certain—it's important to keep as many of the more experienced people working at AOL as possible, especially the cheerleaders.

What I worry most about are the phrases I began to hear almost constantly about AOL from high-ranking corporate executives at AOL Time Warner—"we need to stabilize it," "we need to bring it under control," "we need to put in a process." I know what they mean—AOL has long been a management mess, chaotic and hard to understand. But in imposing order, I fear that the new managers will also drown out more essential elements of spirit that are harder to reignite. AOL has already suffered from too many khaki-wearing MBAs with little feel for the product. It needs more dreamers.

Problem: Lack of Product Innovation

Simply put, AOL has long ignored its basic product offering to consumers. It has inexplicably allowed its software to atrophy, despite the periodic and noisy rollouts of new versions. But AOL should have assessed its product more honestly. Aside from a few fluffy new features, very little of substance has been added to the main dial-up product for years now. Amazon makes more improvements to its online commerce tools in one day than AOL makes in hundreds.

And therein lies the problem: The Web continues to both innovate and simplify, getting closer to becoming one big version of AOL. Even AOL's chat areas, once a major attraction (especially for sex chat), seem poor compared to the more sophisticated tools now available on the Web. And AOL's email tools remain weak in comparison to Yahoo's, relying too much on adding more and more silly icons. The service also continues to be impossible to navigate beyond the front screen—hasn't anyone at AOL ever heard of a table of contents?

And don't get me started on the spam issue—I know it's hard to fix, but fix it anyway. Without better spam filters—and soon—AOL will lose its two most important constituencies, women and children.

Solution: AOL's product guru, David Gang, who is hard at work on this problem, was pretty blunt. "We have let our product get shitty," he said. "But if you put out a great product at a great price, consumers will buy it." *Uh-huh.* First, as Miller also noted, AOL has to "innovate the essential and blow away with the basic." By that, he's referring to updating and improving the stalwart parts of AOL—email, news, chat, IM tools, and anti-spam tools. After that, AOL has to slowly lace in new stuff being used on the Web, clean up its clutter, and help its users find what they want. As everyone races to the next new thing, AOL needs to be a fast follower.

AOL has certainly ramped up its metabolism, finally making meaningful changes in its latest version—9.0—in mid-2003. Coming quickly on the heels of the weak rollout of 8.0, AOL has added important anti-virus software, stronger spam filters, and parental control tools, better ability to personalize screens, improved mail management, sassier communications and chat features and well-integrated multi-media offerings. That's good for AOL, except these changes were *years* overdue and already present in a plethora of other competing services. AOL now has to keep pace and even surprise its users again if it wants to keep them using the service. It is not the jalopy that its rivals like to call it, but neither is it offering that new-car feeling.

Problem: Lack of Customer Service, Declines in Subscribers

More and more, these two issues have gone hand in hand. For years, AOL—well known for abusing any member who had a problem—always had a willing pool of new customers it could keep marketing to in order to replace those who churned off the system. This is obviously no longer the case, as the numbers of prospects AOL can draw from have dwindled and are going negative in the important U.S. market.

This dial-up market, as everyone knows by now, is static as more and more consumers replace their slower connections with faster—and pricier—broadband ones. On the opposite end, low-cost dial-up services are proliferating and growing by stealing business from AOL.

Millions will leave the service over the next two years, this is a near certainty. There will be a level at which AOL will stop bleeding customers, since many people—including myself—like to have a dial-up alternative for traveling and others are satisfied with the AOL experience. But AOL's future lies in keeping happy the current customers it has and generating more incremental revenues per member, rather than nabbing new ones.

Solution: There's no magic here, except to increase customer service initiatives to turn around what AOL insiders tell me is very low member satisfaction. Instead of rolling out new versions—a practice the tech industry is addicted to—AOL now says it will be adding useful features and tools on a daily basis and improving problems more regularly. This is a good thing. The AOL customer, I suspect, does not want to be wowed as much as well served, and the simple ability to get through to the company goes a long way.

New ways of marketing to customers are also needed, and I'd drastically cut the marketing budget and funnel the money to more useful research and development projects. Others disagree, noting that AOL must remain a ubiquitous marketer like Coca-Cola. But I think that money is better spent on other more worthwhile initiatives that would have a big impact. Why not, as one former AOL executive suggested, appoint a central "Spam Czar," whose only job is to rid the service of those irksome emails? Dumping pop-ups is a good first step, but ending AOL's annoying inability to mesh with lots of other popular Web applications would be a much better one. And what about a price cut?

Problem: Loss of Community Roots

One of AOL's greatest accomplishments was recognizing how important its robust online community was to its users. This was how AOL got popular in the first place and how it roared past other competitors. A lot of AOL's "genius," in fact, actually lay in simply getting out of the way of customers and letting them define the service. When people get online—much as those online quilters I met at AOL had done long ago—they do what they want and in ways that are impossible to program. No media company can control this, and they shouldn't even try. The proliferation of Web logs, or "blogs," in which people post their own diaries, opinions, and reactions to other blogs, is the latest iteration of this trend, and it has exploded in popularity and has had huge impact on politics and culture. Inexplicably, AOL was nowhere in this space, until its rollout of blog tools in mid-2003. What took so long?

Author and law professor Lawrence Lessig has dubbed this compelling community activity the "social commons," a right of society to have content thrive in the public domain without interference from big media. Lessig sees big media as a danger to this kind of development, and he's right that most users ultimately coalesce around fewer and fewer big destinations. AOL didn't help matters by pushing more features that attempt to guide users to their ad-supported (and too often ad-programmed) sites inside the service, rather than rely on members to lead the way.

Solution: AOL should sell itself as a space where people meet, rather than a place where they get all sorts of programming shoved down their throats. Let a thousand Web flowers bloom. It's a lot harder than it looks, but AOL has got to take down every barrier it has constructed and let people do what they want. By providing the best tools for online engagement, AOL will become a needed part of that dialogue.

Many sites on the Web are now perfecting increasingly sophisticated tools for interaction—aimed mostly at teens, which has been AOL's most loyal user base. One application being developed at Microsoft, for example, called NetGen, allows teens to form groups as easily as they might create a real, live party, with the ability to program music, chat, and share information easily. Another site called Second Life is an exciting online community created by its members. In comparison, AOL's current tools had become antiquated, although similar changes are now being made. Here, AOL should lead the pack. The new "Super Buddy" animated icons in 9.0 are a step in the right direction, but are still not enough to hold ever-fickle teens.

Problem: Diminution of Brand

Other than Martha Stewart and the fine folks over at Enron, is there any other brand that has gotten more dinged than AOL in the past few years? It's almost pathetic how badly one of the online indus-try's best-known monikers has gotten slapped around externally and, worst of all, internally. While Ted Leonsis argued to me that con-sumers distinguish between "AOL the service and AOL the company," I'm not so sure about that. And internal polls by AOL of its members confirm that the troubles of the corporation are badly hurting the ser-vice. Right now, with the spate of investigation and lawsuits, the sto-ries of internal bickering, and a general feeling that the company is under siege, the brand has been getting a workout.

Solution: I am not sure why it took so long for someone to make Ted Turner and all those bellyachers at Time Warner happy (and per-haps even shut them up) by pulling AOL off the corporate name and returning it back to Time Warner, so the inevitable sign can go up at the eventual ribbon-cutting of the new headquarters at Columbus Circle in Manhattan. Such a move was planned to occur in the fall of 2003, when the company hoped to settle its government problems. The move was also being delayed until after the rollout of 9.0 to avoid linking it with the inexorable spate of media stories sure to rehash the merger-from-hell story line when the news was unveiled. Word began to leak out that the name change would happen in the summer of 2003. So expect it to happen sooner.

Interestingly, those running the online service were the most aggressive in pushing for the name change and for a good reason, especially AOL CEO Jon Miller, who urged Dick Parsons to give him back the brand. Removing those three letters from the front of the corporate moniker would presumably allow the AOL brand to again refer solely to the well-known online service, where it belongs. And it will enable its executives to craft new definitions of its products, sepa-rate from the main company and away from the image of the disas-trous merger. A great brand, which is hard to create, is one of AOL's great assets and needs to be protected at all costs.

Problem: Decline in Ad Sales

One of the canards of current coverage is that AOL's ad sales are doomed. Well, that's true of the old mega-deal efforts that made no business sense for clients, who were only buying in hope of an IPO pop and little else. The confusion between ads and programming also got woefully confusing, so much so that a billboard on a highway was more honest than AOL's tacky infomercial approach. That practice has thankfully stopped—mostly because no one wants to buy these kinds of slots anymore. As Leonsis delicately noted to me, "I think we have taken the service back from the unnatural acts which we were performing."

But there is no question AOL has had to start from scratch in remaking its reputation in the ad community. Yahoo has already been at that task for years now and so AOL is going to be doling out a lot of apologies for its dot-com arrogance and swaggering behavior. Its ad staff is also in the midst of wrenching changes and has to shift into a more traditional structure that has been required in the new economic paradigm. Again, this is basic block-and-tackling work that has to occur before AOL can really move forward in any meaningful way, something which Don Logan excels at.

Solution: Ad sales online are going to grow and grow big—just not as quickly as many had hoped. But the trends are moving upward as both big and small advertisers continue their experimentation with video and audio, as well as highly targeted ads, in the more robust broadband environment. There is no real killer app here, just simple tactical moves to see what works best and where. Even the once-hyped focus on "niche" or one-on-one advertising—that is, ads that are directed specifically to a person depending on their online usage patterns—is one arena that advertisers will eventually figure out how to do right. The real game these days is in much smaller transactions, like paid search, that is pulling in buckets of revenues for sites like Yahoo and Google and also in online classified ads, where Barry Diller and eBay rule. AOL missed these major trends in its pursuits of giant deals, but it's still not too late to enter the market in a big way. Online classifieds are still growing, taking market share from newspapers, and it's a market AOL has largely ignored.

At the annual gathering of media moguls at Herb Allen's retreat and schmoozefest in Sun Valley, Idaho, in the spring of 2003, Yahoo's Terry Semel stood up and made a declaration to those gathered that the huge online portal would rule the fast-growing market for making big bucks off searching for information online. He made the first step to delivering on that boast within the same week when he announced that Yahoo would fork over $1.63 billion to acquire one of the leading paid-search companies, Overture. Contextual advertising has become a lucrative arena that is sure to become even more so (and more competitive, too). As the Web business turns back to its very roots and embraces the one basic idea on which the commercial Web was founded—the ability to find everything about anything anytime and anywhere—AOL must be a leader.

Problem: Whither Content

AOL got a lot of press in the spring of 2003 when it announced recent deals with other Time Warner divisions to carry exclusive premium content on the service. That included magazine content, the possibility of an online comedy show from HBO, and other stuff. The idea seems to have gotten out there, unfortunately helped by a vague comment by Dick Parsons, that AOL would rule by creating hits like HBO does.

That's not entirely true, since AOL and most others on the Web realize the original content game is a questionable proposition for a lot of reasons. These include the difficulty of creating new online material that people actually want to pay for, even as the wholesale illegal downloading of existing content continues. This is all still being sorted out, and will change as broadband usage becomes widespread, but it remains a costly and uncertain endeavor. So far, very little in online content creation has been lucrative, despite constant refrains that content will inevitably be king. For now, it's much less lofty royalty in the Web realm.

Solution: I think I'm pretty safe in predicting that there will be no hit like the Warner Bros.–produced television hit *Friends* on AOL, or anywhere on the Web, for many years to come (if at all). I'm also certain that AOL shouldn't even bother to attempt any major content initiatives, even with the able help of proven creators like Warner Bros. and Time Inc. Making special content available is an okay strategy, as long as it does not cost AOL too much. But it doesn't seem to be what users really want from their online experience.

A better bet seems to be the kind of event- and news-driven packages of content—created by media professionals—that is being successfully sold by RealNetworks and Yahoo. AOL has been trying to get into this arena with its very admirable "First Look" at music and movies, but it's still not clear that this is why anyone signs on to AOL. With so much free information available on the Web, AOL's power to point and add context and navigation seems a more useful direction. For Time Warner divisions, of course, using AOL seems like a good strategy for now, but its efforts will remain more glacial. "I don't have wild expectations," said Time Inc.'s Editorial Director John Huey about the magazine unit's digital aims. "It will be a part of our business, but I'm not sure it's a *big* part." Huey's right: Someday the Internet will surely kill the media company's businesses, just not *this* week.

Problem: Need for Personalization

For years, AOL has tried to add personalization features to its offerings, but it has done it in such a half-hearted and thin-featured way that all efforts have been dismal. More personalization is definitely needed, as evidenced by the popularity of such tools on pretty much every successful Web site on the planet. One of the great things about the Web is the ability individuals have to program for themselves, since presumably no one knows you as well as you do. AOL has long gone against the grain by foisting the same Britney Spears–heavy front screen on everyone who passes through its service. It's recently tried to offer a handful of still-strict screen choices designed by AOL, but that's not the same. I am certain AOL has done 237 studies on how people prefer this mainstream approach, but I'm going to have to disagree. They don't.

AOL's new "QuickViews" feature in 9.0 is a step in the right direction, allowing members to create menus of information that are easily accessible as the cursor rolls over different icons of the main screen. And there are other tools coming that allow more user control, although AOL still seems loathe to turn over the keys to the service completely to those who deserve to drive—the customers.

Solution: Let the people decide on what they want on their front screen by allowing them the widest range of choices about what should be featured there. AOL can still control the many offerings of news or colors or weather or whatever, but the user should have much more control over his or her own experience. In this way, AOL can begin to suggest new features that users may never have known about, since AOL has so little information about their preferences. I mean this in the nicest way, but AOL programmers are inexperienced and not media savvy enough. By giving this power to users, it solves a myriad of problems and eliminates Britney from the lives of those who are less interested in her. Or not interested in her at all. "At some point, there has to develop an editorial culture at AOL," said Time Inc.'s Editor-in-Chief Norm Pearlstine. "Although I am not sure anyone knows what that means."

I'll tell Norm what it means—only each individual customer of AOL can define the editorial culture of the company for himself or herself. When trying to figure out how to reinvigorate the service in 2002, some executives pondered whether or not AOL had a definitive "voice" like the increasingly popular conservative ranting on Fox News. AOL, in fact, has tens of millions of voices and should keep it that way. Searching for a common editorial mindset seems like a giant waste of time for a place as disparate as AOL.

Problem: Will People Buy Premium Services?

Over the years AOL has basically sold one product for one price—its bundled online service and access package. Now Miller and others are talking about disaggregating the service, selling bits and pieces of it—such as an offering that provides special phone management—for various prices. While it's an idea that pretty much every other competitor has been rolling out for more than a year, it's still an unproven product strategy that might be more trouble than it is worth. AOL users are used to buying a single product and these extensions are risky, because they provide customers the opportunity to reconsider the worth of every part of AOL.

More troublesome is that this tends to dredge up a habit that has floated around AOL for far too long—that of treating customers as objects to always be leveraged in some manner. AOL executives used to talk incessantly about "renting subscribers" to other companies and recent attempts to foist a range of a la carte services has the same feel to it. As long as "What can we squeeze out of our members?" is the tone, AOL will lose subscribers.

Solution: More promising to me is giving AOL users more and more benefits as a privilege of membership. While it has done this on a small scale, AOL has never really leveraged its power to offer its members special deals all over the landscape. While purchasing clubs and other members-only groups are a specialized business, providing AOL members more and more reasons to stay with the service and to use it more extensively seems like good business. An AOL membership is a subscription—like a Time Inc. magazine—but the relationship AOL has with its subscribers has so much more opportunity for intimacy and interaction. AOL used to have a much better rapport with its users and needs to do so again. Could AOL offer a serious airline miles program? Or major discount at retailers used heavily by customers? Or give its users some kind of "cash" it could spend on the service? The phone alert—which tells you who is calling you when your phone is engaged on AOL—seems minor and will not matter once more people have broadband.

The real point is to treat customers with much more respect and to find ways to reward them for loyalty. Treating members like cows to be milked is not an image that will sustain AOL. As one former executive who was always bothered by the lack of customer focus said: "Those that serve, lead."

Problem: Lack of Broadband Strategy

Broadband has taken center stage of the "survival of AOL" debate, sucking up all the attention paid by Wall Street and the press, and becoming the only metric that AOL is apparently being judged by. It has indeed become a pimple on the face of a beautiful lady. Critics have fixated on the lower margins that AOL suffers in the broadband environment compared with the higher percentage of fees that cable and telephone carriers can charge. And, indeed, AOL is no longer in the position of getting lucrative deals as a reseller of access. In addition, many worry about the software challenges and their associated costs that AOL faces as it rolls out its broadband product. In other words, the broadband experience for AOL is one that is costly, full of headaches, and rife with risk.

And, the same thinking goes, it's unlikely to succeed, since cable and phone operators now have competitive options for consumers and are no longer captive to AOL. A range of other Web services is now easy to cobble together that offers the same kind of experience and ease of use. What, many ask, is the point of AOL at all when the Web in concert with broadband has it all?

Solution: So what? Broadband is where the market is going and is the space that AOL has to adapt to and serve. Any company with tens of millions of dial-up customers has to find a way to transition over as many as possible to broadband, and they stand a much better chance of doing so than of finding new users. Rather than bang its head against a closed door, AOL has finally seemed to realize that cable and telephone companies are simply not going to give away the store to them in this shift to high-speed after having seen how AOL took advantage of telephone companies in the dial-up arena. Rather than try to push services like Road Runner out of the way, AOL has to make a product that people want to pay for on top of it. While some think they can't, I don't believe it's a foregone conclusion that everyone will junk AOL for whatever the cable company offers. Cable and telephone companies are notoriously bad about creating compelling consumer offerings, and that gives AOL a big opportunity to shine. No matter how trendy they become, cable companies are still easy to compete with, given their slow-moving nature and customer-abusive tendencies.

AOL's first efforts at a new broadband product are a good start. All it needs to have are several must-have applications or services that are hard to replicate. For a long time, for example, IM was one of those kinds of thing for the dial-up AOL service, keeping people coming back month after month. And dial-up is also not as big a disadvantage as people think. People who travel with a laptop, for example, can always easily connect to AOL wherever they might be and use broadband at home—a fact AOL should sell more strongly. AOL need not define itself by its access options, especially since it simply does not control the most important future ones, so it should just stress its ubiquity. AOL should be AOL no matter how you sign up.

Problem: AOL's Place in the Digital Lifestyle

Becoming a part of people's lives in a constant state of connection is the paradigm everything will ultimately revolve around. But AOL jumped on this trend too soon with its ill-conceived AOL Anywhere effort. Rolled out before there was clarity on how it was going to work, and created out of fear of Microsoft more than anything else, the initiatives produced a bad AOL TV service, a bad AOL on BlackBerry pager service, a bad AOL on cell phone experience, and a bad AOL on network computer service. Its other investments related to digital video recorders, satellites, and other alternative delivery systems were a waste of time, effort, and money. AOL primarily remains a creature of the personal computer and I think it always will be, no matter how much its executives wish it could be otherwise.

AOL has also always paid lip service to the idea of seamless integration of popular services—and then has done almost nothing to realize it. Its arrangement with Kodak on digital pictures was clunky; the music services it backed were badly executed; its efforts at online billing were weak.

Solution: AOL should simply embrace its PC beachhead and make its service the best experience possible for its users, who are increasingly going to be using their computers as an all-purpose entertainment and information device. AOL should take a page from what Steve Jobs has been doing at Apple Computer with its various attempts to actually succeed at seamlessly creating a digital lifestyle for its users. In that albeit small universe, the digital camera works perfectly with the computer, the iPod music player works easily with the computer and software, and now the stellar music service works in tandem with the computer, the software, and the iPod.

Apple is surely aided in the fact that it makes and sells both the hardware and system software, but its efforts are pointing the way to the essential value of a single design environment that helps consumers in getting all their many devices to work together. AOL's original value proposition was built around the single promise of ease-of-use in the interactive space. It is in one of the better positions to continue to push this role as more and more features and devices add complexity to a customer's world. For example, wouldn't AOL be a natural candidate to stitch together the billing and operational issues that come from the myriad wireless networks that are popping up nationwide? But, instead of AOL, that's being done by entrepreneurs like Sky Dayton at Boingo. The list of what it could do to help consumers navigate the increasing complexity of the connected life is endless. Such a service would be invaluable, especially if AOL could successfully play the role of a neutral party.

Problem: You've Got Jail

There is little good news in either the government investigations or the dozens of shareholder lawsuits that the online unit faces. With the division under scrutiny, these issues will continue to cast a dark cloud over its future prospects until they are settled in some fashion. What is there to say? This situation, which is of AOL's own making, stinks, and it has taken on a life of its own that now seems uncontrollable. While a lot of the charges may ultimately be unproven, that really does not matter now.

The many investigations of AOL are a tarnish that will never go away and, in many ways, part of a fast-and-loose culture that has been in place from its founding. While some at AOL still feel the company is paying the price for the sins of the whole dot-com industry, there is no question that AOL was the biggest and baddest player in the boom and deserves to get scrutinized the most carefully.

Solution: Stop arguing with the government and settle immediately, if possible. The fact of the matter is that the government, which has gone this far, has got to find AOL guilty of something and a price will be exacted. While I am aware of the complexities of the situation, it is in everyone's best interests—including the government's—to get this stuff in the rearview mirror. The company can take a longer-term view on the lawsuits, which hinge in part on the government investigations. But investors should be prepared to suffer some big payouts. While the *Wall Street Journal* recently estimated that lawsuits could cost AOL Time Warner $1 billion or more, other more realistic observers put the figure in this catfight at $5 billion.

The company should pay the price and move on. While some will say that AOL got off too easy and others will think it was overly pilloried, none of it really matters, since AOL's focus needs to be on the next iteration of the industry. After all, that's precisely what AOL's longtime foe Microsoft did. It was facing much more serious charges from the government related to its monopolistic practices only a few years back. Today, it is considered dominant once again. And the government trial of Microsoft, surely Bill Gates's worst moment, feels like a distant memory.

Problem: Live Free or Die

In the broader scheme of things after the investigations and lawsuits are over, being under the umbrella of AOL Time Warner right now appears to be of minimal benefit for either AOL or the larger company. Without an iron fist at the top forcing synergies that might make some sense, there's just no reason for AOL to be attached to Time Warner. While some at Time Warner now posit that having an online unit as a division makes it a stronger media company in the future, I am not sure the overall angry attitude toward AOL will ever turn around substantially enough to give AOL a real chance to thrive. Company divisions can and should work opportunistically with lots of online players, no matter their affiliation, so helping AOL is not a priority.

AOL, of course, suffers much more, most of all in its ability to be nimble. At this point it can hardly innovate or spend much-needed money on research and development; it cannot make any really substantial acquisitions that others in the Web space are making; it cannot cut prices; and it cannot do anything risky or new without a feeling that the upper echelons are watching. In fact, the company has been in talks to start selling off pieces of the online service not integral to the business. That gives its competitors a lot of space to excel. "If Microsoft ever embraced the customer, it would all be over," AOL's marketing legend Jan Brandt noted to me in 2003. "The strategy of Time Warner is to milk the failure of vision, so what Microsoft could not do to AOL, we are going to do to ourselves."

Solution: Brandt has a point; it has ultimately been AOL that has suffered in this merger more than any other part of the company, despite all the Time Warner kvetching. It probably deserves that. But the AOL division currently has an inexplicable negative value on Wall Street, which seems ridiculous given the potential it still has. If Time Warner has no real and profound ideas on assimilation—other than using AOL as a conduit of content—it should, as Steve Case has reportedly been advocating, "integrate or liberate."

I've talked to many at the company, and this does not seem to be a current option. The general idea is that selling after all the trouble is foolish, an emotional decision that would be akin to a fire sale. After riding it all the way down, the argument goes, why not wait to see what happens rather than give in to an act of desperation? Why not just pretty it up and see if it can be stabilized first? One major investor certainly had this view. "My attitude is why sell it at the bottom?" said Gordon Crawford. "There are still a lot of great companies to be built based on the Internet."

That's fair enough, if the Time Warner side of the company truly has the commitment to put aside all its anger and let AOL's strengths rise to the surface. For all its negatives, the rise of the online service is a remarkable accomplishment that shouldn't be discounted because of serious errors made along the way. I'm certain that any Internet operator—like Barry Diller, for example, who is still sniffing around along with many others—knows the value of AOL even in its current straits. Frankly, I'd sell it to him or anyone else who understands this basic point. Jerry Levin was right about one thing—Time Warner does not have either the DNA or the passion for the vagaries of the online space that defies logic.

Maybe that's why some at AOL refuse to leave the stage, such as Ted Leonsis. "I'm like that guy at movies—the credits have rolled, the janitors are sweeping up, and I am still sitting there," he said. He paused and raised his bushy eyebrows dramatically, as if to wonder why that was.

Finally, the most important question I could actually answer. After all the troubles, Ted Leonsis was still in love—and it was a profound love—with the digital future and the promise it still might bring.

And, I might add, so was I.

INDEX